Proletariat
Culture and Lifestyle
in the 19th Century

Proletariat

Culture and Lifestyle in the 19th Century

Edited
by Dietrich Mühlberg

Edition Leipzig

Texts, illustrations and compilation:
Wolfgang Bagger, Tobias Böhm, Isolde Dietrich,
Horst Groschopp, Günter Kracht, Ludwig Martienssen,
Dietrich Mühlberg, Anneliese Neef, Herbert Pietsch,
Horst W. Rohls

In collaboration with:
Dagmar Claus, Edith Broszynski-Schwabe,
Ani Dimitrova, Franz Johannson, Christa Lorenz,
Heinz Marohn, Rainer Mischke

Translated from the German by Katherine Vanovitch

The proletariat: culture and lifestyle in the
19th century / ed. by Dietrich Mühlberg.
[Transl. from the German by Katherine Vano-
vitch]. – 1. Aufl. – [Leipzig]: Edition
Leipzig, 1988. – 275 S.: 297 Ill. (z. T. farb.)
EST: Proletariat ‹engl.›

© Edition Leipzig 1988
Lic. No.: 600/78/88
Design: Horst Schuster
in collaboration with Frank Speckhals
Produced by: Druckerei Fortschritt Erfurt
Printed in the German Democratic Republic
Order No.: 594 652 9
ISBN: 3-361-00224-9
09800

Contents

1 A razor blade manufactory in
France, late 18th century. Manufacture brought many craftsmen together
under one roof and a single management. As an early form of concentrated production, it laid the
technological and economic foundations for factory-based industry.

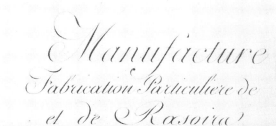

Manufacture d'Nationale

Fabrication Particulière de *Nécessaires à Barbe*

et de Rasoirs *d'a Acier Fin*

The only Manufacture in France of good Razors of melted steel in the same manner as that of Sheffield in Yorkshire

19th-century Industrial Capitalism and the Formation of the Working Class

Workers' history, and with it the history of a specific workers' culture and lifestyle, begins with the Industrial Revolution in England. This was the dawn of a radical upheaval in patterns of production from the late 18th century onwards which gave birth, economically and socially, to the modern proletariat. Up until this point, a colourful hotchpotch of lower classes had existed side by side in various conditions of dependence upon their exploiters: day labourers, serfs and landless peasants, beggars and vagabonds, casual jobbers and inmates of poorhouses, lesser artisans, journeymen, craftsmen who had entered the manufacturing workshops and thus been sucked into the growing division of manual labour, homeworkers who supplied piecework to agents. Now they gradually merged to form a single class, with capitalist wage labour becoming the universal norm.

This process of proletarianization advanced fastest in the classical home of industrial capitalism. By the 1840s England had a mass proletariat in which factory workers were the dominant group. In Belgium, France, Prussia, Saxony and other countries, it took longer for the differences in lifestyle between various forms of dependent labour to disappear. Pre-industrial wage labour was more widespread and survived for several decades longer.

Not until the upswing in factory-based industry after 1850 could the Continent lay claim to a proletariat of social significance, but here, too, an urban industrial proletariat eventually emerged as the dominant strand of capitalist wage labour. This group was, henceforth, to exert a major influence on the work and lifestyle of the class as a whole and on class organizations which began to function on a national basis with specifically defined aims. That is why a cultural history of working-class life in the 19th century is inevitably bound to focus on the industrial proletariat and its development.

From "Fourth Estate" to Modern Proletariat

"Discovering" the proletariat By the close of the 18th century there were already indications, in England at least, that a "new estate" was evolving from the subordinate populace of disintegrating feudal society. Public attention was aroused by the manner in which the workers and *ouvriers* were now rebelling against their masters. Governments and the urban establishment were accustomed by this stage to collective resistance and communal acts of despair, but organized political activity took them by surprise. Bewildered, they responded with military force. In 1819 the mounted yeomanry, still basking in the victory of Waterloo, trampled demonstrating workers underfoot as they assembled at St. Peter's Fields in Manchester to claim the right of suffrage. Twelve years later, when the silk-weavers of Lyons demanded a minimum of material security, the newly installed July Monarchy in Paris, which had toppled Charles X in the interests of the commercial class, sent in the army to quell the protests. For several days in the autumn of 1831 the weavers had taken control of their town. From their slogan—"Live working or die fighting!"—it was clear that they expected more than mere charity to alleviate the lean years: they were asking society to grant workers the acknowledgement they deserved.

This conscious, organized activity on the part of the workers came as such an intellectual shock to Europe's well-to-do classes that burghers began to change their attitude towards the factory rabble. Striking fear into their hearts with military repression was evidently not enough.

In European government circles, the "helots of the mills" were often regarded as "close allies of subversion" and the "frightful weapon, ever at the ready" of "political vandals"[1]. At the same time, civil servants, industrialists, academics, writers and artists were taking a closer look at the social behaviour of workers, taking England as their specimen. Many of them proposed reforms and studied the ideas of those French socialists who had identified the labouring masses as the proletariat of the new age. Books and pamphlets on the "impoverishment" of the lower strata, on the "condition of the working classes" and on the "social question" multiplied. A new viewpoint was emerging. The inferior classes of olden times, who had never been assumed to have any rights of their own, and the "fourth estate", formerly reduced to a rhetorical phrase, were evidently being acknowledged as the working majority of society.

Any critical observer was now confronted by the picture of a divided nation with two distinct cultures. The concept was used by the Utopian socialist Laponneraye in 1833 in summarizing his impressions of the French population, "divided into two nations, with entirely different interests quite separate from each other, the nation of the privileged and the nation of the unprivileged, or proletarians"[2]. Before the British Conservatives threw in their lot with the industrial bourgeoisie, Disraeli, the future Chancellor of the Exchequer and Prime Minister, wrote reproachfully of "two nations; between whom there is no intercourse and no sympathy; who are as ignorant of each other's habits, thoughts, and feelings, as if they were dwellers in different zones, or inhabitants of different planets; who are formed by a different breeding, are fed by a different food, are ordered by different manners, and are not governed by the same laws . . . the rich and the poor"[3]. Friedrich Engels, son of a German factory-owner, took up the same image when he wrote in 1845: "The bourgeoisie has more in common with every other nation of the earth than with the workers in whose midst it lives. The workers speak other dialects, have other thoughts and ideals, other customs and moral principles, a different religion and other politics than those of the bourgeoisie."[4] Yet the conclusions which different writers drew from this same observation varied considerably. Few would have agreed with Friedrich Engels in his description of the English proletariat: "Thus they are two radically dissimilar nations, as unlike as difference of race could make them, of whom we on the Continent have known but one, the bourgeoisie. Yet it is precisely the other, the people, the proletariat, which is by far the more important for the future of England."[5]

A "bestial mob movement" threatens civilization For most bourgeois observers around 1845, however, all the proletariat seemed to hold out for the future was a threat. They certainly did not see it as a class with positive historical potential.

The proletarians, to them, were dependents who owned no means of production and therefore relied on an industrialist to "give" them work. A handful of socially enlightened factory-owners condescended to indulge in a little community partnership from their superior position of wealth, but not even they believed that the proletarians might be capable of contributing productively to cultural developments or of taking independent action. After all, the burghers themselves had almost all the creative forces of society at their disposal and had set out to mould the world to meet their own particular needs.

Their view had its roots in earlier attitudes which the propertied classes had adopted towards their inferiors. Now that the social safeguards which had protected vassals from extreme circumstance under feudal conditions had been eroded away, some well-to-do philanthropists had come forward to assume responsibility for the poor and disinherited. Poverty was to be moderated by charity. Of course, the overwhelming majority of well-heeled middle-class citizens took another point of view. Since the 16th century, primitive accumulation of capital had deprived hundreds of thousands of men and women of their basis for subsistence. Even lesser craftsmen and peasants lived under a constant cloud of looming beggary. As far as this battle for survival was concerned, the new bourgeoisie and the conservatives found themselves in agreement: the rabble generated by this process should be kept short, and the idle poor, riff-raff beyond the law, had no right to claim any support whatsoever. Looting, hunger riots and other manifestations of greed proved that these new paupers were inclined to commit crimes against property, and their swelling ranks began to pose a threat to public order. That is why the owning classes of all countries had welcomed the Poor Laws, which acknowledged pauperism officially and laid down measures for harnessing it. Not for nothing did the British call them "bloody laws".

This legislation turned the cause and effects of poverty upside-down, but the respectable burghers were convinced by its logic. If these people had only themselves to blame for their situation on account of their own laziness, then no penalty was too harsh in order to stamp out their recalcitrance and force them into labour. Brutal pressure was not only legal, but was even regarded as

1 Buss, Franz J., Ritter von: "Speech on the social problem in the Baden Chamber of 25 April 1837," in: *Quellen zur Geschichte der sozialen Frage in Deutschland*. Vol. 1. Ed. by Ernst Schraepler. Göttingen, Berlin (West), Frankfurt am Main, 1955, p. 49.

2 Laponneraye, Albert: "Brief an die Proletarier." Quoted from: Höppner, Joachim, and Waltraud Seidel-Höppner: *Von Babeuf bis Blanqui. Französischer Sozialismus und Kommunismus vor Marx*. Vol. 2: *Texts*. Leipzig, 1975, p. 272.

3 Beaconsfield, Benjamin Disraeli, Earl of: *Sybil, or, The Two Nations*. London, 1845, p. 74.

4 Engels, Friedrich: "The Condition of the Working-Class in England," in: *Marx and Engels Collected Works*. Vol. 4. Moscow, 1975, pp. 419–20. (Afterwards referred to as: MECW/vol./p.)

5 MECW/4/420.

2 "A cobbler's workshop." Painting by Max Liebermann, 1881. The new industries saw the demise of many crafts. Shoemakers confined themselves to repairs.

3 Once a person reached the bottom rung of the social ladder, it was difficult to escape the vicious circle of unemployment, poverty and homelessness. This man lived in a New York cellar for years. Photo by Jacob A. Riis, c. 1890.

humanitarian and godly. It was the only way to deal with these lawless characters who were so suspicious, coarse and cold, hardened by their hopeless destinies. Even once the principle was established that the wealth of nations must be determined by the number of labouring hands, these detached, supercilious tones did not fade. The well-to-do continued to look upon the labourer as crude and difficult to educate, necessary yet despicable. The spread of manufacture, which ushered in the division of manual labour and eroded the craftsman's independence, followed by early mechanical industry, only seemed to increase the workers' poverty and remove every last vestige of humanity from their existence. Would the immense advances in production ever succeed in promoting the producers to some loftier social function? At first, the idea seemed ridiculous. Adam Smith, the father of bourgeois political economics, had already pointed out at the birth of the Industrial Revolution that a highly civilized society and uncivilized labourers were essentially two sides to the same coin. The worker "becomes as stupid and ignorant as it is possible for a human creature to become . . . His dexterity at his own particular trade seems . . . to be acquired at the expense of his intellectual, social, and martial virtues." Unperturbed, he went on

to conclude: "But in every improved and civilized society this is the state into which the labouring poor, that is, the great body of the people, must necessarily fall . . ."[6] The bourgeoisie on the Continent thought similarly. They were at pains to copy British factory methods. The pauperism which inevitably proliferated appeared to be a necessary evil.

Once industrial capitalism had come to determine the fabric of society, and an expanding economy sucked in broader and

6 Smith, Adam: *An Inquiry Into the Nature and Causes of the Wealth of Nations.* Chicago, 1952, pp. 341–42.
7 Harkort, Friedrich: "Brief an die Arbeiter." Quoted from: *Die Eigentumslosen. Der deutsche Pauperismus und die Emanzipationskrise in Darstellungen und Deutungen der zeitgenössischen Literatur.* Ed. by Carl Jantke and Dietrich Hilger. Munich, 1965, pp. 392ff.
8 Cf. for example the bourgeois Liberal Max Wirth in 1863 in: "Über die Verhandlungen des ersten Vereinstages der deutschen Arbeitervereine, abgehalten zu Frankfurt am Main am 7. und 8. Juni 1863."
9 Smiles, Samuel: *Self-Help with illustrations of conduct and perseverance.* London, 1859, p. 284.
10 *Ibid.*, p. 284.
11 Heinrich von Treitschke in his letter to Gustav Schmoller of 7 August 1874, in: *Heinrich von Treitschkes Briefe.* Vol. 3, part 2. Berlin, 1920, p. 398.

broader masses of available labour, with the technological and social conditions of factory work becoming more and more differentiated, proponents of the new bourgeois order began to see the wage labourer in another light. Not that they cast aside their uncompromising detachment and cultural contempt, but they now had important practical grounds for distinguishing between the obedient and diligent worker and the covetous, rebellious proletarian. A classic example of this is supplied by the pioneering German industrialist Friedrich Harkort in 1849, when he defined the distinction between a submissive labourer and one who asserted his rights in the following terms: "I call proletarian one whom his parents neglected in his youth, neither washing nor combing him, not raising him to virtue nor sending him to church or school. He has not learnt his trade, marries without bread and sets imitations of himself into the world who are constantly ready to pounce upon the property of other people . . . I would furthermore designate those proletarians who, though raised by virtuous parents, have been destroyed by the temptations of the great towns; lechers and drunkards who set greater store by a truant Monday than by the Sabbath; prodigal sons without repentance who shrink in horror from law and order."[7] "Virtuous workers" were another matter. They should not allow themselves to think or act like proletarians.

Since the working day in a factory lasted fifteen or sixteen hours, laziness could hardly be claimed any longer as the cause of social misery, and so proletarian neglect was cited in its place. It was lack of culture that made the workers proletarian. They were assured that "nothing divides the diverse classes of society but the difference in their education and knowledge"[8]. Poverty "springs solely from the weakness, self-indulgence, and perverseness of man himself," pontificated Samuel Smiles in a widely recommended volume of homilies.[9] His manual on good conduct was sprinkled with warnings such as that pronounced by the liberal factory-owner John Bright at an assembly of working men in Rochdale in 1847: "There is only one way that is safe for any man, or any number of men, by which they can maintain their present position if it be a good one, or raise themselves above it if it be a bad one—that is, by the practice of the virtues of industry, frugality, temperance, and honesty."[10] If the workers preferred to ignore this counsel and resort to other means by which to better their circumstances, the ideologues predicted the doom of civilization. The Prussian nationalist Heinrich von Treitschke was not the only person to be overwhelmed by "concern for the spiritual values of our culture, which today are threatened by a bestial mob movement"[11]. Gustave Le Bon warned: "Civilizations as yet have only been created and directed by a small intellectual aris-

4 Police detention offered the homeless a certain guarantee against the cold winter. Paupers at the lock-up in Elisabeth Street, New York. Photo by Jacob A. Riis, *c.* 1890.

tocracy, never by crowds. Crowds are only powerful for destruction. Their rule is always tantamount to a barbarian phase. A civilization involves fixed rules, discipline, a passing from the instinctive to the rational state, forethought for the future, an elevated degree of culture—all of them conditions that crowds, left to themselves, have invariably shown themselves incapable of realizing." Human beings, he maintains, then degenerate into barbarians.[12]

All these theories were so distorted by ideological assumptions that they offered no real insight into the evolution of the working class throughout the 19th century. There was a defence mechanism at play which prevented their authors from attaching due credit to those bankrupt craftsmen and peasants who hauled themselves out of destitution and rose from an amorphous rabble of disenfranchised paupers to form an organized proletariat in a process which, in fact, signified social and cultural progress. As a result, the new aspirations of the working masses were perceived as an onslaught on the culture of the élite which was made clear by the bourgeois class in every way.

"The source of all wealth and all culture" To start with, none of the men and women who had been forced by their poverty to accept labour in the spinning or textile mills, brickworks or ore washing were actually proud of this new status. They usually looked upon it as a last resort, or else still hoped that the job would be merely temporary until better conditions for an independent living returned. It took born proletarians several decades to grow accustomed to their position and befriend their role as workers. Former craftsmen found it particularly unpleasant to acknowledge this designation. When a proposal was put to Berlin's biggest popular assembly in the revolutionary year of 1848 that a "league of proletarians" should be founded, there was "such a din that the assembly obliged the speaker to retract the word 'proletarian'".[13]

But as their numbers increased from one generation to the next, as their labour grew more productive and as they began to set the tone on the city streets, so the proletarians sensed the power they might acquire as an organized force and increasingly proclaimed an allegiance to their new "estate". This self-confidence first developed through their work. Many contemporaries noted how this new category of the human race "without property or social ties" was laying claim to an honour conferred simply by labour, and how, unlike the feudal poor, they refused to regard their condition as God-given, but formulated aspirations and set themselves up against the privileged. Workers themselves began to attach a certain cultural status to the designation

5 "Unequal brothers." The worker and the bourgeois were opposite poles in the new social order of the Industrial Revolution. While the man of property revels in his success, the worker in Theodor Hosemann's cartoon (1847), his clothes in rags and his energies spent, challenges the luxury.

Die ungleichen Brüder
«Schämen Sie sich nich, sag' ich, daß ich in des Wetter so zerlumpt rumloofen muß un nischt zu essen habe? Haben Sie denn verjessen, daß ich Ihr Bruder bin?»

Die Republik? Das sind wir!

12 Le Bon, Gustave: *The Crowd. A study of the popular mind.* London, 1846, p. xix.

13 Bernstein, Eduard: *Geschichte der Berliner Arbeiter-Bewegung.* Berlin, 1907, p. 31.

6/7 Politically active workers were lampooned by the bourgeoisie as anti-social elements who wanted to share out wealth without working (left). The working class, meanwhile, saw themselves quite differently as the giants of industry, too strong for all the world's bourgeoisie to shackle. The honest worker symbolizing his class need only unfold his arms to sweep away the pestering potentates. (Illustration on the right from *Der Wahre Jacob*, No. 411, 1902.)

8/9 Foundry workers and their masters 1864. Wage labour and capital, proletariat and bourgeoisie, were opposite poles in the new order. They lent form and face to capitalism and its culture.

11 Mines, pits and coalfields employed many workers, as the new industries pressed urgently for more coal, ore and salt. Photo of 1912.

10 The mine at Patience et Beaujonc. Photo by Gustave Marissiaux, 1904.

ouvrier, Arbeiter, or working man. "Working men" had become "a title of which they are proud, and which is the usual form of address in Chartist meetings"[14]. Another observer commented to his astonishment in 1848: "The world has turned wonderfully on its axis, and those same auxiliary and manual labourers for whom there was once no page in the almanac of social rank now call themselves simply working-men, quite as though the honour of labour belonged to them above all others. In this sense the designation *Arbeiter* may certainly be regarded as testifying to a social revolution."[15]

Organized workers began to see themselves as the backbone of civilization. After all, their labour was the "source of all wealth and all culture"[16]. Their new-found assurance was reflected, not only in the theories propounded by the labour movement, but also in the values for which they lived, the goals they set, and their demonstrative lifestyle. Even their clothes, posture and gesticulation symbolized this self-respect. The imagery adopted by the late 19th-century working-class movement depicts the proletarian as the hero of labour, as Prometheus and Hercules, and as the ally, if not the true patron and protector, of science, education and the arts.

This sense of their own worth was an expression of the social status which workers had achieved. They had mastered the challenge posed by industrial labour. They took the virtue of diligence for granted, like their ability to operate the technology. The capitalist market and urban life had stimulated their demands and encouraged a wider scope of interests. They longed for a life which could offer them the relaxation, leisure and pleasure they deserved after their daily toil. They campaigned for free time and had begun to foster many forms of creative activity which, in future years, would develop on a mass scale: reading, adult education, a taste for excitement and amusement, appreciation of the arts and convivial gatherings, sporting events and group excursions, family life and gardening. They had been through trade-

---

14 MECW/4/529.

15 Riehl, W. Heinrich: "Die Arbeiter. Eine Volksrede aus dem Jahre 1848." Quoted from: *Die Eigentumslosen.* Ed. by Carl Jantke and Dietrich Hilger. Munich, 1965, p. 397.

16 "Programme of the Socialist Workers' Party of Germany," in: *Protokoll des Vereinigungs-Congresses der Sozialdemokraten zu Gotha vom 22. bis 27. Mai 1875,* p. 54.

Emil Winzer & Sohn, Potschappel.

12 This elderly worker was one of the better-placed proletarians around 1895. As a conductor he had a secure contract, a uniform and pension rights, raising him above the status of a factory worker or even a craftsman.

13 This group of railway workers illustrates social differentiation within the proletariat itself, from the old man who works as an unskilled labourer to the foreman bearing the rank of government office. Photo by Emil Winzer, 1911.

union struggles which taught them that unity was the only weapon available to those who have nothing but labour power to place on the market. So it was that solidarity became the noblest value in a moral code shared by potential rivals.

During the course of the 19th century, the workers of the leading industrial nations evolved new cultural patterns and incorporated them into their lifestyle. The key to this development was the infrastructural growth of their class, for whereas workers had initially only achieved any kind of numerical concentration in a few scattered places, they eventually constituted the organized majority of working people with their own internal channels of communication.

They may have differed in their understanding, demands and long-term goals, but they viewed the world with the eyes of confident proletarians. The dominant groups had forged their own way of life, fashioned by industrial labour and structured around a dynamic daily rhythm. It was a life amid masses, geared to the organized defence of common interests, and permeated by a pressure to take advantage of any democratic rights. It was a mode of existence where the emphasis was placed firmly on the future, and so, not surprisingly, class-based organizations drew up alternative strategies for all walks of life. Their proposals and demands covered wages and hours, health and safety, women's employment and children's schooling, housing, local government, general education and the arts, the social organization of labour and an appropriate distribution of its fruits.

For many workers, the dreams of a better life for themselves and their children mingled with a belief that their own society, based on competition, exploitation and insecurity, would have to undergo some radical transformations. Labour organizations in every country sought to obtain influence in the world of politics. National movements grew and forged international alliances. As the 20th century dawned, the working class felt increasingly convinced, not only that they were capable of expressing a valid opinion on matters of national significance, but also that the political future was theirs.

It was a creative process in which the proletarians created many of the ideals, patterns and customs still nurtured by working people today, and which are part and parcel, in all manner of ways, of the cultural traditions of modern societies.

14 Hunger rally in Prague during the First World War. Class confrontation grew in scale along with the social contradictions. Mounted police dispersed the demonstration. Restoring law and order frequently meant injuries and deaths. The police used draconian brutality.

How Factories and Machines Skilled the Worker

Manufacture, in the original sense of the word, paved the way for mechanized industry by breaking down the traditional craft processes into various partial operations, but although the wage labourers employed in manufacture can be designated early proletarians by virtue of their economic status, they were still craftsmen by nature of their work. The Industrial Revolution, however, gave birth to a new type of producer with quite different qualifications who learnt fundamentally new skills in the course of the labour process itself.

The technological revolution began in the textile industry. The spinning jenny invented by James Hargreaves in 1764 was powered by human muscle, but increased the productivity of artisans, homeworkers, cottage textile-making and textile manufactories notably. The transition to the mill system, however, only began in England when "single capitalists began to set up spinning jennies in great buildings and to use water-power for driving them"[17]. It was then simply a matter of time before James Watt's rotating steam engine was fitted to spinning machinery. England took this step in 1785, and the Sieburg spinning mill of Berlin pioneered the move on the Continent in 1797. The first mechanized spinning mill in the United States to be powered by steam began operation in 1827.

Weaving and other fields of production were mechanized soon afterwards. The machinery used consisted of three parts: a motor, the transmission, and the tool, or processing mechanism. This mechanical system determined how co-operative labour was now reorganized within the mill. In early years, various machines stood side by side working in parallel co-operation—first spinning machines and mechanical looms, then machines which combined these functions. Each unit performed all stages in the production process. In the latter half of the 19th century, a new type of factory dominated the key industrial sectors, where a product was processed by a group of specialized machines in turn. When electric motors provided independent drive at the close of the century, it was possible to design these mechanical systems purely to suit the demands of the technological sequence of production. The result was the conveyor belt. The assembly-line methods developed by Taylor and Ford broke up each stage of the process into countless partial operations performed by hand or machine, echoing the fragmentation of craft labour that had been ushered in by the period of manufacture. This opened the door to a future of automatically controlled mechanical systems.

It was a revolution in production technology which lasted over a century and likewise transformed the productive forces of working people. A major difference between the work of a factory hand and that of a craftsman or peasant was that industrial production was applied science in the practical form of technology. At first sight, the cultural implications seemed negative. The actual producer was no longer able, under these conditions, to determine or even structure the production process. That called for engineering staff with a special training. Moreover, the producer was operating technical equipment which had been invented and designed by experts. Workers were, therefore, restricted to making use of the instruments which others placed in front of them. On the other hand, this "materialized science" did require a certain technical understanding on the part of its operators, and an ability to handle the machines sensibly. A minimum, at the very least, of scientific and technical education proved necessary. The bourgeoisie in the industrial countries were quick to realize that the education system was now a factor in economic growth, and so they began to press for improvements in basic schooling and for specific vocational training.

The introduction of technology also meant that "Modern Industry never looks upon and treats the existing form of a process as final. The technical basis of that industry is therefore revolutionary."[18] Production was overhauled at shorter and shorter intervals. As a result, the skills acquired by the proletariat were continually devalued and workers were forced to change their jobs, but this also encouraged workers to be mobile and versatile, obliging them to respond flexibly to new demands.

Whereas the work of a peasant or craftsman had preserved a certain universality, combining physical with mental effort, another new feature of industrial labour was its reduction to the operation of machinery and auxiliary tasks. It called for much less physical exertion, a factor which had posed an insurmountable barrier to the expansion of pre-industrial production methods. Although new types of job demanding great physical effort were repeatedly created, the overall balance shifted in favour of mental energy based on technical knowledge. At first, there seemed to be no limits to the potential growth of mental labour, in contrast to physical effort. But there was a heavy price to pay. The machine imposed its own logic, rhythm and pace on the operator, who functioned like one of its parts. Besides, human labour had to perform the tasks which machines, as yet, were unable to perform, such as carrying heavy loads within the factory. And wherever there were gaps in the process which machines could still not fill, the mill owners bought in the cheapest labour available, one reason for the widespread employment of children in the textile industry and the mines.

17 MECW/4/311.

18 Marx, Karl: *Capital*. Vol. 1. Moscow, 1971, p. 457.

A completely new kind of behaviour was obligatory, and the consequences were unexpected. The machines themselves worked fast, and that called for deep concentration, simultaneous attention to various details, rapid evaluation of observations, quick decision-making, split-second control reactions and reliable calculation of the effects. In other words, the intellectual disposition of the producer was radically transformed. Industrial labour, therefore, stimulated a new rational and aesthetic attitude towards the social and natural environment.

When the industrial bourgeoisie began intensifying production in the period from 1830 (Britain) to 1855 (the German states), the challenge to these production-orientated thinking patterns became fully evident. The pace and output of the machines accelerated tremendously. Efficiency was increased by higher pressure and temperatures, purer raw materials and high-precision tools. To keep abreast of this intensification, workers in the sectors concerned had to acquire far greater vocational skills and a broader technical background knowledge. It was around this time that groups of especially highly-skilled workers emerged. As industrial technology advanced, more and more new job designations came into existence.

On the whole, the transition to factory production and mechanical labour gave rise to cultural effects that were clearly contradictory.

15 Georg Knorr, inventor of the air brake, at the testing apparatus, Berlin, 1909. Like the labourer and the capitalist, the engineer was an essential figure in the industrial environment. These pioneers of the "useful arts" were as fanatical as artists, as zealous as missionaries and as sensitive to responsibility as doctors. Their aim was to design new and better equipment which would supplement and reinforce the natural skills of human labour.

16 Modern industry was applied science. It called for workers who would approach production from the scientific angle. Apprentice workshops in big factories aided the training process. Royal Railway Workshops at Limburg (Lahn) in Germany. Photo of 1912.

17 The new power generated by the steam engine was transferred by open transmission belts, which posed a lethal danger for inattentive, overtired workers who frequently tried to dodge time-consuming safety regulations. At the same time, these transmission belts were a symbol of working-class power, for the worker had only to reach out a hand and all the wheels would stop turning. "Paper-making, floor of Hollanders." Xylograph from *L'Illustration*, Paris, 1874.

18 Burbach Foundry near Saarbrücken. New industrial sites sprang up, each one larger than the last. Foundry and forge chimneys were the most striking addition to the horizon. In the 19th century iron and steel output determined the growth of the other industries, so these smokestacks were genuine symbols of economic potential. Proletarians soon discovered that a belching chimney meant work.

19 Ore was carried to the coal, and sometimes coal to the ore. Railways and steamboats brought them together. But there were some who were still sceptical, as Camphausen's cartoon shows. From *Düsseldorfer Monatshefte*, 1849.

— Habt ihr mich nun begriffen, lieben Leute, könnt ihr euch jetzt die Wirkung der Dampfkraft, diese große Erfindung des neunzehnten Jahrhunderts, wodurch diese Maschine in Bewegung gesetzt wird, erklären?
— Jo, Herr Paster, ävver ehr könnt sage, wat ehr wellt, e Pähd (Pferd) setzt doch dren!

Manufacture

This forerunner of modern factory-based industry, had developed right across Europe. Under this system, artisans worked together in workshops according to a pronounced division of labour. The skills of the craftsman had been fragmented in the extreme by the production process. Each individual performed one partial operation in what had once been a complex activity. "On the one hand, manufacture either introduces division of labour into a process of production, or further develops that division; on the other hand, it unites together handicrafts that were formerly separate. But whatever may have been its particular starting-point, its final point is invariably the same—a productive mechanism whose parts are human beings."[19]

In both cases, the labourers were reduced to mere detail functions, yet at the same time this gave them the chance to become true virtuosos with regard to their specific skill. Their tools were also refined and perfected and the new system of manufacture turned out to be much more efficient than the earlier, simple form of craft labour. This simple form persisted, however, not only to perform highly specialized tasks, but as the major supplier of craft products.

Apart from producing faster and in greater quantities, the manufactories paved the way for the introduction of machines, which combined a simple tool with a form of power that was now independent of human input. In terms of the labouring skills required, too, manufactory hands were a kind of "embryo", although they were replaced by machines rather than the future factory hands, whose task was to supervise and regulate production and not to intervene with their own physical strength or dexterity. As mechanical labour spread, it was the manufactory hands whose skills tended to be devalued. They were often unsuited for factory work precisely because they had preserved their highly specialized craft and had to be paid adequately.

"In enforced periods of quiet, a factory-owner who can no longer discover sufficient quantities of good workers, or who finds it impossible to retain them on account of interrupted production, must turn to the machine market. This will supply him on request and at short notice with iron workers whose activity is cheaper and whose output is usually far superior to that of the skilled labourers previously in his employ, even if the range of products to emerge is somewhat more narrowly limited; a circumstance from which he will soon recover. Today, those states which are cultivating the factory system are advancing rapidly . . . towards perfected mechanofacture."[20]

Women and children man the machines

Some mechanical labour had to be broken down into very rigid stages of the production process. Many machines still required simple back-up. A

19 Marx, Karl: *Capital*. Vol. 1. Moscow, 1971, p. 320.
20 Reuleaux, Franz: *Die Maschine in der Arbeiterfrage*. Minden, 1885, p. 14.

20 The steam engine had long since been invented, but prisoners in England's Gold Bath Fields were still using the treadmill in 1867.

few basic actions to the rhythm of the piston were enough to regulate the flow of steam into the early engines, and this meant that physically weak, unskilled labour could now be employed for the purpose. Women and children were taken on by the factories, opening the floodgates to an enormous reservoir of industrial labour. The biggest numbers of women and children were employed in the textile mills and the mines, but the food, drinks and tobacco industry, brickworks, paper mills, and the chemicals, printing machinery and metalworking sectors also benefited from the cheap labour. In the course of the first half of the 19th century, women and children accounted for most of the increased workforce in those industries. In the cotton mills of England around 1840, women and youngsters under 18 made up three-quarters of the payroll.

Women and children were subjected to the same demands as men. They worked just as many hours and to begin with were not protected from night shifts or direct health hazards. And yet they received lower wages than men for the same work. That was one reason why they often had better chances than men on the employment market. The children were completely defenceless, and women showed less resistance than men to the demands of the work and of their superiors, and these virtues were held in particular esteem. Their small bodies made children more versatile: they could be sent into places which adults would not reach: up chimneys, along pit tunnels, under weaving looms.

21 An English weaving room, *c.* 1835. Even among exclusively female labour men were in command.

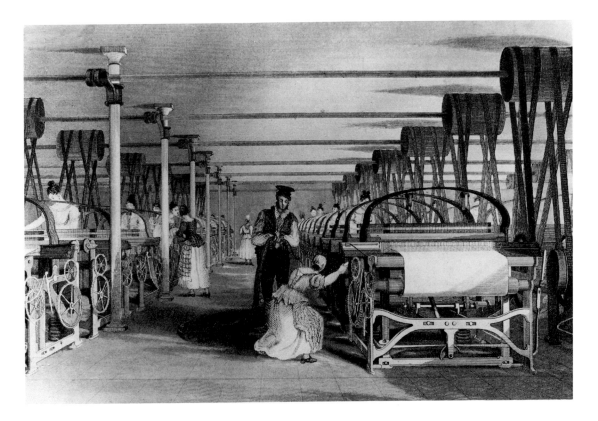

In 1834, a government adviser named Keller wrote a report for his minister which was typical of the situation in Germany. It contained his observations after a tour of Prussia's Rhineland provinces, during which he visited dozens of factories to inspect the conditions of child labour. The author regarded the employment of children not only as natural, but as a charitable blessing. Even so, he took a critical view of their one-sided occupations, the "relative perniciousness" of which was "indisputable". A pin factory employing about 100 children prompted him to comment: "Their tasks are not exactly difficult, yet some of their labours are at least tiring, and others not undangerous. This applies specifically to the casting of the heads. The skill, agility and dexterity of the children in all these labours is astonishing. The tools and machines which they operate are meaningful; the children themselves, who sit working in rows bending forwards and backwards, but all making the same movements and the same sound almost to a beat, strike the observer as if they were machines."

Keller makes similar remarks about the advantages and disadvantages of child labour from a carding tool factory: "The carding machines are used in many other factories, especially in wool and cotton manufactories; their fabrication is very delicate work, the details of which require a very sensitive touch in the fingertips, since the wire that is so densely sewn on very thick leather, the whole resembling an iron brush, must be very fine and specially prepared beforehand to this end. The most delicate labours can only be performed by children, indeed children of the female sex. The work is not unhealthy, except that the eternal monotony of it leaves the children with no prospects or foundations for the future. For common to all these mills is the unfortunate circumstance that the children employed learn nothing more than what is required for the single task entrusted to them at the factory, which in the rarest of cases is complete in itself."[21]

The demands of factory labour A theologian by the name of Paul Göhre took a temporary job as a worker in an older type of machine factory, and thanks to his attentive powers of observation we have the following description of the various demands which factories made on their labour force. Here the spectrum ranged from monotonous manual labour via complete command of all-purpose machinery to the precision work of assembly. One thing which Göhre, writing in 1891, already took for granted was that everyone involved had come to regard mechanical labour at the mill as normal.

First of all, the draughtsman had to "calculate accurately and indicate, using pin and compasses, all the holes to be bored, sur-

22 A worker at his machine, 1906. Who serves whom: the worker the machine or the machine the worker? The man has the pride and self-respect to have his portrait taken in his work environment. He has mastered the modern technology which does not belong to him, however alien and hostile it might once have seemed.

faces to be planed and rough edges to be smoothed on big and small casts alike, according to the often complicated plans which lay before him . . . We then carried the casts to be drilled, faced, cut and shaped according to the foremen's instructions . . . The drill and plane operators stand with scarcely interrupted monotony at their machines, big and small, making them drill holes and more holes, plane surfaces and more surfaces. Again and again they see the steel plane plough and flatten the surfaces, the drill dig into the cast iron as if at play. Again and again they cool the hotspots with soapy water. Again and again they sweep aside the shavings, blow away the sawdust. The only action which calls briefly for a little mental thought and attention is setting up the casts in the proper position for drilling or planing. The draughtsman demands that the holes be exactly vertical and the surfaces exactly horizontal . . .

"The work of the cutters and turners was different yet again. These two types of work, however unlike they may be in detail, resemble one another insofar as they permit the man at the slicer or lathe a greater degree of autonomy and independent action. In knocking out the superfluous iron from surfaces, corners and edges with straight, curving and circular movements, the cutter must follow the lines indicated on the drawings with the utmost accuracy, although the casts have usually been filed down beforehand to a smooth shine. This obliges him to lean forward as he sets the machine in motion, watching and directing its path with unflagging attention. It is the same with the turner, whose task is to shorten pins, shafts, cranks and levers, to shape and to

21 "Reisebericht des Geheimen Regierungsrates Keller, Berlin, an den Staatsminister von Altenstein, Berlin, vom 1. Februar 1834." Quoted from: Kuczynski, Jürgen: *Geschichte des Alltags des deutschen Volkes. Studien 3*. Berlin, 1981, pp. 261ff.

23 James Nasmyth, who invented the steam hammer, recounts that he was obliged to introduce new machinery after a long strike by his operators: "The essential feature of our modern mechanical improvements is the introduction of automatic machine tools. What a mechanic has to do now, and what every young boy can do, is not to work himself, but to supervise the fine work of the machine. The entire class of workers who depend exclusively on their dexterity are now eliminated. I used to employ four boys to each mechanic. Thanks to this new combination of machines I have reduced the number of adult men from 1,500 down to 750. The result has been a significant increase in my profit." Ten years later, in 1861, Krupp introduced the steam hammer to Germany. Here, the steam hammer "Fritz" at Krupp's.

carve grooves, cuts, incisions and points so that the pieces can be attached at once to the new machine with no more than a stroke or two from the fitter's file . . .

"The rubbers-down seemed to me to have an all too pitiable task. These two men were already advanced in years, and from six in the morning till six in the evening, day in day out, they had nothing to do but redrill by hand, in eternal monotony, the crude holes drilled by the machines, until they were clean, smooth and precisely right . . .

"The work of our fitters was a complete contrast to all this. When everything had been drilled, planed down, rounded off, cut and turned as the draughts demanded, when the screws and nuts and bolts and insertable parts had been tempered, and when the few wrought-iron and brass components were assembled, then they were able to begin their work, the actual construction of the machine."[22]

Special-purpose machinery and mass production

The boring, cutting, shaping and facing equipment, presses and stamps of early mechanical engineering and of the incipient electricals industry were in some ways very like the tools of older times. They were universal machines requiring almost the skill of a craftsman from their operators. That is why these jobs were usually filled by skilled artisans who moved to the factories. They were in great demand and often in short supply during the transition to industrial mass production.

High output made it profitable to use a series of special-purpose machines. These did not have to be operated by "factory artisans", as semi-skilled labour was adequate. Two different reactions to this rationalization process are expressed in a letter dated 1872 from the industrialist Werner von Siemens and in the recollections of a Siemens foreman named Jacobi. "Business is so diverse and complex that it has become too big, and the shortage of workers is simply intolerable. We now have empty halls in abundance but can find no workers to fill them. How can anyone meet deadlines under those conditions? We have been seeking zealously for the last year to copy the Americans and do everything with special-purpose machinery, so that we can make good products even with poor workers . . . Now everybody is convinced that our future salvation rests in applying the American methods and that we should alter our entire management in that sense. In future our function should be restricted to mass production. That way we shall be able to satisfy any demand and defeat any competition!" writes Werner von Siemens.[23] But workers who had learnt their skills under the crafts system saw things differently. They resisted the introduction of special-purpose machinery for a long time, and with it the devaluation of their labour qualifications: "As common workers for the most part—and where possible of course the old ones—had to learn how to use the machines and as they were all then paid according to piece rates, the so-called 'American halls' soon became a target of hefty socialist at-

tack. People just did not like the rapid acceleration in their work. It took a long time for the old artisans in the workshop to accept things," recalls Jacobi.[24]

The mass product

In the craft economy, every product had been unique, usually tailored to meet the customer's needs, but the big factories bowed to the laws of series production. Vast quantities of completely identical commodities were now turned out accurately, thanks to expanding markets, free trade, and huge capital investments in the form of raw materials, factories, machines, plant, fittings and long payrolls. Coarse estimates, haggling and bargaining, and arbitrary decisions gave way to standard weights and measures, scientifically defined rules, technical norms and, by the same token, fixed prices, wages and working hours. Modern technology called for binding yardsticks and regulations.

In craft, the separate components did not take final shape until they were fitted together in the ultimate product. This even applied to clocks, mills and looms. It was the same in the early days of mechanical engineering. But that was no way to approach large series of intricate products. The components that would be assembled had to be prefabricated very accurately. They were supplied by other factories, and increasingly from abroad. Observing technical standards and rules was just as much an everyday necessity as weighing, measuring, and testing to ensure that each product conformed to requirements of standard or type. Without these basic procedures in industrial co-operation there would be no guarantees for smooth production or appropriate wares.

It must have been totally alien to the mentality of the small-scale commodity producer to observe industry's technological capacity for reproducing large quantities of identical objects, to see how labour was subjected to strict norms and standards with no variety in content to the outsider's eye, and to watch the rich versatility of craft life being levelled down to a mass of industrial labour. Petty-bourgeois critics of industrial capitalism tended to condemn the impoverishment and one-sided monotony they saw everywhere as a loss. The working-class movement pointed out that if industrial productivity was rising all the time, then proletarians had a right to claim better living standards, but this argument was countered by gruesome images of egalitarian existence: masses of identical human beings would not only work to the same patterns, but live in the same houses, eat the same food, wear the same clothes and ultimately think identical thoughts and feel identical emotions.

22 Göhre, Paul: *Drei Monate Fabrikarbeiter und Handwerksbursche. Eine praktische Studie.* Leipzig, 1891, pp. 48–51.

23 "Werner von Siemens: Letter of 13 March 1872," in: *Werner Siemens.* Berlin, 1916, p. 354.

24 From the memoirs of the foreman Jacobi (Werner von Siemens-Institut Munich). Quoted from: Kocka, Jürgen: *Unternehmensverwaltung und Angestelltenschaft am Beispiel Siemens 1847–1914.* Stuttgart, 1969, p. 126.

24 Big industry meant mass production for ever-expanding markets that were waiting to be captured. This chromolithograph shows a messenger boy shouting the latest information, but as a tool of publicity he was already being replaced by a whole new industry: advertising.

Most sensitive observers of industry's destructive effects were not perspicacious enough to analyze the cultural potential and realize that the uniformity could give birth to completely new opportunities for diversity. That was a hope cherished by the workers. Naturally, they could not share the naive and ruthless optimism of the industrial magnates, for they were on the exploited end of the process and frequently had to bear the personal costs of progress. Besides, many had still not come to terms morally with the disadvantage that their own unique skills as producers were no longer required, so that they could now be replaced by any Tom, Dick or Harry. Nevertheless, the proletarians had a vested interest in stable working and living conditions that were clearly regulated, and standards that would at least remain the same, if not improve. Industrial society offered a new security: factory work was basically similar, wages differed little and had a recognizable value.

Moreover, the goods on sale were cheaper, more reliable and regularly available. Many former luxury articles, such as sugar and coffee, pens and paper, newspapers and books, mirrors and furniture, and numerous other things were no longer so rare among working people. Industrial technology was even creating more and more consumer goods which workers were able to afford as a result of mass production. Examples were lamps, watches and clocks, sewing machines and bicycles.

25 On 1 May 1851 Queen Victoria opened an "industrial exhibition of all nations". This was the first time that capital had put itself on ceremonial display. 14,000 companies vaunted their prowess in 1851. By the second World Exhibition in Paris in 1867 their numbers had risen to 50,000. The biggest exposition of this kind was held in Philadelphia in 1876 to commemorate the Centenary of the United States of America. 130,000 visitors flocked to hear the President open the event.

26 The aim of the Vienna World Exhibition in 1873 was "to promote the cultural life of the day and a complete representation of the industrial economy and its further progress".

World Exhibitions Because of the competition, a firm or a trademark had to establish its reputation among the public, promoting the image of an entrepreneur, technician or inventor, and identifying itself by means of the commodities it offered. The first major exhibition of such wares was held in 1798 on the Champ de Mars in Paris, but was still devoted predominantly to everyday articles from household innovations to clocks, globes and waxen flowers, although there were also steam power units and textile machines on display.

There was no event which projected the new working environment of the industrial proletariat better than the World Exhibitions, the first of which took place in London in 1851. "This great world congress of products and producers . . . by displaying, narrowly confined within a small space, the whole mass of the productive forces of modern industry"[25], demonstrated the economic potential of the industrial bourgeoisie, and also their pretensions to power. Yet at the same time the industrial plant on view—printing and textile machinery, steam hammers and railway telegraphy—showed what complicated apparatus the workers had under their daily command. The sheer quantity of the industrial goods exhibited, and their low price, illustrated the labour potential of the industrial proletariat.

The Exhibition Hall itself, a crystal palace of iron and glass in London's Hyde Park that had been designed, fabricated and assembled in only eight months, was an example to the world of the colossal tasks which proletarians, working to a co-ordinated plan involving production, transport, construction and installation, were capable of completing in a very short period. Over six million inquisitive visitors poured into the Crystal Palace between 1 May and 15 October, and to the majority it naturally symbolized the power and inventiveness of the industrialists. It only occurred to the socialists among them that here amid the collection of machines and products a material had been created "for the building of a new society . . . At a future exhibition the bourgeois will perhaps no longer figure as owners of these productive forces but only as their ciceroni."[26]

To begin with, there were few workers among the visitors, even on Mondays to Thursdays, which were cheaper. Few firms followed the example set by the Admiralty, which gave its dockers a week's leave for the purpose. It was only on later occasions that more workers took advantage of the cheap excursions organized by the railway companies in conjunction with exhibition shareholders. Governments and entrepreneurs on the Continent had not had the courage to send working-class delegations to this first exhibition so soon after the Revolution of 1848/49.

But 1851 in London was just the beginning. World Exhibitions have caught the human imagination for over a century. No work of art ever proved so attractive as aluminium, the gas engine, aniline dyes, the typewriter and sewing machine, the lift, telephone, car, camera, ice-cream machine, electric floodlight, phonograph, elevated railway or escalator. Here was proof that applied science could outwit nature. "Prometheus Unbound" was evident in technological change and industrial development. Whatever the trade, the transition from "manufacere" to "macchinofacere", from manual to mechanical labour, was an exciting process for people of all social strata.

How Industrial Capital Moulded
the Wage Labourer

Industrial labour had imposed a totally new kind of discipline on the workforce. Of course, the toiling populace had always been expected to be obedient, dutiful, well-behaved and ready to play an unquestioning role in the production process. Their work was strictly regulated by the guild, the family as a productive unit, the abbey, estate, poorhouse or workhouse, and anyone who failed to accept the rules could depend on severe sanctions. And yet human nature had always been taken into account. Individuals set their own pace and output and usually saw the direct results of their effort. Ultimately, too, provisions were made for anyone unable to work.

The transition to capitalism changed all that. Public opinion now regarded poverty as the fault of the victim. Work became a duty. Productive activity was rated higher than leisure and enjoyment. People were expected to provide for their upkeep by their own endeavours. The spectrum of disciplinary measures ranged from the religious commandments of a Protestant work ethic, the pangs of hunger and pressure to take work in a manufactory, via factory regulations, overseers and notices advertising the virtuous use of machines and time, right across to the worker's own internalization of this new behaviour code.

In Britain, Enclosure and the Poor Laws had laid unique historical foundations: paupers were not to be maintained by the labour of others under penalty of death. In 1791 the French National Assembly voted through a law proposed by the member Le Chapelier, who represented the interests of the wealthy bourgeoisie, prohibiting strikes and associations and making work compulsory.

Diligence prevailed in its capitalist form against a backcloth of starvation and sweat, torments and tears. The modern factory

25 Marx, Karl, and Friedrich Engels in *Review* (May to October 1850), in: MECW/10/500.
26 *Ibid.*

which now set the tone did not mean simply that workers were recompensed in the form of wages: a new approach to life and to work was developing. Its features were disciplined labour, hard work, acquiescence to the regime, and a desire for impressive performance. At first labour power was used extensively, but as time went by more intensive forms were adopted. If workers wanted to keep their jobs, they had to concentrate harder, invest greater speed and accuracy—and above all do more work.

Discipline, co-operation and organization had been drummed into the proletariat by capitalism using external coercion, competition and more subtle methods, and what they had learnt at the factory gradually became a habit. Workers knew how to hit back successfully with the tools that had been forced upon them. Conscious self-discipline and dependable labour held the seeds of proletarian superiority. The working class had thus acquired important aspects of its confidence and culture.

Work enforcement in manufacturing days The new labour discipline had its roots in abbey statutes, villenage, guild regulations and the military drill of mercenary armies. It began to evolve in the 14th and 15th centuries, when competition sprang up in Italy, Flanders and England between the small producers of the cloth-making guilds on the one hand, and a network of agents and scattered manufactories on the other. Bankrupt chief wardens, unemployed journeymen, and jobless rural artisans fell prey to the economic pressure of commercial capital, which worked these wage slaves to the bone. But it was not for another 100 years at least that manufacture, as a system of co-operation based on division of labour, was really born.

The larger workshops were often obliged to resort to force in order to acquire enough artisans. But it was not only the press gangs that provoked hands to resist or flee. Craftsmen objected to the very idea of dividing and restructuring their labour and equated the whole business with a treadmill or galley of slaves. They were told how fast to work and how much to produce. Again and again, the workers in the manufactories rejected these coercive regulations. In the late 17th century France was already witnessing numerous strikes, acts of sabotage, pilfering and demonstration. Workers everywhere were obliged to better their situation by means of theft and deception. Riots and rebellions were commonplace. Colbert, Minister of Finance to Louis XIV, set up a special economic police force, responsible for law and order in the manufactories. Overseers made sure that the workers observed their hours and produced sufficient articles to adequate standard. Violating the rules could mean spending your free days in prison.

The situation varied, however, from one country to the next, for the capitalists were still not influential enough to assume control over the whole lives of these early proletarians. In Catholic countries the ecclesiastical calendar was still fully observed, and the obsession with work in Lutheran, Calvinist and Pietist thinking

was unknown. In 18th-century England, workers at the manufactories usually only appeared four days a week. If they had earned enough money, then they did not see "sufficient reason that they should work the other two days for the capitalist"[27]. In 1783, Frederick II of Prussia issued an edict banning "St. Monday", and in England, too, there were rigorous measures to round up workers to come in on that day. In France and other Catholic countries, Church holidays were soon considerably reduced. But it was not until the era of large-scale industry that capital really "succeeded in seizing for itself, by the payment of the weekly value of labour power, the whole week of the labourer"[28], which meant that strict labour discipline could be enforced every day.

The factory as a new working environment People who arrived from the countryside to take a factory job were astounded at first by the sight of dozens or hundreds of men and women working their countless machines to a common purpose. Even to a journeyman, homeworker or manufactory hand, the size of the plant was gigantic and the pace of labour incredible. Contemporary accounts often refer to the factory as an artificial organism demanding the unprecedented subjugation of the individual. Life changed radically. Johann Eberhard Dewald, a journeyman who took employment at a tanning factory in 1837, wrote from

27 The king decrees an end to Saint Monday. A resolute policy on labour time erased many Church holidays and also Monday truancy. The interests of capital and the pressures of technology prevailed against the common rights of workers.

EDICT,

wegen

Abstellung einiger Mißbräuche

besonders

des sogenandten

Blauen Montages

bey

den Handwerkern.

De Dato Berlin, den 24. Martii 1783.

Gedruckt bey George Jacob Decker, Königl. Hofbuchdrucker.

Prague lamenting the transformation: "But what was new to me and I had never come across was that I was not to lodge with the master. And an awkward business it would have been, too, finding common lodgings for all the journeymen at Pollak's factory, especially as not a few were married and had children. In fact, in a factory like this one, things are altogether different from in the shop of a craftsmaster, and there is no sticking together among the journeymen. Each goes his own way and does not spare much thought to the others. Behaviour worthy of a guild is not to be found among any of my colleagues, and there is no company to be kept as among decent journeymen. Moreover, I do not like the work, for everyone must perform the same task all the long day, and so loses sight of the whole. I suppose that is how things must be in a factory, yet I cannot put my heart into it and always feel I am only half pursuing my trade. For that reason I hoped to leave again soon."[29]

Loss of the familiar, comprehensible order is clearly a cause for lament. Even though "Pollak's factory" was by nature still more or less a manufactory, journeyman Dewald found it hard to find his feet in this new mode of production. Fifty years later the socially committed curate Paul Göhre returned from his excursion into the proletarian world with quite different impressions. He actually compared the ironware factory on the outskirts of the German town Chemnitz where he worked briefly in 1890 to a church. Like God's house, the factory was a place where large numbers of people were taught to behave, where they were expected to acquiesce and subjugate their own feelings, an institution of power and wealth. Whereas the church had its sacristy, wrote Göhre, here there was the engine room with a "stone monster" issuing forth its tremendous energies across the whole floor and causing dozens of powerful machines and hundreds of workers to move. A great chimney soared aloft on one side. Mighty sounds vibrated incessantly through the hall: not chiming bells or organ pipes, but fitters hammering and filing, machines creaking and pounding, wheels turning and squeaking.

"At the windows along the two long walls stood the fitters' vices; by the pillars which supported the galleries, where one could always find space and a half-sufficient light, were instruments big and small; the biggest, a huge drill, lay right across the entire hall . . . Under the ceilings formed by the galleries ran the long shafts which spun constantly, driven by the steam engine, feeding the tools via belt pulleys and connecting driving belts, all with the force of unceasing motion . . . This was the workplace of a hundred and twenty to a hundred and fifty people as they went about their daily duties, bare, desolate, black, devoid of all comfort, shattered by a never-ending nerve-racking din of harshly mingling tones. And yet there was a kind of nobility and poetry about it . . . the poetry of a grandiose and intricate mechanism running steadily and tirelessly, the nobility of human labour, performed here day in day out at a single spot by over a hundred people in their struggle for bread, life and enjoyment."[30]

28 A Berlin factory. The architecture behind the decorative façade met all the demands of modern production.

27 Marx, Karl: *Capital*. Vol. 1. Moscow, 1971, p. 260.
28 *Ibid*.
29 *Biedermeier auf Walze. Aufzeichnungen und Briefe des Handwerksburschen Johann Eberhard Dewald, 1836–1838*. Ed. by G. M. Hofmann. Berlin, 1936, p. 101f.
30 Göhre, Paul: *Drei Monate Fabrikarbeiter und Handwerksbursche. Eine praktische Studie*. Leipzig, 1891, pp. 42ff.

Machines as teachers Manual work and the division of craft labour soon imposed limits on rising productivity, so that however keen the exploitation, however strict the control, and however long the working day, output could not increase, even with additional hands and the occasional use of simple machines. Capital was greedy for more labour, but its appetite could no longer be satisfied. There was only one solution: overcoming the inherent restrictions of manual labour called for mechanization, a transition to mechanized production, the application of modern science to technology and organization. This industrial mode enabled more goods to be produced more cheaply.

Until then human labourers had moulded natural materials with the assistance of tools which effectively reinforced their own energies, but now the tools were operated by machine. Human labour was only required to attend, service, monitor and carry out any other functions which the machines themselves could not perform. The new machines were self-actors, automata, which enabled workers for the first time to stand "alongside" the direct production process. They no longer needed to propel their tools with their own bodily force; their task now was to supervise and control a device that was powered by technology.

Workers were no longer subjected to the same physical strains, but instead they had to exert themselves in a new way. A machine, particularly a processing machine, was not merely more economical: it kept going until it wore out, never feeling hungry, thirsty, tired or simply unwilling, and it forced the human beings who worked around it to follow suit. They had to adopt an "artificial" rhythm, concentrate harder, observe a more rigid schedule, accept a new kind of work, integrating themselves into an inflexible pattern which demanded the unaccustomed suppression of their own inclinations. The traditional methods of bullying and threats were not going to achieve that. From the factory-owners' point of view workers had to be cured of messy habits, unmethodical working techniques, carelessness, laziness, bad timekeeping, lackadaisical performance and other such vices. Overseers alone could not exercise adequate control. There was a need for general "factory rules" which did not specify precise instructions for every situation as under pre-industrial conditions.

The authority of the machine—and of the wage system—actually proved to be far more effective. Deficiencies could no longer be patched over by hand, and working off lost hours no longer made up for a stoppage. Every infringement of the factory rules was immediately apparent and the penalties ranged from fines and docked wages to lock-outs and dismissals. A worker risked life and limb by not concentrating on the machine's movements. A tool could always be laid aside, but a machine could not simply be stopped and started in accordance with arbitrary decisions. Anyone who failed to observe the regulations fell literally into the works, under open transmissions, stamps, mechanical levers, presses and rollers. Money, time and technology all imposed pressures, and combined with that all-pervasive fear of making the wrong move they created a discipline quite unlike that of former times.

29 The machine room at Richard Hartmann's in Chemnitz (now Karl-Marx-Stadt). The Industrial Revolution gave birth to large-scale industry as a new technical and material basis for society. There is a stark contrast between productive methods and human labour on this shop floor and the scene in the manufacturing workshop.

30 "The Iron Rolling Mill." One of the earliest great artistic impressions of the industrial world of labour. Painting by Adolph Menzel, 1875.

31/32 Machines tamed the labourer. Workers could neither stop them nor afford to make superfluous gestures. Telling jokes and stories, singing and whistling were strictly forbidden at work. Anyway the noise of the factory and the pressure to work fast were prohibitive.

Time for a break To begin with, industrialists had a distinct preference for workers who clocked in on time and then worked as long as they possibly could for the lowest wages conceivable. As time passed, however, it became clear that there were limits to extensive use of labour power of this kind. Humans and machines evidently did not follow the same rhythms. All attempts to adapt the producers to the merciless march of the machines over a longer period of time were doomed to failure. The working day of 14 to 16 hours which was not uncommon in early years made several lengthy breaks necessary. As the equipment grew more expensive, so these interruptions became costlier, hindering efficient utilization of the plant.

This had never been regarded as a problem in pre-industrial circumstances. Taking a rest, a break or a lunchtime nap were established rights. Work was also interrupted for bad weather, dusk, exhaustion of natural energy reserves, and many other reasons. That was the mentality which the first generation of workers brought with them to the factories. At first the owners were obliged to accept the fact. They merely tried to organize standard breaktimes, restrict excessive stoppages, and ensure a minimum of interaction and teamwork among the workforce.

Opposing interests were expressed in the conflict over work times. Whereas the workers needed rest to restore their modest energy, and therefore insisted on their right to breaks, the factory-owner had a crucial interest in "closer filling up of the pores of the working-day"[31]. Labour intensification was essential to efficient management. The employers had realized by this stage— even backing their observations up with experiments—that with advanced technology workers could be induced to produce more in less time. If the excessively long working day was reduced somewhat, breaks could be disposed of almost entirely, creating a period of pure, tense performance.

By the same token, this intensive exploitation of labour power prompted the trade unions to demand a legally enforced reduction in the working day. Otherwise non-working hours would be nowhere near sufficient to replenish spent energies.

A provisional solution was found by compromise. Capital agreed to a law limiting the working day and in return won a free hand to introduce every conceivable productivity-raising measure within the factory. Labour representatives had obtained a quantity of free time after work which employees were able to spend as they chose.

This new situation was reflected in a changed attitude to breaks. Proletarians no longer insisted on long breaks, in fact

31 Marx, Karl: *Capital*. Vol. 1. Moscow, 1971, p. 386.

they even called for restrictions. In their view, long interruptions only lengthened the working day and reduced the spare time which they had come to value so deeply. Social reformers interpreted this as a sign that class antagonism was dying out. Both parties stood to gain because "high wages and short working hours went hand in hand with far more intensive performance,"[32] wrote the social politician Lujo Brentano. But reciprocal concessions did not blind either side to the realities. It was obvious that shorter breaks in work and more differentiated rewards, as the piece rate system began to spread, ultimately ensured that workers were truly being squeezed of all their energy. New forms of labour organization curtailed any idling and dawdling, chats between workmates and distractions of whatever kind. Even though certain breaks had to be respected and maintained as part of social labour time, they were taken into precise account as a cost factor.

Punctuality "Time is money", said the factory-owners, and they meant more than the formality of measuring the working day with a stopwatch and hooter. For one thing, the workers kept an eye on one another to make sure that no one took time out at the others' expense, especially during shift changes, at the conveyor belt, and when the team was being paid piece rates. For another, there were supervisory staff whose task was to assert pressure and discipline.

One Berlin worker describes her experiences in a letter: "In 1898 the light bulb factory moved to Helmholtzstrasse in Charlottenburg. Our manager at the time, *Herr* Remané, had his room on the ground floor, and he often used to be standing there at seven in the morning before hours began, enjoying the sight of the workforce, which was then about 400 men and women, hurrying to start their labour punctually. Once I came five minutes late, and a fierce pounding at the window instructed me to come to *Herr* Remané to be reprimanded. The gist of it was: it was disgraceful not to start work on time, anyway it was not worth coming five minutes late, next time I ought to have a proper lie in, and he hoped nothing of the kind would happen again. I apologized that I had to come from the south-west of the city, taking the overhead railway from the station Hallisches Tor to Zoo, and walking the rest of the way. Nonsense, came the answer, I come from Tempelhof by bicycle and I am punctual . . . One day I was going past the engine room when I heard *Herr* Remané scolding. The minders had provoked his displeasure, for they were standing ready to leave the room before the bell had rung. I heard *Herr* Remané say: If I ever catch you again, you can all fetch your cards."[33]

32 Brentano, Lujo: *Über das Verhältnis von Arbeitslohn und Arbeitszeit zur Arbeitsleistung.* 2nd, completely revised edition. Leipzig, 1913, p.26.
33 Osram-Archiv 0.27, Stadtarchiv der Hauptstadt der DDR, Berlin.

33 Works canteen, *c.* 1895. Everyone needs a break, but when and how long did not depend on how tired, hungry or thirsty a worker was: clocks, bells and hooters gave the order.

34 A workmeter. Time-clocks re-placed overseers. Unbroken automat-ic monitoring was the ideal. The "psychograph" was attached to machines like a tachometer, gauging output at all times.

35 Lunch break at AEG. Hundreds of workers left the factory within the space of a few minutes for a hot meal at home or in the pub. Photo of 1906.

Factory Sergeant-Majors A factory resembled the Church or Army with its strict hierarchy, and the foreman had a special role to play. He asserted shop-floor discipline and distributed the work, but he was also the intermediary between the owners and the workers. "Although they often came from simple working-class origins, yet rarely from the same factory, their social superiority was clear for all to see, both during working hours and particularly outside. They did not wear proper working clothes but, even during working hours, the usual fashionable jacket, tie and white shirt. They were the link between the workers and the higher-ranking officials in the establishment up to the directors; they are—I know of no better comparison—the factory sergeant-majors. They perform the detailed technical management of the factory, with a guiding responsibility to the directors in these matters and as regards the character of each individual worker; they kept a check on all the workers and, more important, influenced the hourly wage and specifically the piece rate which each would get. They helped determine the pace of the work and it lay in their power to ensure, when business was poor, that hands were kept on and not dismissed. If reductions really were made, here again they would have a say in who should go; finally they were in a position to remove many a badly formed cast inconspicuously

and to cover up for bungling. All in all, as far as both the workers and the directors were concerned, they were the most important people in the factory . . ."[34]

Cultivating needs Efficient organization, strict controls and zealous overseers may have been important factors in maintaining a disciplined labour force, but the key motive for this general diligence was to be found outside the factory. Once it was established everywhere that the only way for people without property to acquire the means of existence was by paying for them with money, need became the decisive force behind regular attendance at work.

This reflects the dual nature of capital. On the one hand, a capitalist expects his own workers to be thrifty and content with poor wages. On the other, workers should be acquisitive consumers who were encouraged to spend as much as possible on the goods which the market offers them. Karl Marx was referring to just this dual nature of capital when he wrote of its "civilizing effect". This view was later echoed by bourgeois social politicians: "The best worker in the world today is the one with the greatest needs."[35] Practical experience had shown often enough by this time that whenever capital was confronted with relatively unde-

36 During the First World War many skilled workers acquired overseer status in the arms factories. They did not have to fight at the front and their wages did not fall quickly. Many of them adopted the airs of a small employer, sporting a collar and tie to supervise prisoners of war, unskilled workers or women. AEG in Berlin hired Turks as cheap labour. Photo *c.* 1915.

manding workers and attempted to discipline them into steady employment, orders, laws, whips, factory regulations, overseers and stop-clocks all failed miserably. The only answer was to nurture previously unknown needs and lure these people away from their simple mode of living.

There is a classic and highly tendentious formulation of this process in the memoirs of the German inventor and industrialist Werner von Siemens. He describes a visit to his brother and business partner in the Caucasus, where it was proving repeatedly difficult to find reliable workers among the local population who would appear at the factory every day. Some of the people were nomadic, others lived in mud huts, and they were not prepared to bow to the severe labour discipline. "As the people there have very modest needs in life, they have no reason to work much. If they have earned enough money to guarantee their upkeep for a number of weeks, they stop working and rest. The only answer so far has been to accustom these people to needs which can only be satisfied by constant work. The lever to this was the innate desire of the female sex for an agreeable family life and their easily aroused vanity and dressiness. Once a number of simple workers' houses had been built and a few working couples had been found to live there, the women soon took pleasure in the greater comfort and pleasantness of these homes. It suited the menfolk, too, that they did not constantly have to patch their roofs against the rain. Arrangements were then made for the women to purchase all kinds of little gadgets to make domestic life more comfortable and themselves more attractive to their husbands. They soon developed a taste for carpets and mirrors, improved their toilette, in short, acquired needs which their husbands, who were also quite happy with the situation, were now obliged to satisfy. This aroused the envy of the women still dwelling in caves, so it did not take long before there was a universal clamour for the workers' houses, which of course meant having to build homes for all permanent workers. I can only recommend most emphatically that we should proceed the same way in realizing our colonial aspirations. A man without needs is hostile to all civilized development. He will never be the grateful recipient of social and religious civilization until needs have been aroused in him and until he is accustomed to working for their fulfilment."[36]

What wages mean to the worker   Siemens's idyllic interpretation of colonial exploitation contains some observations of a fundamental kind. They indicate the cultural potential implied in developing those needs which preserved the worker's dependence on capital. This dependence was as wide-ranging as the needs which bred it: work could vouchsafe the bare necessities of existence, or it could broaden the horizons of a person's needs and enjoyment substantially, by means of a secure wage as big as capital was prepared to offer.

So it was that workers found themselves caught up in a strange relationship with capital: they themselves were obliged to fight for the right to exploited employment. Any other demands would have lain outside the realm of the capitalist market and the bourgeois view of justice. A few craftsmen managed to build their small firms into industrial enterprises, but journeymen rarely found a path to success. There were isolated cases of dishwashers becoming millionaires, but the mass of workers simply had to accept any job they could get, toil and sweat, put up a decent showing for their pains, obey the will of the machine and the instructions of their superiors, and go back to the factory day by day if the wages were all right. Work became the proletarian's prime need, simply because there was no option. Idleness was intolerable because it cost money to eat sufficiently, keep a roof over one's head, raise children, stay healthy, acquire some education, indulge in a little pleasure and join any organizations. In the long run, some kind of regular wage was essential.

Your pay and your pride   "The dull compulsion of economic relations," wrote Karl Marx, sealed "the subjection of the labourer to the capitalist."[37] At the same time, it made him assert himself within this dependent situation. Nobody would achieve much single-handed. Associations of workers formed in factories and trades to win a fitting recompense for their labours.

Writer Georg Weerth provides an early account of how organized working-class struggle influenced the labourers' own sense of identity and their attitudes towards the level of their wages and the masters who paid them. He went to England in 1843 as a clerk for a German textile company, and was able to draw on a wealth of experience in comparing the view of British proletarians with that of their German contemporaries. The British workers already looked back upon several decades of trade-union campaigning for better wages and a fixed working day. They had organized mass strikes and drafted a political manifesto of their own in the form of the People's Charter of 1838. Marx was later to call "the English factory workers" the "champions . . . of the modern working class generally"[38].

The German states were backward industrially, and there was no practical movement to match this as yet. Not surprisingly, the awareness of the German workers lagged behind, too. "The payment of wages is always a solemn moment in the factories. The factory-owners and factory overseers stand behind the tables, looking down with dark gravity and a certain dignified contempt on the indistinguishable ragged figures who step up to the table one after the other to take their trivial reward for the week's labour, and probably even to thank their masters for paying them

---

34 Göhre, Paul: *Drei Monate Fabrikarbeiter und Handwerksbursche. Eine praktische Studie*. Leipzig, 1891, p. 83.

35 Schulze-Gävernitz, Gerhart von: *Der Grossbetrieb—ein wirtschaftlicher und socialer Fortschritt*. Leipzig, 1892, p. 65.

36 Siemens, Werner von: *Lebenserinnerungen*. Berlin, 1892, p. 216.

37 Marx, Karl: *Capital*. Vol. 1. Moscow, 1971, p. 689.

38 *Ibid.*, p. 283.

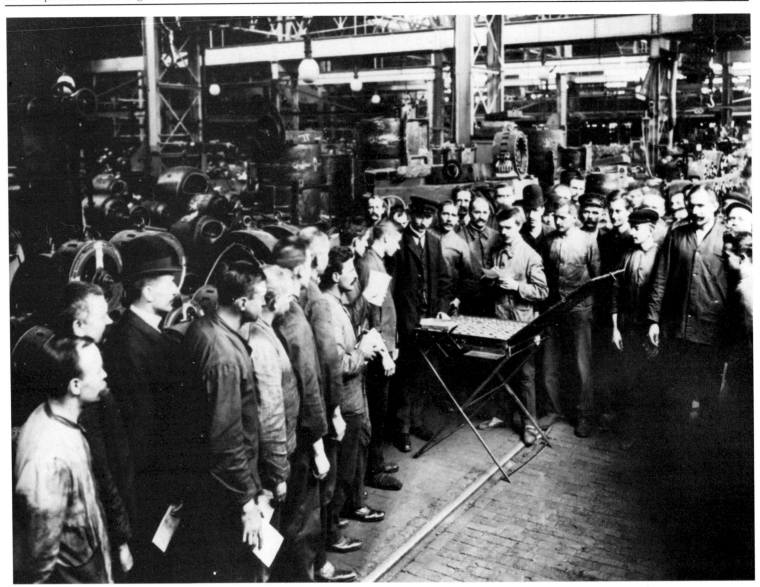

37 Payday at AEG, Berlin, 1911. Whether workers were on piece rates or an hourly wage, their pay was based on the value of labour power, not the value of the product. Wage systems were elaborated to spur the workers on and disguise their exploitation. Even so, payday was a cause for celebration.

as poorly as possible. Only in England, where we often witnessed the payment of wages, the whole transaction assumes a more positive air for the worker: the English proletariat are much more conscious than in any other country of their value in relation to the bourgeoisie. They know that the bosses cannot survive without the workers and that in the near future the hour will strike for these two classes to settle their accounts more precisely. And so most English workers step in front of their masters with a curt pride, with no greeting, no flicker of expression, stiff and serious. They watch the money being counted out coin by coin, check it over, sweep it slowly and deliberately into the other hand, turn on their heels without a word of gratitude or greeting, and leave the room as stiff, as serious, as proud as they were upon entering.

"In Germany, of course, the business is completely different, and the whole scene still bears the marks of the Middle Ages; in our country, the worker lives in fear of his master, and it is rare for the poor devil to forget to thank him profusely for the few pennies his labours have deserved."[39]

Ford and efficiency. In the latter half of the 19th century, capitalists in all the industrial countries had begun to discover the worker as a consumer with a wallet. There were commercial prospects in everything: food, spirits, cotton, light bulbs, bicycles, newspapers, rented accommodation. But no one was as thorough or as successful as Henry Ford in using this as a lever to boost his labourers' dedication to their labour. When he introduced the first conveyor belt into the car industry in Detroit in 1911, he was considering working-class needs on two counts. Firstly, the assembly line only paid off with real mass production. But the luxury cars manufactured hitherto had been aimed at an exclusive circle of customers. So Ford adapted his output to utility vehicles within the financial reach of the farmers and rural and urban workers who composed over 80 per cent of the United States' population. Secondly, he was obliged to pay relatively high wages in order to obtain disciplined workers for challenging but monotonous labour. He hoped that these wages would enable them to dream of owning their own car. "One of the difficulties in Europe is that the workman is not expected to buy what he makes."[40] In his view, this meant failing to take advantage of the most effective element in capitalist labour discipline, whereby workers internalize the external pressures on them to work hard and set themselves the aims of finding jobs, earning well and being able to afford as much as possible. "Efficiency is merely the doing of work in the best way you know rather than in the worst way . . . It is the training of the worker and the giving to him of power so that he may earn more and live more comfortably. The

39 Weerth, Georg: *Fragment eines Romans*, in: *Sämtliche Werke*. Ed. by Bruno Kaiser. Vol. 2. Berlin, 1956, p. 226.
40 Ford, Henry: *Today and Tomorrow*. In collaboration with Samuel Crowther. London, 1926, p. 154.

38 The pressure of technology based on new management methods: the Ford assembly line. The pressure of needs was also new, with workers part of the financial equation in their role as consumers of cheap mass products. Photo of 1913.

39 Modern office equipment gave many women access to the world of work. This big London office around 1900 adopted similar regulations to a factory.

40 Manchester building site, *c*. 1895. A brick and a slap of mortar: heavy manual work prevailed in construction for years, although in 1851 the construction of the Crystal Palace in London, a gigantic structure of iron and glass, had demonstrated a new kind of technology.

41 Carpenters at a topping-off ceremony in Hamburg, 1912. Carpenters belonged to the labour aristocracy. The clothing is only one aspect of their strong guild traditions. The building boom before 1914 supplied them with constant, well-paid work. The Woodworkers' Union was one of the richest and most influential in Germany.

Chinese coolie working through long hours for a few cents a day is not happier than the American workman with his own home and automobile. The one is a slave, the other is a free man."[41]

Factory boss Henry Ford was able to claim this with the full pathos of conviction because the relatively high wages he paid did not damage his profits. He had introduced the conveyor-belt system because of the pressures of competition, and it had supplied him with a new, technological means to discipline his labour. He needed highly motivated workers willing to achieve big outputs in order to carry out his motto: Make the most of your power, your material and your time![42]

From rule of thumb to a "scientific" system of sweating

Scientific management calculated everything in economic terms and investigated all the costs which arose in production. Its main aim was optimum utilization of human labour power. Whereas it was a relatively easy matter to quantify expenditure on raw materials, energy, machinery, storage and transport, the human factor was more difficult to pin down. There were too many unknowns affecting the supply of human energy, the specific, disciplined work process, the speed and precision of human actions. It had not yet been ascertained just how much tension and stamina could be expected of the labourer, how quickly he or she would tire and how long was required to recover. Knowledge rested solely on practical experience.

Frederick W. Taylor, an American engineer, manager and future business consultant, opened up new horizons. In 1903 he published his pioneering work *A Piece-Rate System*, outlining rules for scientific management which he himself had tried out and which facilitated the calculation of the human factor in production. The principles involved were very simple, but added together they restricted the little remaining autonomy of the machine operator, and whatever opportunity there still was for sidestepping discipline, to such an extent that the intensity of labour could be directly calculated and organized.

Essentially, Taylor tackled rational labour on four fronts. To begin with, the chronological sequence of every work process and the human actions required followed hard and fast rules. Unnecessary movements, which wasted both time and energy, had been discovered on film and were subsequently eliminated. Secondly, every worker was matched to the most suitable job, with direct training in the most rational approach. Thirdly, bonuses were paid for speed and precise observation of instructions. The prospects of reward proved to be a far more effective disciplinary measure than the fines listed in old-style factory regulations. Fi-

41 Ford, Henry: *Today and Tomorrow*. In collaboration with Samuel Crowther. London, 1926, p. 154.
42 *Ibid.*, p. 160.
43 Lenin, Vladimir Ilyich: "A 'scientific' system of sweating," in: *Collected Works*. Vol. 18. Moscow, 1963, pp. 594–95.

42 A factory manager's office in 1910. The industrious proletarian and the capitalist at the helm.

nally, there was a rigorous demarcation between practical and mental labour, with all thought removed from the production process. Of course, this created a certain "idiocy of factory work" and also an army of industrial office workers. However, Taylor did not succeed in undermining the production worker's specific mode of thinking: in the long run, in fact, he inadvertently set it rolling.

This "'scientific' system of sweating"[43] introduced a new element into capitalist labour discipline. Accounts and progress reports, norms, timekeeping, target contests, incentives and unconditional acquiescence during the working day were no longer dependent on the whims of owners or labourers. The old methods had been based heavily on experience, and now they were being replaced by rational, scientific principles. In this sense, although Taylor served the interests of capital with this ruthless exploitation of the working class, he was also paving the way for a major cultural transformation. It was now possible to deduce the most economic and productive methods of working and to apply these findings universally. It was the birth of the modern labour sciences.

The wage ruse Wage systems were effective disciplinary tools devised to boost productivity. Over the various stages of capitalism, money and competition have assumed different forms in order to exert pressure on workers to invest greater effort in their labours, always bearing in mind the specific needs of working-class life.

The advent of money wages signified a big cultural change. It was the first time in history that working people had an equivalent at their disposal which, at least in the abstract, entitled them to whatever was on offer. Admittedly, to begin with it was just enough to ensure a meagre existence, but a proletarian craving had been aroused to afford more. And soon enough the market was offering almost anything for cash.

In pre-industrial times it was customary to pay for labour in kind, with "free" board and lodging. Cash was the exception. Indeed, early factory-owners tried to limit their workers' freedom of movement by setting up truck and cottage systems, paying a portion of the wage in coupons for use in company shops—cheques, too, were introduced early in the United States—or withholding rent for company accommodation. This restricted the workers' choice, as they could not buy or live where they pleased, but were tied to the facilities provided by their employers at prices above the average. It was not long, however, before industrial wages were paid completely in money, although there were repeated attempts to find loopholes in the laws against truck.

Wages were one of the main subjects of working-class conversation. After all, they immediately affected daily life. Paydays were a cause for celebration or an exceptional treat. Nothing fired the workers' hearts more than wage levels. For that reason, the labour movement usually grew out of the struggle for wages, with negotiations on standard pay and piece rates. Whether to opt for pay by the hour or pay by output was a constant topic for discussion.

In the first half of the 19th century, when exploitation normally took on extensive forms, factories calculated wages according to the hours worked and settled up by the day or week. Piece rates were adopted as machinery began to set the pace for labour, as well as in sectors, such as mining, where the workers could not be kept under constant supervision. This system spread with the transition to more intensive forms of exploitation. It acted as an incentive to work faster because it created the impression that a worker's individual efforts could influence wages. Workers on piece rates tended to be under the illusion that they were being rewarded in relation to a tangible output. Tasks calling for specialized skills were excluded from this system, as were duties of a supervisory nature, either because this kind of work could not be defined by quantity or weight, or because pressure of time would encourage shoddy work or neglect.

Individual and collective piece rates were the major stimulus to productivity on the conveyor belt—however advanced the mechanization—where the quantity and quality of output depended heavily on the conduct of the workforce. Once modern technology in the most advanced sectors of industry, such as chemicals, could ensure a steady flow of output which was not directly subject to individual effort, the owners began replacing piece rates by time bonuses. Nevertheless, the capitalists continued using piece rates, complicated bonus systems and other carefully devised incentives to step up the productivity pressure, bribe certain sections of the workforce, play shop-floor workers off against office workers, and generally maintain discipline over their employees, whichever system they were geared to follow.

The workers themselves had various arguments for and against piece rates. Young, single men and women regarded the system as a chance to line their pockets relatively quickly without any skills. Family breadwinners burdened with worry were forced in any case to work fast and accept the negotiated agreement if they had no occupational alternative. At the same time, however, they could see how this exploitation drained them, sapping their energies over the years so that they could no longer compete with more productive youngsters, had to be content with the worst-paid jobs and were always the first to face unemployment. The effects of the piece rate were crippling, if not fatal, for it forced workers into frenzied competition among themselves, provoking a high rate of accidents, early disability, and severe, widespread occupational disease.

Every conceivable disciplinary method had now been applied, from the initial drift of ruined artisans into the manufactories down to the "internalization" of industrial virtues. The process of taming factory labour lasted several generations, and by the end of it reliable, precisely measured productivity had become the norm. External coercion gave way to the self-discipline of the workers, "small cogs in a big wheel" for whom the overall pattern of production was lost from sight. But however much they assimilated the rules, the nature of their work did not change: it remained a burden, and workers did not cease to resist their exploitation.

In spite of their twofold freedom, wage labourers in 19th-century industrial capitalism were tough, disciplined people who demanded a just wage, who regarded work as a need, a right and a duty, and who took care of their own upkeep by purchasing goods and services. By the time this long historical revolution was over, they had evolved that acquisitive spirit and, at least embryonically, the all-round needs and abilities that were to form the basis for production and wealth, but which were kept in check by capitalist relations and ultimately strove to burst free.

After Work

How proletarians lived and how they developed as personalities did not solely depend on the nature of their labour, but also on the form which civil society as a whole had taken with the evolution of capitalism. The counterpart to the sphere of productive activity was a now clearly separate realm outside work where workers could recover their energies and pursue their private life. It was defined by the manner in which they acquired necessary consumer goods, patterns of settlement and housing, relations between the sexes and generations, and, closely interwoven with this, forms of individual recreation. Pervading everything was an inescapable spatial and temporal organization of life, which also shaped communication and intercourse between proletarians.

These elementary conditions of proletarian existence, as part of the capitalist organization of civil society, constituted the rigid framework within which the workers developed their strategies for life and their forms of conduct, both individual and collective. These, together with working conditions in the broadest sense, provided the basis for what the class was able to fashion over the years in terms of its own unique identity.

Social relations themselves, however, were not static; they were changing constantly at an unprecedented rate. Although the basic characteristics remained the same, the conditions of proletarian life modified from one generation to the next. The relatively rapid flux of circumstances handicapped the cultivation of a specific lifestyle of any permanence and undermined much social experience. This basic situation explains why workers were prepared to introduce radical, even revolutionary changes, and also why they sought to protect their achievements and not expose them to risk.

Another feature peculiar to capitalist society was that the producers were obliged to act with personal independence, while their social bonds assumed the objective form of economic necessity: dependence on the market for labour and dependence on the market for commodities required to subsist.

With social relations now on a more objectified plane, working people acquired broader scope for action and decision, even with regard to the basic conditions of life outside work. The proletarian was required to lead a more conscious life. Careers no longer followed the pre-ordained pattern from goatherd to chief farm hand, from apprentice to journeyman, and people did not spend their whole lives in the place where they were born, at the mercy of the master and supping at his table. A proletarian life was directly affected by the demand for labour and the conditions of hire. Income had to be allocated carefully for upkeep, but the wage labourer could choose free of external economic pressures whom to live with, where to settle, how much to eat and drink, how to dress and how to relax. Nevertheless, under capitalist conditions this new-found personal liberty meant a loss of security and a permanent reliance on one's own resources.

19th-century capitalist society created a legal, communicative, geographical and material basis which enabled workers to determine privately the reproduction of their own labour power and of the next generation of labour. It was easier for them to marry and run a home now that restrictions had been lifted on marriage and settlement, transport and communication had been industrialized, mass housing proceeded apace and a broad range of commodities could be purchased. Proletarians accordingly developed their own specific behaviour patterns and priorities with regard to daily life, the family and consumption. As capitalist industry made more complicated, intensive demands on labour, so the needs which workers evolved and were able to fulfil step by step gained in substance.

Space and Time

As a driving force in the capitalist industry of their own nations, the workers were also links in an international chain, with both positive and negative effects. Progress in the British textile trade left the labour of German weavers worthless. If the stock exchange crashed in Paris or Brussels, workers were thrown out of their jobs right across Europe. Expropriation of peasant land in Ireland and Germany forced the dispossessed to depart for the "New World", encouraging the rapid economic prosperity of the United States. Capitalists compensated for the wage concessions wrung out of them by workers in the "mother country" by extracting superprofits from cheap colonial labour. Chinese workers brought in by the railway companies depressed the wages of unskilled Americans. Although the mass of workers had no real insight into the connexions, they certainly felt the tangible influence which far-flung events exerted on their lives. This was a prime motive for the formation of national labour organizations and the internationalism which imbued such movements.

But industrial wage labour also opened up new spaces in a very immediate way for all who were concerned with it. The rigorous temporal division between work and the rest of life created a distinct social sphere. Its basic geography and activities were initially imposed by earlier traditions unsuited to the new way of life. As in the course of time specific patterns of working-class existence took shape this self-defined sphere was not merely filled, but expanded wherever possible.

Wage labour at the mill gave the producer a new understanding of time in two senses. Selling one's life in portions at fluctuating prices encouraged not only a conscious awareness of the value of one's time, but even careful calculation about how best to spend it. At the same time, although producers resisted the increasingly rational use of labour time in the factory, they learnt to think economically about time themselves. By reducing the time one invested in a thing, one could actually win more time. This universally acknowledged principle began to assert itself outside work, too. Taking pleasure in speed and acceleration was a constructive expression of this new attitude. Idioms reflected the workers' contempt for preindustrial inefficiency with regard to the clock. And so it was that private activities also began to be measured in terms of time.

It was not merely the working environment which stimulated this sense of space and time. Technological advances in transport and communications were also decisive. Industrial production for a universal market required the industrialized passage of freight, information and people, all of which could be regarded as commodities. "The production of cheap means of transport and communication was the condition for production founded on capital."[44] Capital tore down the local barriers to intercourse,

---

44 Marx, Karl: *Grundrisse der Kritik der politischen Ökonomie*. Berlin, 1953, p. 423.

43 Mail coach and wayfarer. During the three centuries before the Industrial Revolution, the transport of raw materials, goods and people rose steadily. Freight routes were extended and road traffic by horse and carriage increased above all. In the early days of capitalism wage labourers could hardly afford to travel by coach. Like itinerant journeymen they went on foot. Modern proletarians did not acquire their characteristic mobility until the railway became a means of mass transport.

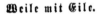

Weile mit Eile.

44 "Miner against a pit landscape."
The railway train constructed by Blen-
kinsop in 1811 was still only used for
industrial cargoes in the British coalfields. Miners walked to work. Col-
oured lithograph by Ernst Kaufmann,
1814.

45 The through train from New York to San Francisco, which symbolized the technological subjugation of an entire continent. Railways and telegraph wires opened up vast territories, linking communities, shortening distances and accelerating the pace of economic and social change.

conquered the world for its market, and constantly reduced movement between places to a minimum. It sought "at the same time a greater geographical expansion of the market and the greatest possible elimination of space by means of time"[45].

Proletarians experienced these changes as pressure or opportunity to move from town to town, as crowds streaming in all directions, as a growing choice of goods changing hands, a swelling river of information, a flood of visual and acoustic stimulation, a flux of fleeting impressions, fast rhythms, dwindling times and distances, spatial gains permitted by modern transport, many phenomena occurring simultaneously, worldwide communication.

The workers accepted the clock and the telegraph, the device for measuring time and the instrument of communication, as symbols of progress.

Industrial traffic and mobility By the mid-19th century North America and most European countries had built up a transport industry, based on steam ships, railways and the telegraph, which was putting the carters and bargemen out of business. Thanks to this industrialized transport, the means of industrialization themselves—steam engines, machine tools, plant, specialists, and ancillary labour—had access to every region of the globe. It was not only the labouring hordes hired by railway companies and the nomadic troops of builders and navvies that roamed from one country to the next as the "light cavalry of capital" (Marx). Whatever territory capital trod was incorporated into one enormous market for labour.

Soaring emigration from Europe to the United States of America illustrates the proportions which mass mobility had assumed as a result of these new means of communication. Up until 1845 about 100,000 settlers a year reached the United States, but this figure soon rose to 300,000. By the eighties about 750,000 immigrants arrived annually, and after 1900 the American labour market was absorbing 1 to 1.4 million new candidates each year.

First of all, this trans-Atlantic migration was a geographical redistribution of agrarian labour power. Although Europe's expanding industries could not absorb all the surplus rural population, internal migration far exceeded emigration. Millions of young villagers in all the industrial countries flooded into the towns and new centres of industry. Many of them continued to work in their old trade or entered the construction and transport sectors, where no special skills were usually required. Others entered domestic service. The ranks of the urban factory proletariat were then swollen dramatically in the second generation by the families of these newcomers.

"Journeys" of this kind were by no means commonplace for working people. Many were driven by hunger to leave their familiar surroundings and set off for strange parts. The fare usually cost them all their meagre possessions. Lots of them carried the debts for years and found it difficult to improve their financial situation. And yet transport technology opened up new horizons even for simple folk, loosening their dependence on social relations at home. Regional and national lifestyles mixed as a result of this movement. The mobility of skilled industrial workers spread elements of proletarian lifestyle throughout the capitalist world, encouraging workers to adopt forms of struggle and thought from one another.

45 Marx, Karl: *Grundrisse der Kritik der politischen Ökonomie*. Berlin, 1953, p. 423.

46 Rush hour 1888: third-class coach on the Berlin Ring. A daily journey by rail or tram was a new communicative experience for workers. Because the railway conveyed everyone regardless of estate, it was expected to act as a democratic influence, but in fact it simply made the new class distinctions more obvious. In 1847 people of every class caught the train to the Epsom Races. The classes in railway carriages, station restaurants and waiting rooms reflected the economic structure of capitalist society.

"A tireless schoolmaster of equality" The railway, to begin with, inspired greater social dreams among democrats and socialists than any other technological achievement. All were convinced that it would break down not only geographical, but also social barriers, eliminating differences in status. Constantin Pecqueur, a disciple of Saint-Simon, wrote in the thirties: "It is the same train, the same force, which carries both great and small, rich and poor; in general, therefore, the railways will function as a tireless schoolmaster of equality and fraternity."[46] The emphatic resistance of the conservatives demonstrates just how widespread such views were. Like other monarchs, Ernst August of Hanover opposed the construction of railways: "I want no railway in my country. I will not have every tailor or cobbler travelling as fast as I can."[47]

True enough, the democratic railway deprived the aristocracy of their privilege of fast travel. Yet the socialist hopes that had been placed in the iron horse soon proved utopian; indeed, although this mode of transport was open to all, carriages were divided into classes which seemed to symbolize the social hierarchy based on money. Nonetheless, a number of Saint-Simonians clung to their ideals, trying their hand as pioneers of the new means of transport: Ferdinand Lesseps built the Suez Canal, the Pereire brothers financed railway construction across Europe, Paulin Talabot designed railway networks and ports.

Socialists had several reasons for approving of the railways. The railway companies were the biggest enterprises of their day, and their management posed an unprecedented technical, economic and social challenge, particularly when the government took the mainline network under its wing, as it did in France and Prussia on grounds of military strategy. These huge mass enterprises could not be run without borrowing methods from the armed forces and state bureaucracy. In the heyday of "free enterprise", here was evidence that social labour could be organized usefully and accurately even on a very large scale. The railways also provided a graphic example to everyone of the degree to which relations had been socialized. That is why the German Marxist Wilhelm Bracke used the organizational forms of the railway (and the postal service) in his political writings as a model for future communist society, an idea that was soon to be taken up by Lenin.

The railway metaphor was a feature of the labour-movement idiom until the turn of the century, for the onward march of progress was symbolized in this impressive mechanical ensemble fuelled by the inexhaustible power of steam technology. Marx called revolutions the "locomotives of history". Wilhelm Liebknecht used the same image to illustrate the "natural inevitability" of a future working-class victory: ". . . any attempt to restrain this movement is as hopeless and futile as the attempt of

47 "Full steam ahead!" Cartoon from *Der Wahre Jacob*, 1892. The combination of technological power and tireless, irresistible motion made the railway a symbol of progress, and not only for the industrial bourgeoisie. The industrial proletariat compared the labour movement with a locomotive hurtling forwards and crushing every obstacle in its path.

48 The junction on Berlin's Landwehrkanal where the elevated railway crossed the canal, the railway and the road, postcard *c.* 1918. The expanding network of city transport pushed urban boundaries out into the surrounding countryside and permitted hitherto unknown concentrations of workers. The main task of the industrialized public transport system was to ensure food supplies and to ferry people to and from work.

a bull to halt the locomotive hurtling towards it. The locomotive will crush him as it pursues its path, just as the labour movement will pursue its path over every obstacle."[48]

Everyday industrial transport During the latter half of the 19th century, towns grew at a rate never witnessed before. As a rule, this meant that the workers also had further to travel each day between home and work. Soon the distance for many was more than an hour's walk (about two miles as the crow flies). The need for urban transport increased. Hackney cabs were rivalled by horse-drawn "omnibuses" and horse-drawn trams. But both forms of transport were too expensive for most workers.

Two technical innovations altered this state of affairs. During the nineties, the bicycle, now fitted with air-filled rubber tyres, evolved from an exclusive sporting commodity into a mass product turned out in series which even workers could afford. For many years, it was to be the most popular mode of private transport. The cyclist could travel about six miles to work in an hour. Workers thus became more mobile, improving their odds on the labour market. Capitalists whose employees lived in industrial villages and who were anxious to preserve a constant, dependent workforce by building housing estates tried to prevent the spread of the bicycle by imposing a "luxury tax". The stratagem was doomed to failure. It only reinforced the symbolic value which workers attached to the first machine that lay within their financial means and increased their independence, not only in finding a job, but also during leisure hours.

At the same time, another form of public transport had been found in the big cities to overcome the inadequate power and speed of the horse. Werner von Siemens introduced the first electrical tramcar in Berlin in 1881. Twenty years later, the horse-drawn tram had almost vanished from the world's great towns. By 1913 over 100 German towns had an electric tram system. Mass travel over greater distances was catered for by suburban train services, and cities began constructing underground railways (London 1890, Budapest 1896, Glasgow 1897, Paris 1900). The distance which workers could now travel in an hour rose as an overall result to 12 to 18 miles as the crow flies.

Faster, cheaper transport enabled workers to come and go across great cities. This permitted a broad network of workers' organizations to function permanently. Rallies turned into mass demonstrations with hundreds of thousands of people taking part.

Early days of mass tourism Trains and steam ships gave birth to a new form of travel: mass tourism. It was still the prerogative of the well-heeled classes to spend the summer months at a spa or to join an organized pleasure tour through various different countries. The British bourgeoisie, who pioneered the new

46 Pecqueur, Constantin: *Economie sociale.* Vol. 1. Paris, 1839, p. 336.
47 Lins, W.: *Die thüringischen Eisenbahnverhältnisse in ihrer geschichtlichen Entwicklung und gegenwärtigen Lage.* Jena, 1910, p. 11.
48 Liebknecht, Wilhelm: *Kleine politische Schriften.* Leipzig, 1976, p. 129.

49 A cheap tramcar for workers in
London after 1890.

modes of transport, also set the fashion for fleeing the world of industry to seek "pure nature" by the sea or in the mountains. The first Alpine association was founded in London in 1857. The English made a winter sport of skiing, while Thomas Cook set up a new kind of business: a travel agency.

But a Sunday outing by train did not only bring pleasure; it could be dangerous as well, as the poet Heinrich Heine recounts in his description of the first major railway accident on 6 May 1842, when nearly 150 people were killed. Although Heine called the railway a "providential event which has set humanity on a fresh tack, changing the colour and shape of life" and heralding "new relations, joys and hardships", he also reflected ironically upon the new kind of disaster which accompanied mechanized transport: "I can visualize the amazement with which inhabitants of the Realm of Shades observed the new arrivals on 6 May, the polished Sunday faces, students, grisettes, young married couples, pleasure-seeking apothecaries, philistines of every hue who saw the fountains at Versailles and then, instead of returning to Paris where the table was laid for lunch, suddenly plunged into the Underworld! And crippled, boiled and charred into the bargain! 'Was it a war that served you so vilely?'—'Oh no, we are at peace and have just been out for a spin.'"[49]

Mass tourism began in Britain during the World Exhibition of 1851 in London. Day trips were arranged, and the railways laid on special trains. Trade associations, technical wonders and sporting contests everywhere began to attract the crowds, who travelled by train. The revenue from third-class passengers rose slowly but surely. By the end of the century urban workers were quite accustomed to tourist excursions. True, these were mostly still limited to day trips by a suburban train, a pleasure steamer or bicycle tours, but it was already clear that tourism offered a permanent form for satisfying the growing need for recreation unleashed by the pressures of work. This was one reason for a new demand: minimum annual leave. It is indicative, too, that working-class organizations soon made excursions, always gregarious affairs, into a regular feature of their leisure programmes, and in the nineties workers began forming their own tourist associations.

Industrial daylight Artificial light had already been used to supplement natural daylight in the craft workshops of the 16th century. The working day was no longer determined by the sun, but by mechanical clocks. The only limits to the artificial day were those imposed by the strength and running costs of the oil lamps, the form of lighting in common use.

The sheer size of the industrial workplace and the division of labour called for a new solution. This was developed by the British coal industry. Gas lamps were fitted in a Soho smithy in 1802 and a Manchester spinning mill in 1805. The urban gas

50 Advertisement for the German electric company AEG, 1888. Thanks to the artificial light produced by industry, working hours no longer depended on the sun, and more use could also be made of free time. After the arc light, gas light and paraffin lamp, electric light bulbs overcame the last natural barriers between day and night. This was the technical key to a time continuum which increased disposable time in the same way that railways increased disposable space. The winged wheel, a traditional railway symbol in Germany, was incorporated into the AEG graphics to suggest the link between winning time and conquering space.

49 Heine, Heinrich: "Lutetia," in: *Werke und Briefe*. Berlin, 1980, p. 454f. and p. 478.

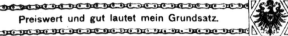

51 Bells and sirens could no longer summon the urban worker to labour. Workers had to observe their own timetable, and for that they needed an alarm clock for the home and a pocket watch to catch a scheduled train. Alarms: the working-class clock. Advertisement of 1912.

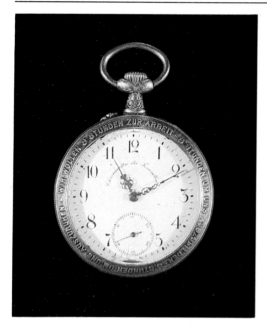

52 The wall clock and private pocket watch symbolized the conscious dichotomy of lifestyle. This "worker's chronometer" of 1890 is inscribed with the labour-movement demand for "eight hours to work, eight hours to learn, eight hours to rest".

smoke-filled rooms, not even halls, but frequently the cramped interiors of the public house."[50]

The invention of the generator, the construction of big power stations and a transmission technology for electricity brought a new form of energy which could be distributed and regulated at will. Apart from increasing and diversifying the applications of technological power at work, it came to influence life as a whole. Electricity was useful to the working class: it lit their streets, shops and pubs, fuelled their trams and urban train networks, cooled their beer and ice cream and illuminated their cinematographs. From the early 20th century onwards, electricity also began to "industrialize" the worker's household energy supply, providing light, heat, refrigeration and motor power.

boards born in England spread to other industrial countries, and factories and homes were linked by a web of piping to a central point of production. Working-class homes were still dependent on the oil lamp, which Argand had improved, but soon acquired the petroleum lamp, a lighting device made industrially which burned a technical fuel. Gaslight, and from 1886 incandescent gas lamps, spread to the urban tenement blocks in the latter half of the 19th century.

As a result of these industrial developments in lighting technology, the rhythm of daily life and of production was no longer dependent on natural daylight. Life contained more active hours. The working day could be doubled and trebled, and after clocking off there was no need to follow the cattle to bed like peasants and rural workers. The labour movement recognized the cultural progress implicit in this, while at the same time criticizing the fact that exceedingly long working hours forced proletarians to make day out of night in an unnatural manner. Karl Kautsky wrote in 1910: "The city dweller shortens his life by adding to his daily labours some nocturnal hours of company or politics or attendance at shows. But if he were to renounce this, then he would be degraded like the peasant to a simple beast of burden, reducing the length of his real life beyond working hours to almost nothing." Kautsky declared that socialist society would shorten the working week and abolish night work for waiters, cooks, musicians, actors, cab drivers and tram conductors. Opportunities for entertainment would be available during the natural day: "In the daytime, pleasure and sociability also entice people more into the open, into nature, into the fresh air, whereas pleasure and sociability by night crowd people into closed,

50 Kautsky, Karl: *Die Vermehrung und Entwicklung in Natur und Gesellschaft.* Stuttgart, 1910, p. 245.

Goods and Services, Basics and Luxuries

In the 19th century, the peasants who belonged to an estate and craft journeymen still received their daily meals and bed in the house of the farmer or master. They were also allocated cloth produced in the household. Only a small proportion of their wages was paid in coinage. Even farm workers who lived independently took some payment in kind, as did brewery workers and miners.

These material forms of reward were soon irrelevant to proletarians. The contract which they entered on sale of their labour was based on cash and calculated by the hour. Even if they did not actually see the colour of all their money, as in the truck and cottage systems, they were recompensed for their work by a financial equivalent. This money a wage labourer received was the only means for him to purchase food, clothing and shelter. This applied above all to the industrial proletariat in the big cities, where there were fewer and fewer opportunities for producing home-made articles, and consumer wares had to be bought. Some forms of self-provision, however, did persist. Workers in industrialized rural communities still sometimes owned their own houses and managed to continue farming or gardening on the side.

Wage labour did not guarantee a life-time job. The benefits of personal independence and mobility were offset by instability and an insecure livelihood. The "liberty" to sell one's labour for the best price possible implied a dependence on bullish business or bad management. Jobs often had to be sought anew, and that might even mean moving house.

If the main breadwinner was ill, the whole family suffered. Long-term unemployment could prove fatal, and there was no provision for old age. For these reasons proletarians were frequently obliged to pawn possessions. They had nothing else to fall back on. A weekly or fortnightly wage packet did not make long-term planning or saving feasible. Money was needed to satisfy present requirements: rent, food, clothes. And if the wage packet was occasionally fatter than usual, the "extra" was spent on celebration.

The market adapted to its new customers. "In the great towns of England everything may be had of the best, but it costs money . . ." reported Friedrich Engels in 1844.[51] As the factories, towns and proletariat grew, the production of consumer goods became more diverse. The first goods available on a truly mass scale and within the proletarian budget were potatoes, cotton and spirits, the cheapest and shoddiest wares on offer.

An explosion of consumer goods and mass consumption hit all the industrial countries in the late 19th century. By the turn of the century the spectrum of commodities on sale was already far more differentiated, especially with regard to food, clothing and such little extras as tobacco, chocolate and other semi-luxuries. Shops and department stores sprouted, making these products accessible everywhere, at all times and to all comers. Industrial mass production kept prices down, so that even workers aspired to many things which now fell within their financial grasp. Thanks to rising labour intensity towards the end of the century, most sectors of industry were paying higher wages, and proletarians were by all accounts potential customers. Urban and young workers in particular developed a wider range of more sophisticated needs. This trend indicates standards and values that were geared towards consumption, and these had to be placed in perspective against the worker's own performance and the income which could appropriately be demanded.

It was a process of learning, which created a new consumer awareness, but which involved older and rural proletarians to a lesser extent. Their needs remained modest, even when their earnings improved. But not even they acquired a taste for petty-bourgeois thrift, preferring to spend more on their old, familiar habits.

What could a worker afford? For industrial wage labourers there was a close link between age, which affected health and fitness, and living standards. Leaving aside the ups and downs of the economy and income differentials defined by skills, every working-class life went through a phase of establishment, a

53 Pawned tools returned free of charge during the Paris Commune of 1871.

---

51 MECW/4/368.

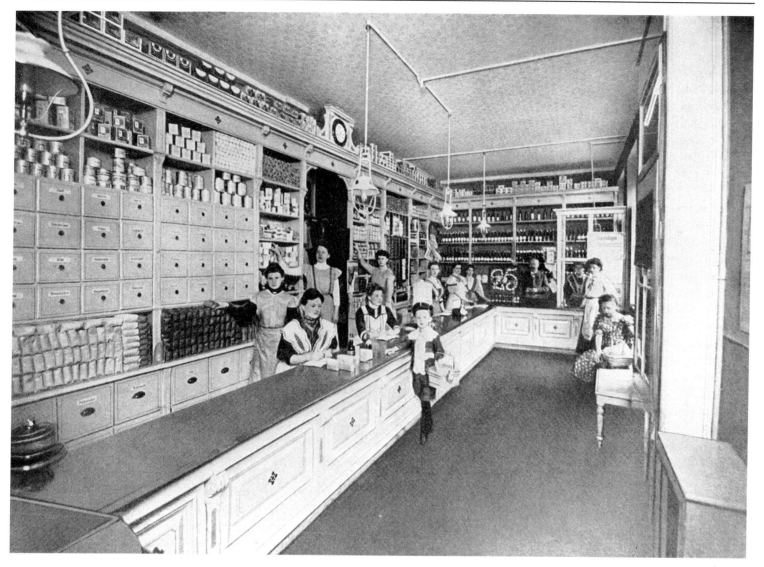

54 Inside a co-operative shop, Leipzig 1909. There was a small shop for everyday items in almost every working-class block. It also sold "colonial wares", coveted luxuries such as cocoa, chocolate, cigars, tea and coffee.

period of vitality and experience when wages reached their maximum level, and then an impoverishment wrought by age.

Workers earned most between the ages of 25 and 40. These were also the years of greatest social differentiation between proletarians. The key factors were varying employment opportunities, the intensity and stamina invested in labour, and family size. In most cases, however, this wage plateau did not last beyond the age of 45.

Young men and women under thirty paid very little for their accommodation. Instead they acquired more personal effects: better clothes, jewellery, watches, possibly books. These possessions functioned indirectly as savings, for in lean times they could be pawned. Marriage brought a brief improvement in living standards if the wife went on earning. Besides, sharing cut everyday costs. This was the time to buy household goods, linen and furniture. Young working-class families put off moving into a bigger home for as long as they could, but as children arrived it was inevitable. The higher rent put a considerable strain on the purse, especially as the cost of upkeep was rising and the mother brought in no income. Most of the budgetary research in the advanced industrial countries which dates from the end of the last century is based on this pattern of working-class income and expenditure, where the man was earning fully, the woman providing a smaller supplement, and several children required feeding into adulthood. Comparisons show that spending habits did not vary much with workers of different incomes. Rent and food drained most of the resources. Only when the household had purchased meat, sausage, animal fats, bread, and alcohol could the remainder be allocated on other things. These essentials devoured far more of the budget than the next items: clothes, shoes, household utensils, heating, light, recreation, education, health and body care.

Additional income or rising wages rarely led to any radical alteration in consumption or housing conditions. As a rule, most of the working people stuck to their habits, partly, no doubt, because they were justifiably unwilling to rely on their good fortune persisting.

The department store The stock of a village or general store was like the daily needs of its customers: a colourful hotchpotch for all its modest scope. Crammed together on the shelves were herrings, hams and sausages, paper and ink, linen and woollen goods, soap, sweets, tobacco, petroleum, dyes, tools and wooden utensils. The storekeeper was often an innkeeper, too. Even in the big industrial towns with their expanding population, these all-round shops fulfilled their purpose well. Working-class wives found almost everything they needed at the corner shop, and at a pinch they could even have credit. In working-class districts on the Continent, almost every tenement block had its "dwarf" store. Specialist shops entered the scene, and in busier streets they stood door to door, from the basement

to the first floor, attracting passers-by with window displays, signs, posters, and banners.

From the middle of the century big cities like Paris, London, Vienna, and Berlin built huge central markets which catered for a substantial share of daily needs. Many traders kept a stall here, offering a broad range of fresh vegetables, meat, fish, groceries, and other useful wares.

But it was the department stores which came to symbolize modern urban retailing in the latter half of the 19th century. France set the tone as the biggest shops in Europe opened their doors. The *grands magasins* of Paris—Bon Marché, Louvre Magasin, Belle Jardinière, Samaritaine, Dyfayel, Printemps, Pygmalion, Maison dorée—were models of entrepreneurial spirit and bonus systems. Similar establishments were founded in London, with William Whiteley and Harrods, and in leading German cities, with Tietz, Wertheim, A. Jandorf & Cie., Gebr. Barasch, and Messow & Waldschmidt. In the United States of America, these stores assumed even bigger proportions. The biggest in the whole world was Marshall Field & Co., which occupied a complete square in Chicago. Other giant stores were Grand Leader in St. Louis, John Wanamaker in Philadelphia and New York, and Macy's, Simpson and Crawford, and Saks, also in New York. The city's dominant department store, Siegel, Cooper & Co., aimed its publicity at a "public without discrimination of class", raking in profits from everyone's needs, "the cheap ones of the working-class woman, and the extravagant ones of the millionaire's wife"[52]. Just as in Europe, the American emporia had grown out of insignificant little outfits on the proceeds from working-class custom. By the end of the century they were nothing less than palaces, architectural masterpieces containing marvels of interior design. The economic aim of the department stores was to make huge profits out of mass turnover. This meant they could sell their wares more cheaply than small-scale retailers, thereby attracting workers. This new commercial principle generated a new approach to shopping. Prices were fixed and goods were only sold for cash. There was no bargaining or chalking up on slates. Sales staff were not permitted to reduce the price or offer credit.

There was plenty of time to inspect the wares on display without compulsion to buy. Orders for individually tailored goods were not accepted. "Cut-price bargains", "special offers", "clearance sales" and discount, as well as free gifts for customers who spent a certain sum and cheap beer in the refreshment rooms, encouraged people to spend their money on unplanned items simply because they were inexpensive and readily available, rather than urgently required. The department stores used these methods to promote new products, whose popularity spread to the proletariat. This not only applied to fashionable

52 Wussow, O. E. von: *Geschichte und Entwicklung der Warenhäuser.* Berlin, 1906, p. 30.

55 World and trade exhibitions demonstrated economic productivity in general, but the big department stores which opened around this time actually displayed the gamut of mass-produced industrial commodities to a broad consumer public. Bon Marché, founded by Boncivant and Vidan in 1852, promised to make shopping worthwhile. Mass turnover guaranteed fat profits from low prices.

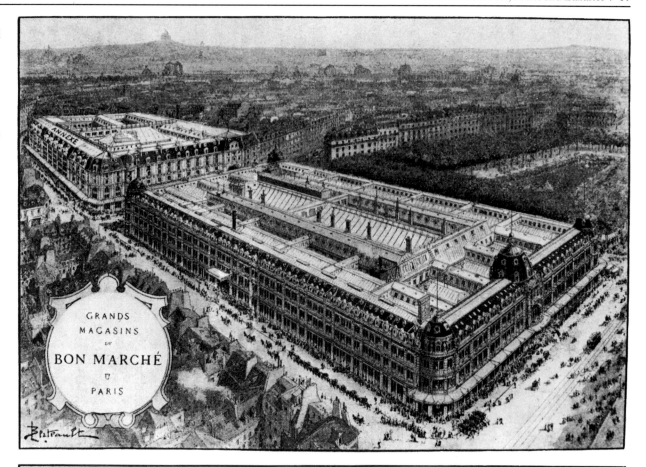

56 Marshall Field department store, Chicago. "The fundamental principle of the modern department store is to open up untrodden realms of consumption to great popular masses in hitherto unsuspected ways, far beyond the framework of customary business, and to enable industry to achieve production, in the broadest sense of the word, such as never witnessed before." (O. E. von Wussow)

57 People's kitchen, Munich, 1889. There was space for four hundred people and a plate of soup cost 5 pfen- nigs. These public kitchens were cru- cial to mass catering in the big cities.

wonders such as tinned vegetables and toilet paper, but equally to clothes, linen and household goods.

Hire purchase and loan establishments offered serious competition to the big stores as far as working-class clients were concerned, for the purchaser could enter a contract to buy with little or no money at all.

Moreover, more and more proletarians were shopping from co-operatives which they founded themselves as a defence against swindling and profiteering. The products on sale, especially food, were purchased directly from the producer. This meant doing without the intermediate trade, so that realistic, low prices could be passed on to members without a fat commission.

Daily diet "Mostly the main meal consisted of potatoes in every possible form, which is why the rhyme went round: Spuds for breakfast, spuds in the stew, spuds in their jackets your whole life through. Pearl barley, millet, peas and beans were sometimes dished up for variety. On Fridays, when the food money was running out, the six of us ate 20 pfennigs' worth of black pudding and liver sausage with sauerkraut and mash. On Saturdays, when we were almost broke, there was herring. These simple meals were enough for us. To make up for it, Sunday was meat day with a pound of pork that cost 60 pfennigs and potato dumplings, although Mum was pleased if a tiny piece of the meat was left over for Monday."[53]

That was the diet of a family consisting of a Silesian factory worker, his homeworking wife and four children, and the de-

scription is typical in many ways for proletarian life around 1900. Similar meals were dished up on working-class tables in other countries: potatoes, herring, pork, bread, syrup, chicory coffee or tea, soup, low-fat cheese, margarine, innards, cheap sausage, lard. The industrial countries of Europe regarded it as a great advance in the field of popular nutrition that the 19th century had driven away the spectre of famine. Annual per capita consumption of meat doubled in England and Germany between 1800 and 1900. This was the period when American workers developed a taste for a daily steak. The consumption of sugar rose tenfold over the second half of the century. Milk production expanded from around 1870, and by the turn of the century workers could afford fruit and vegetables (tropical fruits excepted). The changing demands of labour itself, the need to maintain a lasting output of energy, and patterns of urban food supply all affected the eating habits of proletarians, starting with dwellers of big cities. Shopping and restaurants brought them into contact with new foods which they learnt to accept.

British, Dutch and Scandinavian workers adapted to the working day by postponing their main meal until the evening, whereas German workers clung to their square lunch. Going home at midday was only possible in smaller industrial communities. Elsewhere a solution had to be improvised rather than relinquish the habit. Some workers took a ready-made meal with them. Sometimes wives or children brought food down to the mill during the break, or else workers would find a tavern near their work. Canteens were introduced in factories that were either very big or a long way out of town.

In many families, women prepared meals the evening before. Where that proved impossible, throwing together a quick evening meal was easier now that prepared foods were on sale. Any single worker or wife rushing home from the factory could open a tin or prepare a soup from soup powders like those invented by the Swiss miller Julius Maggi. Stalls selling soups and snacks, and fast-service restaurants proliferated in working-class districts. They offered cheap meals, and it became quite customary to buy something to eat and drink in passing.

Little extras In feudal society, where rights were conferred according to estate, laws governing the use of luxuries and clothes had curtailed adornment and indulgence of the palate among the common people. Now consumption was regulated by money alone. Workers were allowed to desire whatever they could afford, although that, of course, fell a long way short of courtly dissipation and bourgeois opulence.

The cities at the turn of the century provided a broad off-the-peg range of consumer goods and services which went beyond the bare essentials and yet were already tempting working-class

53 *Deutsche Kindheiten. Autobiografische Zeugnisse 1700–1900.* Ed. by Irene Hardach-Pinke and Gerd Hardach. Kronberg (Taunus), 1978, p. 198.

58 "Lunch break at Borsig's factory." Painting by Hans Baluschek. 1911.

59 A mobile refreshment stall on Berlin's Potsdamer Platz, 1908. Hot drinks were sold in winter and cool lemonade in summer. There were long queues at breakfast and lunch time.

custom. It was primarily young and better-paid workers, male and female, who visited bars, music halls and theatres for stimulating drinks, meals, entertainment, pleasure and even education. Workers with big families and married working women stayed behind for lack of time and money.

Semi-luxury foods and drinks were among the few joys of day-to-day working-class life. They were tangible aims, and neither circumspicious thrift nor a petty-bourgeois love of showy possessions prevented workers from spending any "extra" pay on pleasurable treats. Intensive labour with its additional mental strains reinforced their desire for diversion, variety and stimulation.

Around 1900 cheap alcohol still topped the bill for proletarians in Europe and North America, followed by tobacco and coffee. Working-class women shared the latter, considering it a modest privilege.

Now that workers could rely on their staple foods, they began to develop more sophisticated dietary habits. Sweets and white bread were no longer entirely beyond their reach, and fresh meat was regarded as the yardstick of prosperity. In former times, meat had always been boiled to make a soup, but now it was seasoned and roast. More ways of preparing food called for more kitchen utensils, crockery and cutlery. Recipe books soon found their way on to the shelves of working-class homes. A trend towards adopting the customs and pleasures of the more comfortable strata became apparent in every field of consumption, from food and clothes to furnishings.

Bourgeois contemporaries were morally scathing about this "mania" for rich foods and an immaculate household. They called it "wasteful" and "pretentious", and made disdainful remarks about the cheap, poor-quality "substitutes" which these greedy workers fell for as a result of their lack of education and good taste. Even so, as producers and businessmen, it was they who would derive most profit from the trade.

Boiler suit and top hat Bourgeois observers were particularly suspicious to note how difficult it had become to distinguish between the gait of a worker on the city streets and the gait of a more "superior" person. German workers in particular were so well-dressed when they went out walking on a Sunday with their wives and children that they did not betray their "status" at all. Photographs of Social Democratic rallies reveal demonstrators in dark suits and white dickeys bearing hats, pocket watches and canes. But even an everyday street scene showed how much the demand for a variety of fine clothes had been satisfied. The sales girls of London, the seamstresses of Paris and Berlin, and the Polish miners who emigrated to the Ruhr were all famous for their fashionable flair. Adelheid Popp wrote of her days as a factory girl in Vienna: "If I only did not feel hungry, I never even considered of what my food consisted. I only wanted to be well dressed, so that if I went to church on Sunday no one should guess I was a factory

60 Advertisements for every conceivable commodity appeared everywhere to seduce the consumer.

worker."[54] At that time, this meant: "a pretty, light dress, elegant shoes, a silk sunshade, pretty gloves, and, crowning all, a hat trimmed with flowers"[55]. Nor was there any need to make these clothes for oneself. They could be bought off the peg from the hire purchase man, the flea market or the department store. With a few routine snips of cheap material, the rag trade now enabled the lady proletarian to keep up with the latest fashions. Many could afford 1.90 marks for a blouse modelled on the "Parisian cocotte" or "British costume designs".

Because urban workers had considerably more contact with public life than their fellows in smaller communities, fine clothes played a much bigger part in their priorities. They took advantage of city anonymity and began to camouflage their status, which society as a whole did not rate highly. Even at the turn of the century, many young workers in Berlin were already changing in the factory so that they did not have to walk down the streets in their "work clobber". This behaviour was patchy at first and, as with eating habits, a general norm was nowhere established. Traditions and rural customs were still an influence. But one thing which industrial wage labourers never did was to adopt a costume, like the craftsmen, to reflect their trade. To begin with, they wore their old clothes at work, but these wore out too rapidly. The manufactured cottonwear which arrived in its place is still predominant today during factory labour, from the cotton silk made in Manchester and common among British workers to the indestructible blue jeans which Levi Strauss & Co. began producing in San Francisco in 1850.

61 Off-the-peg garments in every price range. Urban workers were attracted by the opportunity to purchase fashion by instalment. Advertisement.

Proletarian Liquor

None of the commodities which proletarians were free to purchase for their private needs caused as many social problems as brandy. It became a pejorative symbol of proletarian lifestyle. The bourgeoisie believed that the threat which the proletariat posed to society had its roots in alcoholism. Since the 16th century they had gained enough experience themselves to know how dependence on drink could lead to poverty, physical degeneration, prostitution, violence and crime. Now they ascribed inebriation to the uncontrolled "lower social classes".

Unbridled drunkenness ran directly counter to the bourgeois ideal of sober calculation and untiring labour for the increase of wealth. To the outraged burgher, booze was a sign of untrammelled individual absenteeism, an escape from order and thrift, diligence and acquiescence. That is why bourgeois observers and social reformers not only exaggerated working-class alcoholism substantially, but also left the real social causes shrouded in mystery. The only people who openly stated the reasons for the first generations of proletarians discovering a taste for alcohol were radical critics of capitalism and the brandy-makers lobby: "Anyone who wants to abolish alcohol must first find the millions to pay for everyone to be happy and independent."[56]

Sure enough, the bourgeoisie themselves had laid the foundations for the alcohol they reviled to become a social danger. The social instability which drove working people to drink had been created by primitive accumulation, the growth of an excessive agrarian population which forced many peasants to relinquish their roots, extensive exploitation and the surge to the towns. Consumption of alcohol on a mass scale then became common when brandy producers increased their output tremendously in the late 18th century. This was because potatoes, an important ingredient, were available at the time in large quantities. Distilling, which until then had been pursued on a small scale or as a sideline among the rural population, now evolved into an efficient industry. More and more liquor came onto the market, prices fell, and Europe was flooded above all by potato-based schnapps from Prussia. Mining magnates, estate owners and many factory bosses made use of this concentrated alcohol for trucking, payment in kind or the servants' table. It reaped them a double benefit by cutting wages and temporarily boosting energies. The workers' senses were dulled a little to their excessively long day and the constant admonishing by overseers. Thus drinking alcohol became a habit among wage labourers in many industries. Even women, who had traditionally been excluded from boozing, began to drink when they entered the factories. "This method of allocating a portion of wages as brandy spread quickly, and it was soon adopted by employers in transport and construction, the owners of coal pits and iron mines, and of brickworks . . . in Germany, too . . . It is indicative that brandy drinking in Germany first spread among miners, and this is where truck was first forbidden."[57]

Alcohol was partially banished from the labour process once technological advances and the transition to intensive exploitation necessitated a new industrial labour discipline. In many fields of production the physical strains were reduced, and greater intellectual attentiveness called for sober workers. But capital continued to take advantage of alcoholic stimulation for many years to come in the mines, on building sites, at ports, at sea and in agrarian production. In 1907 the trades inspector for the German towns of Lüneburg and Stade wrote: "There is a certain connexion between alcohol abuse and the manner in which the workers are occupied, insofar as physically strenuous labour and work in a hot and dusty air are a greater temptation to the consumption of alcoholic beverages, which is therefore observed to be highest in peat and brickworks, cement factories, ship yards and sugar factories."[58] A report from brickworks in the Potsdam region elaborates: "It is not rare for workers to drink up to two litres of schnapps a day and to spend up to a third of their income on alcoholic beverages."[59]

By the dawn of the 20th century, however, most European and North American workers were no longer consuming so much alcohol, either as nourishment or drug. Alcohol had been promoted in status to one of the "little extras", and "social drinking" had become the dominant context.

Drinking in company All the societies where capitalism gave rise to the proletariat during the 19th century had already been acquainted with alcohol as a staple element of daily diet and as a euphoric drug. Because of the intoxicating effects, however, special social rules had always been applied to its consumption. What kind of alcohol a person drank and how much of it were matters of social status. Alcohol was a special feature of holidays and celebrations which distinguished them from everyday routine. Christenings, weddings and funerals, confirmations and harvest festivals were all occasions for a little inebriation. The drink flowed, too, during regular highlights of guild life. Rituals like the toast and the round helped to forge group identity and made the boundaries of social distinction clear. There was a general cultural significance to the rules about when to drink and

54 Popp, Adelheid: *The Autobiography of a Working Woman* (Translated by E.C. Harvey). London, 1912, p. 67.

55 *Ibid.*, p. 75.

56 Bauer, Paul: *Haben die Kampfmethoden der Abstinenten einen einwandfreien wissenschaftlichen und kulturellen Wert?* Berlin, 1911, p. 2.

57 Stehr, A.H.: *Alkoholgenuss und wirtschaftliche Arbeit.* Jena, 1904, pp. 70, 72.

58 Quoted from: Wurm, Emanuel: *Die Alkoholgefahr. Ihre Ursachen und ihre Bekämpfung.* Hamburg, 1912, p. 95.

59 Quoted from: *Der abstinente Arbeiter.* No. 14 of 16 July 1908.

GIN LANE.

Gin cursed Fiend, with Fury fraught.
Makes human Race a Prey.
It enters by a deadly Draught,
And steals our Life away.

Virtue and Truth, driv'n to Despair.
It's Rage compells to fly.
But cherishes, with hellish Care.
Theft, Murder, Perjury.

Damn'd Cup! that on the Vitals preys.
That liquid Fire contains,
Which Madness to the Heart conveys.
And rolls it thro' the Veins.

62/63 The engravings "Gin Lane" and "Beer Street" by the English moralist William Hogarth must be one of the most famous attacks on alcoholism. They were his effective contribution to the parliamentary debate about the Gin Tax in 1750. The bourgeoisie had turned the country into the world's biggest warehouse and its most outrageous slum. The petty bourgeoisie were protesting in despair against pauperization. Alcohol destroyed a person's resistance and aggravated the dangers of social failure. In Gin Lane, Kilman the distiller's only prosperous neighbours are the pawnbroker and the undertaker. In Beer Street opposite, the crafts and trades are healthy. The idea was to dispel alcoholism by reverting to the traditional commoner's drink, beer, which was more nourishing, more refreshing and less inebriating.

BEER STREET.

Beer, happy Produce of our Isle
Can sinewy Strength impart,
And wearied with Fatigue and Toil
Can chear each manly Heart.

Labour and Art upheld by Thee
Successfully advance,
We quaff Thy balmy Juice with Glee
And Water leave to France.

Genius of Health, thy grateful Taste
Rivals the Cup of Jove,
And warms each English generous Breast
With Liberty and Love.

64 George Cruik-shank's "Gin Palace." The bar turned drinking into an industry in England. Hard liquor was doled out on a mass scale without communication at the long counter. In Anglo-American countries the bar replaced the seating arrangement traditional in taverns and became a typical feature of many catering establishments. Bars also appeared in the working-class quarters of French cities.

65 Opium smokers in Chinatown, San Francisco, 1893. In England opium was considered a remedy for almost anything and was often cheaper than alcohol. Paupers used it as a euphoric anaesthetic. There are reports devoted to opium addiction among working women in Paris and New York. For the Chinese coolies imported to build America's railways, opium was the only relaxation they could afford.

when not to drink alcohol, for they kept drunkenness in check and set the symbolic seal on major social adjustments in life. The majority of the people accepted these rules.

When capitalism destroyed the old social structures, these cultural patterns were also eroded, and alcoholic drinks, starting with the swift and strong effects of brandy, became a mass commodity. Every individual was free to get tipsy, and to begin with, the time and place were irrelevant. It was not so much exuberance as constant physical and psychological misery which provoked the proletarianized populace to drink even during their work-free hours, forever seeking the delights of strong liquor. It was the only thing which liberated them from their misery for a brief while.

Two properties of alcohol served this behaviour. Not only was it within the grasp of all proletarians and available at any time; it was also in itself a material form of pleasure. Its enjoyment did not call for any previous knowledge or skill, nor was the drinker obliged to make any preparations, search out company or attend a particular venue. Alcohol offered such unqualified opportunity for pleasure, and was so freely accessible, that special social norms were necessary to govern private consumption. Proletarians were quick to discover this for themselves. Unbridled drinking caused long-term damage to labour power, plunged families into deeper poverty and often broke them up. Workers who fled from squalid housing into the pub to fritter away their money lost every chance they had of bettering their lot themselves. Alcoholics rarely joined working-class organizations. Workers' autobiographies describe the reactions of such fellows as ranging from helpless fatalism to sectarian retreat.

Patterns of consumption appropriate to the living conditions of industrial wage labourers evolved slowly. The pre-industrial drinking rhythms determined by holidays and celebrations gave way to weekly paydays. Finishing work was another cause for a drink. A strong drink on the way home to symbolize stepping out of factory coercion into self-defined leisure is still customary today. In earlier days, it was a brief affair. A worker stopped off at the distillery without being sucked into social drinking. In Britain urban public houses, the gin palaces of the 19th century, exploited the situation: the old inn was converted into a liquor bar, with a long counter where hundreds of customers could be served each hour and drained their glasses standing up.

An additional regular framework for social drinking was provided wherever the links between workers were strong, where family ties were preserved, and where workers spent their free time at clubs or in trade unions and political parties. This placed drinking under social control, and gradually made inroads on the mass boozing which took place after work and on payday.

60 Böhmert, Viktor: *Der Branntwein in den Fabriken.* Leipzig, 1889, p. 12.
61 Quoted from: Jeggle, Utz: "Alkohol und Industrialisierung," in: *Rausch, Ekstase, Mystik.* Ed. by Hubert Cancik. Dusseldorf, 1978, p. 91.

The pressures, challenges and temptations which prompted workers to reach for a bottle and glass were manifold. Budget studies in some European countries illustrate that wage increases encouraged greater spending on alcohol. In Germany, consumption reached its peak in the seventies; in France, where spirits had not managed to displace wine, it was in the nineties. Afterwards the general trend was down. By the end of the industrialization stage, proletarian lifestyle had begun to stabilize and the urban milieu offered other leisure activities which grew in popularity. Workers had learnt how to take their alcohol. It was no longer their foremost and—along with sexual activity—their only form of pleasure.

Spirits bow to beer When technologically advanced companies set about maximalizing productivity during set working hours and exploiting labour more intensively, the factory-owners altered their attitudes to alcohol. The findings of Germany's first investigation into brandy drinking in the factories, written in 1885, make this clear: "Drinkers are of no use in industrial work, for they weaken quickly, are slow in their labour, unreliable, argumentative, frequently prey to illness and cannot in the long term be protected against the dangers of machinery in operation."[60]

Krupp of Essen stopped free schnapps for workers in 1866, and in 1910 drinking beer was forbidden in the cast iron factory. The pattern is typical: beer, with its greater nutritional value and milder intoxicating effects, replaced spirits, and then, in the leading sectors of industry, beer made way for coffee, tea and soft drinks. Of course, the spirits industry put up resistance. Chancellor Bismarck, representing the interests of the landed aristocracy east of the Elbe, who derived some of their income from distilling, sought to price beer out of the workers' reach with his intervention in the Distillers' Tax debate in Parliament in 1881: ". . . in my view beer should be taxed higher relative to brandy, for it is by comparison the drink of a somewhat wealthier class, while brandy is the drink of the celebrated poor man"[61].

The pressure to turn up sober at work did not lead to greater consumption of alcohol outside the factory, but actually encouraged its decline. Rising real wages and lengthier free time enabled better-paid workers to afford beer. This tendency was enhanced in Germany by resilient inn-keeping traditions, for tippling at the bar had never taken root. Even when beer halls modelled on the British counter system began to spread, they retained a number of tables where communication with other customers could continue.

Beer became a status symbol for the most prosperous groups of workers, whereas unskilled workers and new immigrants to the cities did not normally change to beer in richer periods; they simply drank more spirits. In Germany, the pub with its draft beer soon became the focus for meetings of organized workers. Gradually, the growing demands made by class organizations in

66 A committed Social Democrat, painted by Ludwig Knaus, 1877. The artist found it natural to depict this German activist in the tavern. His accessories include the obligatory newspapers and a beer tankard, indicating the labour movement's disapproval of strong spirits.

The weapons of reaction.

The weapons of the proletariat.

67 Georg Wilke's poster for the working-class temperance movement in Germany, *c.* 1910, contrasts the weapons of reaction (booze in all its forms) with those of the proletariat (books and a clear head). The labour movement opposed liquor wherever it was widespread among workers. Intoxication and political enlightenment could not be reconciled. Even so, the temperance movement could not persuade workers to become completely teetotal.

terms of political activity and education banished beer into the more sociable sphere of a worker's spare time.

Soft drinks Industrialization and urbanization made it difficult in all the countries concerned to supply pure drinking water. This encouraged the consumption of drinks made with boiled water: coffee, coffee substitute, and tea. The German industrialist Borsig had milk bars set up on his site. The growing popularity of beer was also due to some extent to a greater demand for hygienic drinks. The first industrially made soft drinks appeared in the thirties. In 1833 John Matthews mixed water with carbonic acid to obtain fizzy carbonated water, a kind of artificial mineral water. In the forties, the French began mixing fruit juice and syrup with soda. Struve was the first industrial concern to produce this *limonade gazeuse*.

As alcohol was banished from the workplace, railway companies, big industrial complexes and co-operative societies began serving their own soda and lemonade. This stimulated new drinking habits among the working masses during their spare time, too. Soon refreshment stands, lemonade sellers and soda fountains were part of the industrial townscape.

When apothecary Dr. John Pemperton offered his coca cola syrup to the drug stores of Atlanta in 1886, his patent only brought him 25 dollars a year. By 1916 Candler, who took over his business, was ringing up 13 million. In other countries, too, the mineral-water industry advanced to become a powerful rival to the brewers and distillers. In 1907 Franz Hartmann converted his company into Sinalco-A. G. Detmold with a share capital of one million marks, and in his first years of dealing he was handing out 18-per-cent dividends.

The Worker and His Wife

The wage labourer's personal liberty brought a privilege previously denied to many working people of no property: the opportunity to start a family. As the ranks of the proletariat swelled and legal, economic and religious barriers were removed, the number of marriages rose in all the industrial nations of Europe.

Compared with the large households of peasants or craftsmen, productive units which catered for many of their own needs, the family life of a capitalist wage labourer provided a completely new framework for running a household and cohabitation. The material basis for sustaining the family was financed by one or more members in employment outside the home. Men, women and children could all sell their labour on the capitalist market. The only functions of a private family household were to renew spent labour power each day and to raise the next generation of workers. All the activities connected with this were regarded, even in proletarian families, as the woman's duty. Although women's employment outside the home was possible on a large scale, and many women did take jobs, the traditional division of labour between men and women was initially preserved.

The working-class wife's most important tasks were to look after her husband and children. The man went out to work and was the "breadwinner". His wages provided the main source of income for family upkeep. However, a father's wages rarely sufficed to feed his relatives, so that older children and, in particular, working-class wives supplemented the family budget with their own wage labour. There were periods when the whole family depended on the woman's job for naked survival. It went without saying that she still had to do the housework as well. On the one hand, this division of responsibilities established the social and cultural prospects which awaited men and women. Many workers never questioned the polarities it implied: the authority and pleasure on the side of the man, who was orientated to life outside the home, and a double burden of work for women, as well as minority and sacrifice. On the other hand, however, the conditions of proletarian life and work held the seeds for challenging traditional family hierarchies and the social inferiority of working women.

Women's fundamental opportunity for taking paid employment in social production was the key to their economic independence. Moreover, as capitalist production intensified labour, the work which women performed in the home to restore labour power was upgraded, both by their husbands and by capital.

Marriage It was the aspiration of young male workers of every nation to "take a wife", while proletarian girls regarded it as a matter of course that they would marry and bear children. For both parties, marriage was the only way to end an uncomfortable and expensive lodger's existence or to escape the authority of parents or, in the case of servants, their masters.

A desire for a home and children, a need to feel secure, looked after and loved, were personal motives for hastening the issue. But economic reasons were just as powerful an argument for living with a partner as emotional ones. Under urban conditions, food, shelter, pleasure, entertainment and services of all kinds were only available for money, so that a small family household was the cheapest and most dependable material framework for daily existence. Income could be used as efficiently as possible for the necessities of life, and security was there to cover unemployment, sickness, disability and old age, since there were few social measures as yet to cope with such situations.

Personal taste and affection were the prime factors for young proletarians to consider when choosing a partner. Ethnic and religious ties might be important, but not property. Their preparations for marriage were not aimed at concentrating capital, uniting estates or opening the doors to a career. There were also no obstacles to getting to know one another or being together, unlike in "protected" bourgeois circles. The opportunities were diverse: work, the anonymous streets, dances at the weekend and other festivities, and later clubs and societies. But be it down the road or up at the dance, birds of a feather flocked together, and working men almost always "went out" with serving maids or factory girls. Mutual affections could be declared plainly and without prudish euphemisms. "Conquests" and sexual experiences were part of everyday conversation. Courtship involved flirting, muscle-flexing, fetching each other from work, exchanging small presents and invitations out. The desire for care and tenderness was strong. If a couple liked each other, they soon became intimate and slept together. A relationship did not begin with the longer term or marriage in mind. Women and men alike changed their "sweetheart" frequently, intending to enjoy life before they settled down to wed. Women found it harder to take advantage of their liberty as the fear of pregnancy was great. Even working-class mothers sometimes locked their daughters up to save them from the fate of premature maternity. Serving girls lost their position, and single parenthood often forced them into extreme circumstances. This was often the point where a proletarian woman took up prostitution. It was not customary for workers to turn their backs on a girl with an illegitimate baby, and pregnancy was usually a ground for marriage. Matrimony in the eyes of God and the law was not always simultaneous. "Common marriages" without a certificate were accepted.

Most industrial and construction workers and miners married while they were still young. They could take the step as soon as they felt able to feed a family. Wages were the yardstick. Love was a couple's main motive in living together, but other considerations also affected the decision. Many proletarian girls had small savings or had saved something for the bottom drawer, and they wanted a decent, well-paid husband who did not drink or

68 A Berlin worker's marriage certificate. "As for me and my house, we will serve the Lord" (Joshua 24, verse 15). The clergy and capitalists liked workers to lead a godly family life, breeding future workers and loyal subjects.

69 Working-class wives talking on the street as seen by the artist Théophile Alexandre Steinlen. The daily worries which they discussed never ran dry: the landlord's tricks, rising prices, children's illnesses, drunken husbands, pregnancy, looming strikes.

hang around in bad company. She, as a future housewife was expected to spend money wisely, to possess practical skills and work hard, qualities which would help the family overcome its day-to-day problems.

The proletarian housewife Working-class women usually had to look after a big family on their own. If they had worked in a factory before marrying, they did not usually know much about keeping house. Although technical household aids were already on the market, these were still too expensive. The daily round of shopping, cooking, cleaning, washing and mending in cramped housing was hard work, and there was no clocking-off time.

The biggest difficulty was allocating the money. Unlike the bourgeois housewife, who received an allowance from her husband, the proletarian housewife was usually free to spend the entire family budget as she thought fit. This was the custom in France, Britain and Germany in the 19th century. Workers handed over the whole wage packet to their wives, who took all the financial decisions and in most cases even determined how much pocket money was available each week for tobacco and alcohol. This did not mean there were no arguments. Some workers spent their money on drink straight away, while others kept the full sum of their wages secret. The traditional tactics employed to get hold of the money on payday paint the picture. Women waited in ambush at the factory gates or the pub, and some factories even paid wages directly to the women.

Holding the family purse strings meant that the proletarian housewife also had a personal duty to fill everyone's stomachs. When money was short, a mother cut her own rations first, then perhaps the children's, and finally her husband's. He was the major breadwinner, and so he always received the best and biggest portions to keep him fit and strong.

Wage labour for married women One working man's wages were not enough to feed a growing number of children, however clever his wife was with the housekeeping and however modest their demands. The woman had to earn some money, too, and older children mostly went out to work.

Married proletarian women had similar motives for taking a job in all the industrial countries. They reflected the critical stations in the material existence of working-class families: a low-paid or unemployed husband, the sickness, disability or death of the breadwinner, and sometimes his irresponsible taste for alcohol. Not until after the turn of the century, when male wages rose and women were not necessarily forced by sheer poverty to work, did greater expectations and the desire for a higher standard of living become motives. At the time women did not regard paid employment as a personal need or life's ambition. They stayed at home if they could. There are no statistics to show how often working-class women took jobs, for how long, and how intensive their labour was. Different categories of employment

70 The life of a working-class woman centred on the kitchen, domestic chores and a swarm of children. Feeding and raising the whole family was exceedingly strenuous. Photo by Heinrich Lichte & Co., Berlin, 1907.

71 Mothers earned some extra cash by running errands, washing laundry and cleaning. They were seldom able to take better-paid factory jobs because of the long absence from home. Photo by Lewis W. Hine, New York City, 1910.

made it harder to trace an economic pattern, and women often kept quiet about their jobs to the census because it was considered a stigma for a husband not to provide for his family on his own.

Married women preferred jobs which they could combine with their family responsibilities. That restricted their choice to cleaning, washing, delivering messages and other similarly unskilled and badly-paid options within their own neighbourhood. Factory work was better paid, but women with children were rarely in a position to take it because they would be away from home for too long. The exception to this were the English textile workers who had entered the mill in early youth and had no intention of leaving just because they were married. 40 per cent of married women in Blackburn, for example, had jobs in the textile factories in 1901. Yet at the same time the percentage of married women working in industrial cities such as London, Sheffield or Birmingham was only 10 to 20 per cent, considerably lower than the Continental average.[62]

Homeworking In the last third of the 19th century, homeworking for the booming clothing industry became a major source of income for not only German, but also French and Belgian working-class mothers. The American sewing machine had conquered Europe, and many women saved up to buy themselves a Singer. After all, owning a machine for themselves offered a handy opportunity for combining housework and wage labour. However, like any other form of homeworking, sewing did not make life easier for the working-class wife: it was a particularly intensive kind of exploitation which paid the lowest conceivable wages, forced her to work unlimited hours, and placed a considerable burden on the rest of the family and their living space. One Berlin seamstress who worked in a room with one window where her children slept, cried and lay sick told a sociological researcher in 1898: "that the calm, regular work in the factory where she was employed a while had been a real holiday compared with the turbulence and chaos of her household, and often she had found it hard to find the heart to go home. But the infant had always been overfed by its siblings and was constantly ailing, so that she had been forced to give up her work outside. Now she is sewing blouses in her house and earning much less for incomparably longer hours of labour."[63]

The severe conditions depicted in this report were typical for the circumstances of many proletarian women. Most working-class wives were repeatedly obliged to combine housework with wage labour. Only by giving all their mental and physical energy

72 "Three seamstresses." Colour etching by Théophile Alexandre Steinlen. The urban women who cleaned, sewed and washed laundry were not subject to the same restrictions in their behaviour as housemaids, nor were they victims of factory coercion. Their poor wages sometimes forced them into prostitution.

73 "Women discussing at the bar." Lithograph by Théophile Alexandre Steinlen. It was only in the big towns that young waged women acquired a similar independent status and self-confidence to male industrial workers.

62 Cf. Stearns, Peter N.: "Working-Class Women in Britain, 1890–1914," in; *Suffer and Be Still: women in the Victorian Age.* Ed. by Martha J. Vicinus. Bloomington, 1972, p. 110.

63 Dyhrenfurth, Gertrud: *Die hausindustriellen Arbeiterinnen in der Berliner Blusen-, Unterrock-, Schürzen- und Trikotkonfektion.* Leipzig, 1898, p. 67.

74 Homeworking with a sewing machine provided the main source of income for working-class women in Germany, France and Belgium in the last third of the 19th century. Unlimited hours and a cramped flat were the price to be paid for staying with the children. Photo by Heinrich Lichte & Co., Berlin, 1911.

75 Sunday was the only chance a working-class family had to sit down for a meal together. During the week, long hours and shift changes set the pattern. Photo by Lewis W. Hine, New York, East Side, *c.* 1910.

76 Elderly working-class couple, *c.* 1914. When workers married, they looked forward to growing old together in good health, harmony and prosperity. But for many the bitter reality was domestic discord, early widowhood and an old age of material want.

and often neglecting their own well-being could they manage to provide their husbands and children with a decent home and regular meals.

Everyday family life Proletarians did not lead a private life in the bourgeois sense, cut off as a family from the social world about them. Although urban housing conditions were such that a separate, anonymous existence would have been possible even in working-class districts, there was a close-knit web of neighbourly communication and mutual assistance. Working-class families also kept up their contacts with relatives and fellow-workers who did not live too far away. Lodgers, too, were often involved in the life of the family.

A working-class household rarely settled for long in a tenement. Frequent moves were prompted by the search for a better job or a cheaper flat. This mobility, which contemporary cultural observers would label as "rootlessness", meant that many families never forged very deep bonds with their housing environment. They did, however, learn to adapt quickly and make new friends. Gossip, quarrels, arguments and punch-ups were as much a part of normal behaviour among residents of working-class districts as unconditional support in times of hardship and the sharing of joy and pain. Certainly the women stuck together particularly. By day they dominated the stairway, the yard, the street, shops and markets.

It was unlikely that the whole family could be together every day. Daily and weekly rhythms were fixed by the long working day of the father and the grown-up children. It was something quite special for everyone to sit down to a meal together, and even more rare to spend leisure time jointly. When father came home during the week the children were usually in bed, or else were packed off quickly so that he could have some peace.

Unlike the women, men were able to avoid their homes and screaming children and pass the evening at the pub or club. German fathers would at least spend some time with their wives and children on Sundays, joining them on the allotment, on a walk, or in a café out of town. By contrast, it is reported that British men preferred to spend their free days engaged in typically male pastimes such as sport and betting.

Wearing the trousers The accounts of proletarian family life that have come down to us today indicate differences, and to some extent even antitheses, in the conduct of men and women. Working men did indeed expect to enjoy authority and special rights in relation to their wives. They saw themselves as head of the family, and their pride was wounded when the woman had to bring in extra income. They insisted on individual liberties and material advantages within the family which were granted them as breadwinners. These included pocket money, the biggest servings of food, tobacco and alcohol, a place on the sofa, a Sunday afternoon nap and visits to the pub. It was considered "manly" to take your drink, gamble and boast about your sexual prowess. For a long time, working-class men poured scorn on the idea of helping in the home, being careful with money, or spending the evening with the family. Only when the working day became more intense and a relaxed, comfortable home acquired greater value as a sphere of recreation did men begin to take an interest in their flat, household functions and the children.

A woman's daily struggle to keep the family going was never done. Her chores and children kept her indoors. Once in a while she might read a penny novel for her edification, or chat to the neighbour over a cup of coffee. A trip to the big shops or cinema were rarer distractions. She could not expect to have regular free time like her husband.

His visits to the pub, and the money he spent on pleasures and interests which she could not share, were often the bone of marital contention. A man's political commitment would also repeatedly provoke strife. It was not that the women did not understand their husbands or liked to nag, but as mothers of a family they worried about where the wages were going, and what was to become of the breadwinner himself. These were the reasons why labour leaders in different countries called women the worst enemies of a strike.

Most of the signs suggest that working-class women were discriminated against socially and culturally. The law and public morality did not defend them. But their tasks were more important compared with the role of bourgeois women. They had daily responsibilities to fulfil. They influenced their children's upbringing. Occasionally family survival hinged on their earnings. These were contributions which brought proletarian women respect, strengthened their confidence in themselves, and allowed them to grow more independent in their actions.

Sexuality Bourgeois outrage at the immorality of proletarians was very soon countered by the observation that their unworthy situation left them no other pleasures than intoxication by alcohol and the joys of sexual intercourse. Besides, capitalist factories brought men and women together in confined spaces, inevitably stimulating their sexuality and encouraging daily inchastity. The widespread belief that working men and women indulged in unbridled sex had its roots in the principles of official bourgeois sexual morality in the 19th century. It was true that the sexual discipline imposed by the village or guild no longer applied to proletarians, who led their lives as they chose once work was over. Traditional mores, supported by the Christian ethic which decried anything carnal as a sin, had condemned or prohibited extra-marital sexual relations. For a craftsman or peasant, marriage was a long-term, practical partnership determined by economic considerations. The prime need was for teamwork, and this reduced the choice of spouse considerably, for it had to be made within the peer group. Love might grow

77 "Comment on the factory rules: Female employees may not sit down—except on the boss's lap." Cartoon by Adolphe Willette. The sexual harassment of women workers by their factory superiors may have been exaggerated in contemporary complaints. According to pre-industrial concepts of morality, women in independent employment outside the home were indecent and beyond the law. This explains both why their male employers, superiors and fellow-workers overstepped the bounds of privacy, and why the moralists who protested let their prejudice run away with their imaginations.

Kommentar zu einer Fabrikordnung:
Es ist den weiblichen Angestellten verboten sich zu setzen — ausgenommen auf den Schoß des Chefs

78 "True, it would be more agreeable to live from one's securities." Cartoon by M. Dumont, 1897. Class-conscious and conservative proletarians alike disapproved of prostitutes as anti-social elements who preferred not to work. But sometimes there was solidarity in the face of a common enemy, such as interfering police officers, callous profiteers and sanctimonious moral preachers such as this one.

. . . Das ist ja richtig, man würde viel angenehmer von seinen Renten leben . . .

79 "Man—Woman—Chattel."
Charcoal drawing by Hans Baluschek,
1906. Whoring was part of the lumpen
proletariat lifestyle. Sometimes parents profited from their daughter's
trade; the pimps, or "lumpen aristocrats", certainly did.

later out of sexual attraction, but then again it might not. The economic unit was dominated by the man, who sought his own satisfaction and took no account of his wife's sexual needs. This was hardly fertile soil for erotic sensitivity.

Young proletarians were able to choose a partner without concern for economic considerations or social estate. Personal qualities, primarily sexual attraction, were the determining factors. There was also liberty and opportunity, especially in the anonymous city, to experiment with the charms of various partners and establish one's own taste.

Once married, most proletarians confined their sexual activity to the home. In many cases, social circumstances hindered the cultivation of sexual behaviour which could sustain the pleasure and relaxation of both partners in the longer term and deepen the bonds between them. The first obstacle was the division of function within working-class families as decreed by social norms. As the woman had to look after the man at home, it was assumed that she should also be there to satisfy his sexual requirements. This framework enabled traditional behaviour patterns to persist and granted some influence to' the bourgeois concept of "conjugal duty". But even progressively-minded workers who tried to treat their wives more considerately as equal partners had the odds stacked against them.

Housing was cramped and overfilled and did not permit an isolated corner for privacy. Secret, hasty intercourse was the only answer. Overwork, especially on the woman's part, left a couple with little time or energy for tenderness. Fear of pregnancy added a bitter taste, and the only known countermeasure was coitus interruptus. Not until the end of the century could workers afford the sheath. This lack of efficient contraceptives that could be used by proletarians was a key factor preventing the cultivation of sexual pleasure without procreation. The bourgeois could—and did—draw a distinction between conjugal duty and extra-marital sexual delights. Sexual morality in society was determined by this dualism.

Some light is thrown upon the state of proletarian marriage by reactions to a lecture given by the Prussian Minister of Justice, Kirchmann, to the Berlin Workers' Association in 1866. He talked of "communism in nature" and argued the case for families with two children. Not only did Prussian public opinion find this scandalous and immoral, successfully pressing for Kirchmann's dismissal from government office; the workers he had been addressing were also angry and took a negative view of the affair. As they knew nothing about the potential for contraception, they thought they were being told to refrain from marital intercourse. The fledgling labour movement saw this demand for family planning as an attack on working-class rights and also rejected the idea.

The education available to the working class provided no information about the physiology and psychology of sex. Although workers did not attach the same strict tabus to sexuality as did of-

80 "Night Club." Painting by Hans Baluschek, 1900. The moralizing King of Prussia sent in the police to close down Berlin's brothels. The prostitutes of the biggest garrison and university town in the German *Reich* moved into restaurants, variety theatres and night clubs. Waitresses and minor actresses were "remunerated" by the opportunity for prostitution. Many a homeworking seamstress was obliged in the slack season to earn her bread by going "on the streets".

ficial bourgeois opinion, the only way for proletarian men and women to find out more about these matters was to compare experiences with friends and relatives, and this process was itself fraught with prejudices. The situation did not change until the early 20th century, when bourgeois scholars began publishing work in the field of sexual research.

From the turn of the century onwards there are more frequent indications of sexual enlightenment. Workers in several countries were earning more and could afford a separate parents' bedroom. Family planning and fewer children became common. As working-class youth movements were formed, these offered a forum for discussing relations between the sexes. Leisure societies slowly began involving women in their social activities and treating them as equals. Under the influence of petty-bourgeois reformers, workers' associations started paying attention to issues such as healthy living, a new understanding of one's body, and love unsullied by bourgeois hypocrisy and Christian prejudice. The first socialist essays on children's education included views on how to prepare girls and boys for their gender roles in a partnership of equality. All forms of worker education turned to the question of sexual enlightenment. Otto Rühle, whose work in this field set the direction for the German labour movement, outlined a philosophy during a lecture he delivered in 1906: "We love life and invest all our energy in discovering the full wealth of its beauty for our noble enjoyment. We shall also build an altar of honour to that creative life force which is manifested in the act of love, to that life-giving desire which outgrows its very self."[64]

Childhood, Youth and Old Age

The states of childhood and youth were considered to be 19th-century discoveries. It is certainly true that the backcloth against which people grew up had changed in both the ideal and the material sense. For huge sections of the population there was a dividing line between family life and production, between the private sphere and work. It was now possible, in fact necessary, for parents to devote special attention to their children, who had to be raised and educated into youth. This placed a new emotional accent on the relationship, and a specific children's culture emerged. In Germany, the first children's fashions, children's rooms and children's books appeared in bourgeois circles during the mid-century *Biedermeier* period.

As far as peasants were concerned, children were the toilers of the future. That was the way that other working strata had always regarded them, too. As soon as they could walk, they would be drawn without more ado into the adult world, learning their future tasks naturally through experience.

Working-class children were caught between the two extremes. Their position changed during the course of the century as child labour receded, state schools opened, and the proletarian family evolved. Growing up in the family was no longer the same thing as growing into the world of work. Language, morals, opinions and practical skills were now constructed informally and accidentally against a far broader horizon of experience: work, lessons, the street, people outside the family. There was no grand design, such as bourgeois educationalists prescribed, to this process of assimilating values and codes of behaviour which were not only diverse, but often contradictory.

In every industrial country, similar objective conditions, for all the chronological and national variations, encouraged the recognition of childhood as a phase in proletarian life which called for special acknowledgement and forms of activity. Firstly, laws were introduced to protect children from labour; secondly, schooling became compulsory; and thirdly, proletarian family life took shape. At the same time, families became smaller and living standards improved. This provided flourishing capitalism with more effective guarantees for the supply of uninterrupted generations of well-qualified, resilient workers and willing subjects. But until the turn of the century, not much changed in the daily lives of most working-class children. For a long time yet, working-class families had to send their offspring out to earn money as soon as possible. That made it difficult to take account of their emotional and physical development, let alone to respect the law about compulsory schooling, which many parents saw as obstructive and superfluous. The labour movement pressed constantly for limitations on child labour, protective legislation for mothers, and more wages and leisure to improve family conditions.

After the turn of the century, politically active, well-paid, urban, skilled workers were the first to devote more attention to their children's personal development. They had fewer children, insisted that their wives should stay at home, no longer made their offspring take paid jobs, and spent some of their spare time in their company. Illegitimate children, and the children of unemployed, unskilled, auxiliary and rural workers, and especially of homeworkers, remained for many years to come the "victims of triple exploitation" by parents, work and school, as Otto Rühle formulated their plight.

Children alone Towards the end of the 19th century, newspapers repeatedly carried reports of toddlers who had been left alone at home, fed tranquilizers to keep them in a state of semiconsciousness for days, or even died as a result of unattended accidents. These sensational stories illustrated the conditions to which doctors, educationalists and socially committed labour representatives were trying to alert public opinion, the plight of

81 "Woman Knocking." Charcoal drawing by Käthe Kollwitz, 1909. Each new pregnancy and a growing brood increased the cares of the working-class wife. After the turn of the century the average number of children in a family dropped to four, and family planning gradually became the custom.

proletarian children whose mothers worked away from home all day long. It could result in horrendous disaster, and was generally discussed in the same breath as illegitimate babies and factory work for women, but it was a basic problem for all working-class families. Not only were there no social provisions for the infants and dependent children of waged parents, but there was also no individual solution to the problem. The more children a family had, the more urgent it became for the mother to bring in some income. Women only found provisional care for their children during their absence. The little ones stayed on their own, or were looked after by older siblings, grandmothers or neighbours. Crèches and nurseries were rare in all European industrial countries before the First World War. Many urban workers, especially single mothers, separated from their children for lengthy periods, paying foster parents to take them in the country so that they could work and earn unhindered.

The priority was to make sure that everyone had a full stomach, clothes and a roof over their heads. Each new baby placed a considerable economic burden on the family: midwife's fees, loss of the mother's income, greater demand for food, and less space to live in. Under these circumstances, parents and siblings sensed the bitter irony behind every "bundle of joy".

Even if the mother did not take paid employment, or only found a temporary job, she rarely had time to respond to a child's special needs. "I knew no point of brightness, no ray of sunshine, nothing of a comfortable home in which motherly love and care guided my childhood. In spite of this I had a good, self-sacrificing mother, who allowed herself no time for rest and quiet, always driven by necessity and her own desire to bring up her children honestly and to guard them from hunger."[65] Many workers recall their childhood home in similar terms to the Viennese worker Adelheid Popp.

Child labour Before industrialization, growing up, learning and working was all one and the same process for the children of common toilers.

In the early days, wage labouring families could not do without their children's earnings, but now each member had their own job, for labour was sold individually. When industrialization began, mechanical technology in most trades was a great spur to child labour. Small physique, nimble fingers, unformed personalities and defencelessness in the face of unreasonable demands made them highly desirable employees. Many writings exposed the brutal excesses of child exploitation during the birth of industry, and there were protests against this social disgrace. Contemporary engravings show little children down mines, at

64 Rühle, Otto: *Die Aufklärung der Kinder über geschlechtliche Dinge*. Bremen, 1907, p. 7f.
65 Popp, Adelheid: *The Autobiography of a Working Woman* (Translated by E. C. Harvey). London, 1912, p. 67.

82 Opium, the poor man's nurse-maid. Looking after the infants and toddlers was a problem as old as industrialization itself. Working-class parents never found an adequate solution.

textile machines, in paper mills, making glass and so on. Child labour at the mercy of the capitalist market had nothing more in common with the natural relationship through which children were once familiarized with the working environment of a craft or farm. However, as the century passed, it became harder and harder to employ children in factories. There were several reasons for this: the work process was growing more complicated, proletarian struggle was pressurizing increasingly for humane working conditions, and the government objected that children exhausted in this manner at a tender age were later not fit for military service.

Countries passed laws limiting factory work for children. But that did not make child labour impossible. Extraordinarily cruel methods of child exploitation persisted longer in German industry than in France or Britain. And child labour did not disappear completely anywhere in Europe or North America. Children under 14 "drifted" into trades which did not lend themselves so well to statistical analysis or legal regulation. Ruthless exploitation of child labour continued almost unrestricted in agriculture and homeworking until well into the 20th century.

Around 1900 there were about three million children aged 6 to 14 in paid employment in Germany. They boosted family income by taking ancillary jobs in various trades and services. The son of a Silesian factory worker describes his duties graphically: "We children soon had to help with the homeworking, but the monotonous, boring sewing in that poky cubbyhole drove us older ones to look for more varied activity. In the morning before school we delivered the baker's produce for breakfast, in the afternoons newspapers, and between times we crept to the station and put up unfair competition to the regular porters by carrying travellers' suitcases into town . . . At twelve I was already well established as the errand boy for Scheibler's shoe shop in Bäkkerstrasse, sweeping the shop and pavement at six in the morning, cleaning the shoes, fetching breakfast and then trotting off to school at seven o'clock. During the midday break I had to take shoes to be repaired by the master cobblers and collect them again, run errands to the stitcher's, cut leather for soles, and shine enormous boots half as tall as myself until the original brown of the leather was radiant black. This work carried on after school until the shop shut at eight o'clock, and also on Sunday mornings. In return I got one mark a week 'wages', and that mark played a very respectable role in keeping the household on keel. Occasionally my younger brothers and sisters came with me to deliver coal. I could soon carry a basket weighing a hundredweight on my back into the cellar, thereby relieving our mother of this heavy task, which she had taken on for the coal merchant in our house. In the winter, the snow had to be cleared and the ice broken up, too."[66]

66 *Deutsche Kindheiten. Autobiografische Zeugnisse 1700–1900.* Ed. by Irene Hardach-Pinke and Gerd Hardach. Kronberg (Taunus), 1978, p. 199.

83 English children waiting for a warm meal. Facilities for child care and child leisure were slow to spread in the cities.

84 Scrubbing steps in Scunthorpe. Working-class children had to contribute to their upkeep by working. Extensive child labour in factories had fallen. Instead they took on other odd jobs.

85 Exhausted children at a New York evening class. Photo by Jacob A. Riis, *c.* 1890. In the early 20th century child labour still conflicted with compulsory schooling.

This working-class lad was overloaded with daily chores. School, which was supposed to have been compulsory for every child for a long time, was simply an interruption in a chain of labours.

Compulsory schooling   The legal obligation to attend school and legislation protecting children were important steps towards educating and disciplining young proletarians. Schooling systems which would involve all children began to evolve towards the end of the 18th century in those countries which would eventually lead Europe industrially, and the initial intention, born of the Enlightenment, was to "educate the people". As capitalism developed, the educational measures introduced by the authorities were dictated by practical economic and ideological demands. The aim was to ensure a useful army of wage labour with elementary education well into the future, and to uphold religious compliance, submissiveness and patriotism. But many reforms and coercive measures were needed to make children attend school regularly.

The situation was undermined throughout the century by employers who bought child labour and, for many years, by proletarian parents who resisted schooling and believed it distracted their children from earning money. It is impossible to claim unambiguously that all working-class children were observing the law on compulsory schooling even at the turn of the century. As children were supposed to start school just at the age when they were capable of taking a job, it was an exception for proletarian children to attend school without interruption. There were, moreover, other fundamental hurdles which reduced their chances and their motivation for much learning: they had no time for homework, no money for books, or no shoes to leave the house in. In retrospect, pupils came to different conclusions about what school had done for them. Bitter experiences of whipping, cramming and humiliation were predominant, but some children clearly took a pride in what they learnt and were given an appetite for education which stimulated many a worker to discover more than had been offered by the simple syllabus.

"Raised on the streets"   Apart from work, school and the family, working-class children grew up in a fourth important element: the street. They passed through it in the course of their work, on the way to school, and, in their few leisure hours, to play. Atmospheric depictions of Europe's growing cities tell of wandering children's gangs and young people loitering in gateways, by shop windows or at stations. Proletarian children and youths cultivated their reactions, imagination, aims and desires through this daily contact with their peers, tussles with the authorities, and encounters with the goods and pleasures on sale. Justifiable demands for playgrounds, children's facilities and holiday play-schemes were always linked with vehement criticism of this street life and the harmful effects it might have on the youngsters.

86 St. Louis paperboys. Photo by Lewis W. Hine, 1910. Young workers officially entered employment at 14.   Most of them took unskilled jobs in factories, mines, building or the service sector.

And yet this street education was a vital formative experience for young proletarians in a world where they would eventually be forced to assert themselves. Where else could they have learnt such important behaviour as independence, intrepidity, swift reaction, wit, humour, material ambition and assertiveness than in these collective, public forms?

Youth   Childhood ended for working-class girls and boys when they entered full employment, which meant at 14 at the latest.

Most of them found an occupation at the factory that was unskilled or semiskilled, for apprenticeships were not very common. These first years of work were marked by frequent job changes and the constant search for something better. Young job-seekers had to be very mobile in response to the demands of the labour market, which changed according to the state of the economy, the season and regional conditions. In taking to the road, they were not so much concerned, like the journeymen, with gathering trade experience as with selling their labour as lucratively as possible. Healthy young men and women without families had the advantage over older workers. They constituted the bulk of migrant, and also emigrant, labour. Those who did stay at home paid their mothers for board and lodging. Sons in particular often earned more than their less energetic fathers, which enabled them to cast off parental authority at an early age. Daughters, too, were affected, thanks to the spread of factory labour, by the "virtual revolution in the lifestyle of working-class

87 Working-class children were at
home on the street. This photo was
taken in the north of Berlin in 1912 by
Willy Römer.

88 These Berlin lads did not have much free time for their boisterous games. Photo by Willy Römer, 1905.

James Aurig   DRESDEN·BLASEWITZ

89 Maids. Entering "service" was the only alternative to factory work for most girls. Photo by James Aurig, before 1888.

women before marriage"[67]. In the case of British women, at least, there is plenty of evidence for this. They preferred working in factories because the pay was good, but above all because they encountered "more life" there. They relished the opportunity to escape their domestic duties for a while. Their wages enabled them to fulfil aspirations. Part of their money was spent on sweets, clothes, picnics and the music hall. At the same time, many girls on the Continent were still putting all their earnings into the family kitty.

These years before starting a family were the freest, happiest and most lavish in the lives of young working men and women. They could afford to "treat themselves", dress with flair within the bounds of income, enjoy their leisure meeting their friends and taking part in many forms of entertainment.

Early economic independence meant that young people knew exactly where they stood with regard to the older generation. Obviously there were some limits on their activity, and interests had to be mutually respected, but they did not have to put up with being treated like small children. The potential inherent in their independence, their creative ambitions, their time and their expectations made young proletarians a prime target for both political groupings and the commercial gambits of the ruling class. Very soon there was a specific range of goods and entertainments aimed at young consumers, as well as spare-time organizations of a religious and patriotic nature.

On the scrap heap at forty   When the industrial cities first began to grow, they attracted young, healthy, single people. Those who were older or not so fit remained in their rural communities, where there was still traditional social provision for poverty, old age and illness. But there is practically no material to tell us about the lives of wage labourers who had grown old in the cities several generations later.

All their lives they had financed their upkeep by selling their labour. As their output began to fall and age rendered them unfit for work, their subsistence was in jeopardy. Their insecurity could not be overcome either by forms of trade-union assistance, such as disability, widows' or funeral funds, or by the social measures which employers and governments slowly began to introduce. August Bebel described the predicament of German workers in his day: "Millions tremble when they think ahead to their old age, when they will be thrown out on the street. And our industrial system makes people old before their time. The celebrated provisions for old age and disability in the German *Reich* grant but a very meagre substitute. Even their most zealous champions admit as much."[68]

67 Cf. Stearns, Peter N.: "Working-Class Women in Britain, 1890–1914," in: *Suffer and Be Still: women in the Victorian Age.* Ed. by Martha J. Vicinus. Bloomington, 1972, p. 110.
68 Bebel, August: *Die Frau und der Sozialismus.* Stuttgart, 1910, p. 464.

German statistics show that average life expectancy rose during the last decade of the 19th century. At the same time, however, the overall health of the population was declining as labour became more intensive. Factory workers were sapped the quickest, and from the age of 40 their strength diminished noticeably. Their wages dropped, and the chances of finding a different job, or re-entering the market after unemployment, dwindled.

Nevertheless, women and men alike were forced to carry on earning until they died. Few proletarians could set much money aside in better days, and if they did, the sum was intended for a "decent" burial. Many elderly workers depended on public welfare and relief. At worst, they were sent to the poorhouse and given a pauper's funeral.

The solidarity of children and grandchildren was doubtless very important during this period. They supported their relatives as best they could, even if they lived elsewhere.

90 Married couple homeworking, *c.* 1910. Workers had few guarantees in advanced years. Most had to earn their own bread to a ripe old age.

Proletarian Housing

91 Mining community in Freiberg, Saxony. Photo by Karl A. Reymann, c. 1905. Miners were among those workers who lived in houses intended solely as dwellings—unlike craft families—before the Industrial Revolution.

Ever since human communities struck firm roots, patterns of housing and settlement have been determined by the nature of production and how work is organized. Until the dawn of capitalist industrialization, almost all working people lived in houses, cottages or huts which included space for production and trade and often remained within the family for generations. Several generations of the family slept together under one roof along with other members of the household or productive unit. Economic considerations defined the size of the house and its division into living and working quarters, storage space and cattle stalls.

Types of farming, climate, landscape and soil fertility influenced not only the density of population and size of village settlements within a given territory, but also the character and proportions of the local town sustained by the territory in exchange for craft produce. By the end of the feudal age, market towns and the seats of noble courts in more favourable locations were already becoming an important focus for transferable wealth, in the form of money and goods, as well as centres of political power and princely pomp. They also required a growing number of manual labour who had to be accommodated within the town walls.

As industrialization proceeded, capital exerted more and more influence on housing and settlement. The aim was to combine labour, raw materials and sales outlets as effectively as possible. The growth of the various economic sectors now determined the size and location of industrial plant and the character of working-class communities.

The textiles industry established itself in rural areas where the guilds held no sway. This made it easier to drive cottage textile producers to the wall and absorb the resultant labour. The rise of mining and foundries gave birth initially to industrial villages, some of which then merged to create industrial districts without assuming an urban character. Armies of road-builders, canal-builders and railway-builders moved from one hut colony to the next.

The inflow of capital turned small towns into big industrial centres, while the mass influx of workers changed the face of feudal residences. But it was not only the factories and sprawling proletarian housing districts which altered the townscape. Trade, transport and crafts now had to take account of labourers' needs. Settlements with a population of several hundred thousand were no longer rare, and they posed demands of a completely new kind in terms of community services, hygiene, local amenities, medical facilities, schools and communication routes.

The wage labourers who flooded into the towns to find a livelihood had to purchase accommodation like any other form of goods. Job-hunters usually had no more than a bed in a hostel or refuge. Even those with a guaranteed income often had difficul-

92 Friedrich Kaiser's painting (1875) depicts the pace of the economic boom which swept across Germany in the seventies. The dynamism behind the rapid growth of cities symbolized the accelerated rhythms of industrial life.

93 Railway workers' flats in Vienna, built around 1870. Like heavy industries, the railway companies built accommodation for their employees, usually right beside the track. Local building styles were copied: this block resembles a mass urban tenement.

94 Railway construction in the centre of Berlin, *c.* 1880. Tracks carved great swathes through the cities to make room for the modern public transport systems which conveyed hundreds of thousands of people from home to work and back each day.

95 "London poor quarter." Drawing by Gustave Doré, 1876. Classes were strictly segregated in the cities, with clear lines drawn between housing for the upper and middle classes and the working-class communities where the unemployed and unemployable also lived.

ties finding a home of their own, for there was a permanent housing shortage which continued to worsen until the turn of the century, and rents became increasingly exorbitant. Second- and third-generation proletarians had higher expectations of comfort. In spite of the high rents, they preferred to spend a considerable portion of the family budget on better housing conditions: it was important to have one's "own four walls" to arrange as one pleased. Specific proletarian patterns of living developed furthest under urban housing conditions. Workers came into contact with city culture and witnessed the contradiction between the austerity of their own productive existence and the wealth of the bourgeoisie. Thus the big cities became power-houses of class organization.

Industrial workers in village communities   In the late 19th century, British, French and Silesian weavers, Thuringian toymakers and Bohemian glassblowers were still living and working in small houses of their own and farming a little arable land on the side. In France, these patterns of rural proletarian life were only found in traditional silk-worm breeding areas. In the Irish counties, families of tenant farmers ran a cottage tayloring industry. This combination of wage labour and a small-scale natural economy generated a lifestyle which had very little in common with the lives of urban proletarians.

The rural proletariat was inevitably sedentary and isolated. Moving to find a better job meant more than a change of rented quarters; it meant relinquishing a small property which they clung to hand and foot. A home of their own and the compensations of an agricultural sideline became, "under the rule of large-scale industry, not only the worst hindrance to the worker, but the greatest misfortune for the whole working class, the basis for an unexampled depression of wages below their normal level"[69], as Friedrich Engels remarked on analyzing British conditions. This did not only apply to home industry, which was usually periph-

69 Engels, Friedrich: "Preface to the Second Edition of 'The Housing Question'," in: Marx, Karl, and Friedrich Engels: *Selected Works*. Vol. 2. Moscow, 1969, p. 302.

eral. In many areas, a substantial proportion of factory workers commuted from neighbouring villages. This does not only refer to specifically agrarian industries, as the Daimler works in Untertürkheim near Stuttgart in Germany illustrate. Most of its workers came from the rural surroundings. They remained conspicuously rooted in the "soil". The effects of owning a house, preserving strong local bonds and covering a long distance to work proved negative. Their lifestyle was marked by a loss of mobility, poor communication with other workers, and an almost complete lack of free time.

A bed somewhere In pre-industrial times, it was quite normal for young, single labourers in town and country alike to live away from home without accommodation of their own. Journeymen and apprentices lived in the master's household, servants had quarters in their employer's home, and the staff of an inn bedded down on the landlord's premises. This form of accommodation inevitably chained ancillary labour to a kind of family hierarchy which considerably limited personal independence. Not only was strict subordination demanded within the extended household itself, but even going out was subject to strict rules. The traditional battle for the "key of the door" indicates how hard it was for journeymen to conquer a small degree of that celebrated "town freedom".

For the occupational groups concerned, this pattern survived well into the era of industrial capitalism. Those who remained tied by this combination of work and shelter were unacquainted with the strict demarcation between working and non-working hours, and they enjoyed little freedom of movement when it came to leisure.

With the advance of industry, a new form of accommodation without a home emerged: lodging. In this way, even as the housing shortage grew more acute, single workers flocking to the cities quickly found cheap shelter despite their meagre resources. Working-class families often took in a peer as a paying lodger. The newcomer was frequently fully involved in family life, and found not only food and a bed, but also social contact to make settling in town less painful.

If new arrivals in quest of a job could not manage to obtain accommodation in this way, refuges for the homeless provided a temporary bed. These were public institutions which were set up in all the major industrial towns. The doors were open not only to strangers from other parts, but also to the unemployed, dismissed serving maids, and families evicted from their homes for not paying the rent.

These shelters were also a magnet to those who never managed or wanted to strike roots in the town with their own home and family. They wandered without ties from one refuge to the next

96 A proletarian home in London, *c.* 1850. The bed and the fire were the most important things, with only the barest essentials of furniture and equipment.

97 The attic flat of a working woman. Photo by Heinrich Lichte & Co., Berlin, 1916.

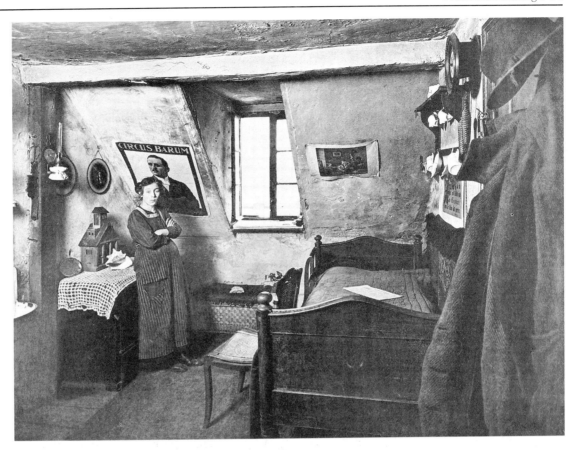

98 This former forge has been converted into a dormitory for unskilled young workers arriving from the country to take on physically strenuous labour. Serving maids slept just as roughly in lofts and other such spartan surroundings. Photo by Heinrich Lichte & Co., Berlin, 1906.

99 "Shacks for evicted tenants."
Drawing by Paul Meyerheim, 1872.
When the housing shortage was at its
most severe, mass evictions of proletarian families with rent in arrears were
not rare. Primitive camps, like this one
outside Berlin, were an example of
self-help.

taking casual jobs, eventually joining the lumpen proletariat or the ranks of criminals.

Houses for workers Prince Albert, Queen Victoria's Prince Consort, designed a working-class house for the first World Exhibition in London that was intended to demonstrate social concern. In fact, the model never went into series construction, but it illustrates the public attention that was devoted to the "Worker Question". Apart from the situation in the factories, bourgeois reformers regarded the poor housing conditions of penned-in workers as a cause of proletarian immorality. Conservative critics of squalid housing were fond of radical solutions. Wherever possible, the proletariat should be kept away from the towns and housed in smaller, almost rural settlements where it would be easier for the police to control in times of conflict. Similar projects proposed owner occupation for workers in the belief that social contradictions would moderate once "propertyless workers are transformed into working property-owners".

The traditions of tied cottages were maintained in Britain and some other countries. Industrialists who set up companies in the countryside and found no other facilities for housing their employees returned constantly to this form. Later on, workers' cottages were even built in industrial cities. The Krupp estates were built in this rural style. They were intended to provide the residents with "middle-class protection from becoming pro-

letarianized in the old working-class districts"[70]. The pit communities of the Ruhr were also a conscious tool of the bosses' social policy. They did act as an effective brake on fluctuation, forming a core of employees who were especially dependent, but they did not vouchsafe untainted good conduct, as the big strikes of 1889, 1905 and 1912 demonstrate.

This housing policy took astute advantage of working-class needs, for in many ways these factory estates complied with the workers' tastes: they drew on familiar elements in the patterns of housing which newcomers had experienced in their original communities; they enabled people with similar backgrounds to live together as neighbours; and they promised a secure home. That is why bourgeois reformers later returned to these models, transforming them into local government projects for green working-class communities.

Urban tenements Barracking was an early form of concentrating labour in a small place, usually by means of non-economic coercion. Towns used these methods when they set up workhouses, and governments for their manufactories. The penal colonies in Australia, Siberia and North America worked on similar principles, herding prisoners together to develop new territory. Councils and governments had the power to dictate

70 Klaphek, Richard: *Siedlungswerk Krupp.* Berlin, 1930, p. 8.

100 Cripplegate in London, *c.* 1855. During economic crisis, unemployment and waves of rent increases, not only the newcomers to the towns, but also many local people could no longer afford a bed and wandered the streets without shelter. If religious organizations or charities did not take them in, local councils were obliged to open refuges where homeless people could stay for short periods at a low charge.

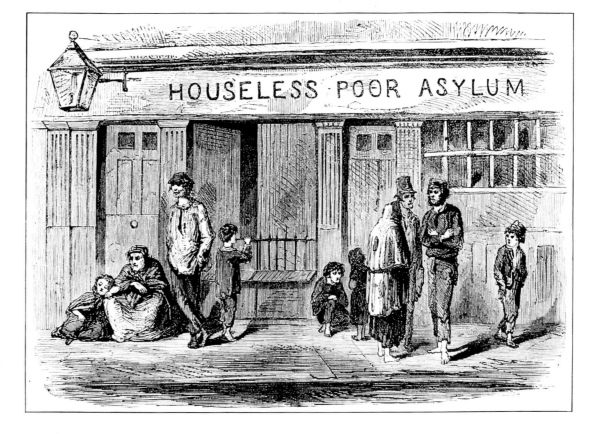

101 A street scene in working-class Berlin, *c.* 1903. Shops on the ground floor, and sometimes in the basement, of the front building served the ten- ants: in this case a baker's and a shoemaker's. It was not customary to photograph everyday life, so everyone adopted a pose for the camera.

102 The yard of a Berlin tenement house. Photo by Heinrich Lichte & Co., 1909. From 1860 onwards, these blocks several storeys high were built on long, thin strips of land. Workers usually lived in the side and rear, with social groups of a higher income brack- et residing out front.

during both working and non-working hours. Later on, factory-owners opened hostels for young, single workers arriving from outside, imposing a military regime aimed at keeping their occupants under constant surveillance. The mass tenements of the 19th century were not at all the same thing, and yet they earned themselves the nickname "rented barracks". In the European cities of the Continent, housing usually consisted of buildings several storeys high divided into numerous self-contained flats. The front block would face the street, and lined up behind were several rear blocks arranged around courtyards. Many critics of housing conditions for working people uncovered disgraceful standards in the tenements. Nevertheless, this form of mass urban rented accommodation can be viewed as an early attempt at rational town planning to cope with a growing number of workers and their families. Compared with village homes or small houses in pre-industrial towns, these blocks were well endowed with tap water, toilets, gas, and later sewage systems and electricity. From a proletarian angle, the housing problem was not going to be solved by covering the country with fragmentary colonies of small houses. The concentrated population of predominantly working-class urban districts was one of the foundations in the latter half of the 19th century on which proletarian lifestyle and class organization were constructed. Logically, then, realistic working-class policy was not opposed to the city as a framework for housing, but to property speculation, exorbitant rents, inadequate inner-city transport, and tardiness in providing the tenements with the civilizing conveniences of the modern age.

New housing standards In the early stage of industrialization, the most important concern of newcomers to the town was to find shelter in order to sleep.

Everywhere, housing for workers was rare and expensive. Nowhere could urban construction keep pace with the rapid growth in population. A bed or a flat devoured a substantial proportion of the individual wage or family income. Whenever earnings were eroded as a result of unemployment, short-time work, illness or another baby, the possible effects were debts to the landlord, pawning possessions, even eviction. So it was always a risk for the worker to take a better flat when wages increased. The situation improved after the turn of the century, with higher real income, relatively secure employment, more leisure time, and a wider variety of recreational needs to compensate for more intensive labour. Choice of housing was also influenced by the growing value attached to family life in the home and greater attention to the children.

However, compared with the overall number of proletarians, only a few well-paid skilled workers could afford significantly better housing at this time. Big industrialists such as Krupp, Siemens and AEG (Allgemeine Elektricitäts-Gesellschaft) responded to this trend by offering company homes to tie these

103 A proletarian moves house. Photo by Willy Römer, Berlin, 1913. Wage labourers were obliged to move more often than any other section of the urban population, owing to rent increases, illness, unemployment or a new job.

104 Sunday in the garden on the outskirts of Berlin, 1905. Better-paid workers like this skilled employee of an electrical company would rent an allotment in a "colony" on the edge of town. Most built themselves a chalet on the site. Thousands of factory and office workers and craft journeymen spent their weekends in their garden.

105 After work: a rest on the sofa, c. 1905. Skilled workers like this Berlin printer were prepared to invest in a comfortable home. A sofa was essential.

more sophisticated home culture among 19th-century bourgeois circles. There were separate rooms for parents and children, boys and girls. Clear lines were drawn between the space designated for social intercourse, sleep, reading, play, eating and cooking. Just as there was a particular time of day for every activity and need, so there was a special room.

For proletarians, too, labour had been removed from the realm of accommodation, fashioning a daily rhythm to match and provoking the development of private life and individual domesticity. This called for a modicum of material prosperity, including a home of one's own.

At the turn of the century, working-class families usually lived in a kitchen-cum-living-room with another small, unheated room. Any additional space was sub-let to a lodger. The women and children spent the day in the warm kitchen. This was the place to cook, eat, wash, study, play and work. The box room was used for sleeping, and it was quite common for some members of the family to make up their beds in the kitchen. Furnishings were scanty.

The first thing which proletarian families lamented was the shortage of beds. It was just about possible, under these cramped conditions, for the adults to restore their spent energy day by day and to watch over the children. It was too much to expect to make oneself comfortable, indulge in individual leisure pursuits or derive any pleasure from family harmony. And yet these were qualities of life which proletarians rated more and more highly as their labour became more skilled and intensive and their need for relaxation and recreation grew. Skilled workers earning better wages wanted better housing standards, and they showed as much by gradually changing their domestic living conditions, with bourgeois family life serving them as a model.

A housewife who stayed at home, no need for lodgers, beds for everyone, separate rooms for parents and children, a parlour with a display cabinet and sofa, ornaments and a framed benediction, lace curtains and china cups were all visible signs that these sections of the working class were demanding higher standards of family life and individual leisure time.

employees to the factory. But local councils and private builders also adjusted to the more differentiated expectations of the working-class population. They built blocks of flats, residential districts and estates with respectable comforts for renting to working-class families in the higher income bracket.

Badly-paid unskilled labourers, homeworkers, employees in the service sector, and single and elderly workers continued living in the urban slums. Their accommodation was acutely overfilled, and the appalling structural conditions were not to improve for many years. These were considered the breeding grounds for two fearsome effects of poor housing: tuberculosis and rickets.

Your own four walls The division between work and the home, the spheres of production and reproduction, had led to a

Proletariat and City

The advanced factory proletariat made the city its home. This geographical and social concentration of productive units and labour became its specific environment. The expansion of the working class went hand in hand with urbanization. Both began in Britain, the cradle of capitalism, where the urban population became the majority in 1851 with 51 per cent. Henceforth the level of industrial development could be measured in terms of urbanization. The only other countries where city dwellers exceeded ten per cent of the population at this time were France, Belgium, Saxony, Prussia and the United States of America.

Every new factory in the countryside bore within it the seeds of a factory town, as Engels observed in 1844 in the light of the "marvellously rapid growth" of English towns. It was not merely towns that grew up, but strings of towns, industrial conurbations, especially in regions rich in raw materials, notably coal, such as Upper Silesia, the English Midlands and the German Ruhr. In 1850 Duisburg and Essen were little backwaters, but by the end of the century they were key industrial centres. Chicago sprouted just as dramatically. About 1830 there were 70 inhabitants, before the great fire of 1871 the total was 300,000, and when the next century began it was the fifth-largest city in the world with a population of 1.7 million. Beef and steel had unleashed this economic boom. The capitals of the major industrial countries counted their residents by the million. London set the ball rolling in 1810, becoming the first city in Europe to register a million inhabitants since the fall of Rome. By 1850 2.6 million Londoners lived in the world's biggest metropolis, which was followed by Paris, New York, Berlin and Vienna. The figures did not just mean industrial progress and wealth. Concentrated poverty and squalor in the cities ignited social unrest of proportions that had never been witnessed before. Factory-owners and politicians alike tried to bring their influence to bear so that the advantages of urban settlement were preserved. After all, the bigger the towns, the more profitable it was for capitalist companies to settle and invest there. The combined benefits of a favourable site for communications, commercial traditions and a mass, versatile res-

106 "St. Pancras Station and Hotel, London." Painting by John O'Connor, 1884. Stations were palatial urban structures which boasted the concentration of wealth and business to incoming travellers. They were imposing gates onto the world.

107 A Berlin working-class district around the Stettin Station. The densely populated townscape was dominated by urban tenements.

ervoir of labour were adjusted to meet the needs of capital. Never in the course of history have there been faster or more radical changes in the character, capacity and structure of towns than in the 19th century.

Living conditions for millions The capitalist cities drew together all the "marvels of civilization" (Engels). Apart from being the focal points of industrial production, they were financial and commercial centres, traffic junctions, seats of local and national government, cauldrons of science, education, art and amusement. Totally new spatial and communicative foundations were laid for urban life, linked inevitably with the size and multiple functions of the community. The process affected sites of production, housing, inner-city transport, supplies, disposal of refuse and sewage, and recreation. Big industry needed its own access to traffic networks, space for factories, and spatial isolation to reduce the impact of noise and dirt.

But more than anything else it needed a vast supply of labour, and systematic provision had to be made for its accommodation. Entire new boroughs appeared where workers would eventually dominate. More tenants were packed into existing quarters, while old districts were pulled down to make room for denser housing. Suburbs and outskirts were developed in the wave of mass-scale construction. Berlin and Vienna were the biggest tenement towns in Europe. In London, Philadelphia and Chicago, many proletarians lived in endless rows of terraced houses. In Paris and New York, enormous blocks of flats were built for workers. The common denominators in all these settlements, be it the north of Berlin or London's East End, were their monotonous appearance and heavy population density. Everyone paid rent and crowded together in the minimum of space in austerely furnished flats with inadequate hygiene.

In the city centres, remote from factory and residential districts, there was hardly any housing or production. Public authorities, banks and insurance companies had their offices here, amid a concentration of department stores, newspapers and entertainment establishments. The biggest and most magnificent buildings belonged to the insurance and industrial companies. The first modern tower blocks were built by a Chicago insurance company (1883), the sewing machine producers Singer (1908) and Woolworth chain stores (1913) in New York. Like these skyscrapers, the Eiffel Tower, built in Paris in 1889 and the world's tallest structure until 1930, represented power and supreme technical accomplishment.

Urban development was propelled forward, and at the same time hindered, by the diverging interests of rival groups of capital. These giant social organisms required some form of order to channel opposing interests and keep the city running smoothly. Property speculators were careful that every square metre was put to a purpose, not only in working-class areas. At the same time, there were laws and plans to observe about building on

108 Budapest Market, *c.* 1900. Similar modern shopping centres modelled on the Parisian Halls opened in other major cities. This was the first step towards hygienic daily supplies of food to millions of city dwellers.

streets and squares, including factors such as alignment, width and height. Main avenues carved furrows through twisty old town centres. In Paris, for example, Baron Haussmann reacted to the June insurrection of 1848 by ordering broad boulevards to be built as "fields of fire" across rebellious working-class districts. Other cities followed suit, adopting the Parisian layout and splendour for their own major thoroughfares. Streets lined with shops and grand monuments, ideal for parades, spacious enough to contain huge crowds and permit the growing flow of traffic, were a typical feature of capitals and other grand cities. Mass transport was a part of urban life, for hundreds of thousands of people had to cover a considerable distance between home and work each day.

Inspiring innovations in technology and organization were also introduced to cater for other everyday needs. Waterworks, sewers, gas boards, electricity stations, refuse collections, slaughterhouses, markets, department stores, arcades, baths and hospitals were among the facilities which made city life feasible, bearable, and even comfortable.

Magnets and "labour-movement hotspots" Towns had always owed their growth to the influx of country dwellers. The population was rising in absolute terms, and as a result of the agrarian revolution vast numbers of rural labourers lost their livelihoods, so that domestic migration assumed an unprecedented momentum in the aspiring industrial lands of Europe.

Immigrants were lured to the big industrial towns by their expectations of a wide, all-round choice of jobs and good earnings. Many left their old homes in the vague hope that they might make a quick and easy fortune in town or establish their independence. There were material and cultural prospects which the countryside could not offer. Discrimination based on property, public scorn and gossip lost their significance to the individual against the proletarian backcloth of the city, where everyone was rated according to the value of their labour and had to fend for themselves. Provincial narrow-mindedness, tedium, superstition, passivity and complacency gave way to matter-of-fact relationships, confidence, and the ambition to achieve and acquire. Since urban wage labourers could choose freely how to run their private lives, their behaviour was determined by a lack of social obligations, mobility, and a variety of stimulation and opportunity. Urban proletarians took the repeated changes in their home, job and trade for granted, just like the rapid succession of impressions and challenges which constituted everyday existence.

Having to pay attention to road traffic, always hurrying, being bombarded with advertisements, lights, noise, throngs and the temptations of superfluous wealth on display were a strain on the nerves of city dwellers, sharpening their senses and provoking new needs. The pace and the atmosphere of the city called for specific reactions, and proletarian demands on life became more differentiated and sophisticated as a result. The city offered every-

109 "London street scene." Drawing by Gustave Doré, *c.* 1875. Every city had its own unique flavour, but everything was in the same state of flux: hectic street life, throngs of people, advertisements and shop windows, pubs, cinemas and dance halls.

110 New York: "Broadway." Engraving, *c.* 1870.

111 London: Trafalgar Square and
St. Martin in the Fields, 1902.

112 New York: East Side. Photo by
Lewis W. Hine, *c.* 1910.

113 New Orleans: St. Charles Street,
c. 1890.

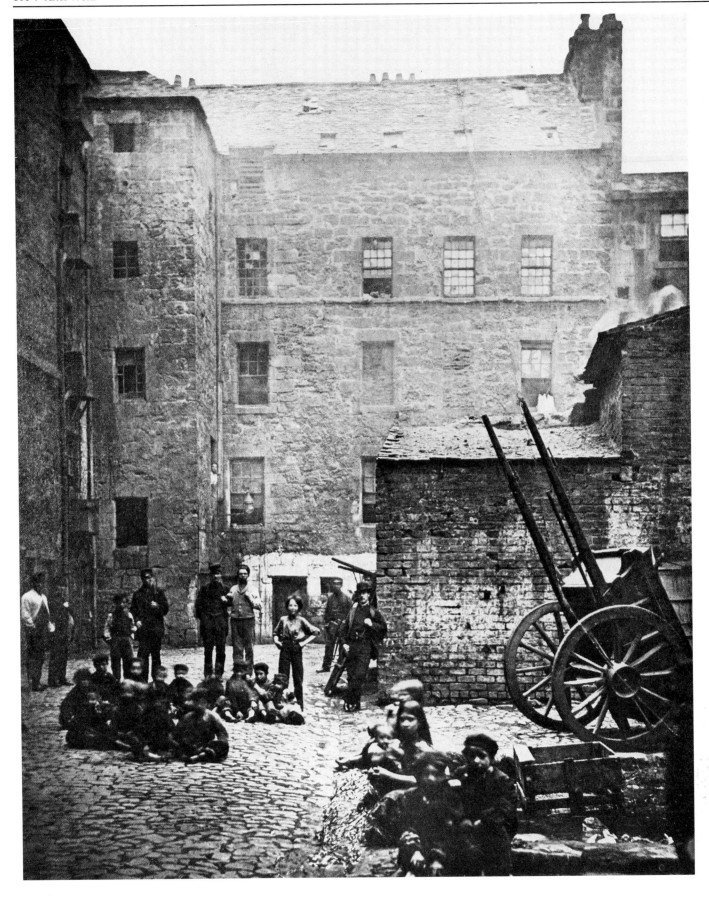

114 A yard in old Glasgow. Photo by Thomas Annan, after 1868.

115 Working-class quarter in Antwerp, *c.* 1900.

116 Working-class street in old Bremen, *c.* 1910. The first newcomers often had to live in the oldest housing, sometimes pre-industrial. The families of those first-generation proletarians stayed here until the houses were demolished. All the accommodation was overcrowded. Children played and neighbours met in the narrow alleyways and yards.

thing and tolerated everything. This is where the "morals and customs of the good old times [were] most completely obliterated", as Engels put it, both in the positive and in the negative sense. It is also where the class antagonisms in capitalist society were experienced most sharply and brought most pugnaciously to the surface.

Just as capital, wealth and power, in all their manifestations, were concentrated in the industrial towns, so the urban proletariat assumed its most differentiated, mass form alongside. The city was a melting pot of casual jobbers and skilled workers, immigrant farm hands and former craftsmen with long local pedigrees, drop-outs and social climbers representing every occupation, background, philosophy and fate within the bounds of working-class existence.

The huge factories and densely populated working-class districts of these great cities were fertile soil for communication between workers, who could observe and compare the full spectrum of working and living conditions, from the most wretched to the most advanced, and then move on to discuss their common reactions and, indeed, actions. Here lay the roots of the bread riots, strikes, demonstrations, and all forms of economic and political class struggle.

During the course of the 19th century, the big European cities of Paris, London, Berlin, Vienna and Petersburg evolved into centres of the organized labour movement. With their mass basis for revolutionary activity they became the headquarters of party leaderships and played host to big national and international meetings of workers.

Village and Colony

At the dawn of the 20th century, the distinctive proletarian type was the skilled industrial worker. He spent over half the day working and travelling there and back, enjoyed a certain amount of regular free time, received a weekly wage, remained a worker all his life, lived in a town, rented a home, bought food and clothing instead of producing them himself, had on average at least two children but no more than six when the appropriate time came, was able to read and write, belonged to a trade union, had the right of suffrage and voted socialist, but was not necessarily a member of any working-class political party.

But this essential type still constituted a minority among the highly differentiated working class. Even so, common features of all proletarians, whatever their differences, were that they owned no machines or factories and so had to sell their labour to acquire the means to live, and that the jobs they performed were those rated less highly by society. As far as these similarities were concerned, workers were a growing group, yet no worker was quite the same as the next when it came to concrete circumstances. There were a whole variety of dissimilarities between them, both new and inherited.

The nature and degree of a worker's individual development hinged on many variable factors: complex or simple labour, with or without machinery, monitoring function or mindless monotony, skilled or unskilled, office or shop floor, blue or white collar, regular worker or unemployed, young or old, female or male, big family or single, decent home or slum, village or city.

In most countries, it was not urban industrial workers, but rural labourers who composed the majority of the working class. Their living conditions were imbued by the legacy of personal dependence on the landowners, the village community and the productive family. They learnt industrial methods and technology later. Pre-proletarian traits of thinking, feeling and living took longer to fade away. They found it harder to join together in a permanent, nationwide association in order to defend their interests. As a rule, therefore, they constituted a source of conservative votes.

The least fortunate workers of all were those in the colonies of industrial capitalist countries. Extreme poverty, trickery and violence had compelled them to enter the proletariat. Their wage labour bore features of forced labour. Their energies were sapped with a particular disregard for scruple. They were as deprived of political rights as the victims of military conquests.

Capital was expanding the working class constantly, turning craftsmen into factory workers, rural workers into urban workers, matriarchal peasants into wage labourers. They all brought views and habits with them from their group of origin, remaining in contact with it through family relationships, and returning if they could, if the demand for labour dropped, or if their strength waned.

In socio-economic terms, wage labourers formed a single class, regardless of occupation, job content, income bracket, race, nation, religion, gender or age. This fact lent common features to their lifestyle and culture. But just as their living conditions varied, so, too, did their opportunities for cultural development and the eventual outcome, as well as their ability and readiness to forge a culture of their own kind. This opened the door to conflicts of interest, both genuine and illusory, between various sections within the working class. Workers with a more advanced standard of living tended to commit themselves to long-term preparations for social change, whereas the unemployed often preferred more radical action in the short term. Many European workers could not see that their relatively high standards of culture were due in part to colonial exploitation by their capitalists. And the First World War showed how national differences could be transformed into arguments why workers ought to defend the advantages, traditions, rights and riches of their own national culture against French, British, German, Russian and other "hereditary enemies", "barbarians" and "bandits".

Rural Labourers

At the turn of the century, rural labourers still constituted an absolute majority compared with all other sections of the proletariat. This rural proletariat was made up of day labourers, serfs, estate workers, smallholders, tenants, farm hands, cowherds, goatherds and shepherds, cowboys, gauchos, vaqueros, sheep-shearers, reapers, plantation workers, hop-pickers, vintagers, rubber gatherers, rice coolies and beet-growers and many more besides. Only in the industrial nations of Europe, such as Britain and Germany, was the number of industrial producers beginning to exceed the number of wage labourers engaged in agriculture. There was a fundamental difference between "agriculture" as a specific productive form using increasingly capitalist methods and the labour of small peasants. Farms (especially in the United States), estates (especially in Germany) and latifundias (especially in Italy and Latin America) were employing more and more wage labourers of a particular kind: rural proletarians. Working conditions changed when cereals were grown on big fields and harvested using threshing machines. Barrack-style accommodation left its mark on housing patterns. Food, clothes and consumer pleasures changed, resembling new proletarian rather than medieval agrarian habits.

As a countryside component of the working class, the rural proletariat represented historical progress. Rural workers were essentially free of roots which might bind them to the soil. Legally they could choose where to sell their labour and whether to turn their backs on the land and enter industry. Unlike peasants

117 "A farm hand's room." Painting by Carl Arp, 1900. Unmarried rural workers slept in dormitories or small, austere rooms of their own near their work. Stable boys would often sleep next-door to their horses.

tied to their land and serfs dependent on their feudal lords, their livelihood had a decisively new basis. They were wage labourers, but with special features.

The wage-labour relationship developed later, more gradually and less purely than in industry. Wages included payment in kind, accommodation rights, permission to till land or graze cattle, fuel and similar benefits. Cash made a very hesitant and always modest entry into a rural worker's budget. Even in the 20th century, some labourers were only paid once or twice a year, on termination of contract or on special occasions. It was extremely rare to be rewarded according to actual results.

In spite of nominal liberty under the law, forms of personal dependence survived for many years. The powers of the *Junker*, *patrón* or boss were absolute, comparable with those of feudal lords. He was more or less free to choose whether to rule the district with kindness or the rod. To some extent, social legislation was not applicable to the rural proletariat, and in remote agrarian regions it was largely ignored. Country workers seldom moved in a time or space outside the estate or even their own narrow sphere of labour. The realms of labour and leisure were not divided, as with the industrial proletariat. Farm hands, dairymaids, cowboys and gauchos lived in servant quarters on the property which employed them. Many bedded down with the cattle for which they were responsible, often living among the beasts for months of the working year, whatever the national characteristics which distinguished them. Day labourers, farm hands, estate workers and similar categories usually inhabited tied cottages near their work. The specific rhythms of agricultural labour left their decisive mark on the lives of rural workers. As agrarian producers, they were particularly dependent on natural processes. Seasons, climate and weather, the animals and the soil influenced their procedures. It was the strength of draught animals, not the power of engines, which still told them how fast to work and when to rest. The evolution of differentiated needs so typical of the urban proletariat was delayed by distorted wage forms, isolation from towns and industry, and the negligible influence of urban communication and consumer variety. Rural workers had simple needs and evaluated products according to how cheap and practicable they were. They rarely had cash to spend, perhaps a few times a year. For a long time they continued to produce food, clothes and other articles for their own use. Working-class families in the countryside hoarded provisions, span yarn and wool, wove, sewed and knitted. They made baskets and their own furniture, and kept a small plot of land. They were close enough to small property ownership to preserve their links with the landowners and the community for varying periods of time. Their mobility was curtailed.

One reaction to this culturally backward lifestyle was the great surge to join the industrial proletariat in the towns. Moreover, opposition to oppressive rural conditions flared up again and again. It was seldom organized, hardly political, and usually of a

118 "Tied cottage." Rural workers and their families usually rented housing from the estate owner or farmer. They rarely possessed a home of their own. Housing was cramped with sparse furniture and poor sanitation. Pigment print by Marie Boehm.

119 All over the world a rural proletariat was taking shape throughout the 19th century. It was determined by national and regional patterns of agriculture. The common feature everywhere was rural poverty, which forced proletarians in the countryside to accept wage labour on big semi-feudal or purely capitalist estates. Rural workers in Peru. Photo of 1865.

spontaneous, individual nature. If corporal punishment was inflicted on rural workers, they often hit back. Labourers setting off for a new life in town would frequently bid farewell to the master by setting his house on fire. Luddite tactics would be adopted by workers who regarded the new threshing machines and other equipment as an assault on the value of their labour. Sometimes they agreed among themselves to work slowly, or else refused to work altogether. In the grain-growing regions of Europe, breaking contract became a mass phenomenon.

Harvest Agricultural labour called for muscle power, stamina and empirical dexterity. It usually took place in the open and depended on the weather. This description of the harvest written by a rural worker named Franz Rehbein conveys an impression of the agrarian work process: "As far as the eye could see it was the same picture, one cornfield after the other full of busy men, women and children … While the harvest lasted the day labourer had but one motto: sweat and toil. You could see why they said piece rates were lethal. You drive yourself so hard that you wish there were twenty-eight hours to the day and not just twenty-four. In good weather, get on with the job. Of course the reaper's legs are almost always wet with dew from the knee down until eight or nine in the morning, but then things get moving. The binders are far worse off, as the dew-laden sheaves drench their clothes all down the front while they tie them. In binding it is the hands that suffer most, for the wet dew makes them soft and sensitive and they look like the hands of a washerwoman elbow deep in water all day long. The nails come loose and cause pain, the fingertips get damaged, hands are often wounded by the sharp stubble, or the flattened blades cut the fingers. But once the dew has dried out, the thistles begin to prick, and the higher the sun climbs into the sky, the sharper they become. For the first few days the binder's hands often sting so badly that she hardly knows what to do with them, and only afterwards when they are quite full of thistles and stubble wounds do her senses gradually numb. How often I have felt secretly sorry for my wife. But what's the use? You cannot afford to be sensitive in the country, or you earn nothing, and you have to take advantage of harvest time … At last, late in the evening when your weary limbs are almost refusing to carry on, the day's work is done. The sun has long since set and a misty evening darkness settles over the fields, and only then a halt is called. After all, nature demands her due and the body must gather fresh strength."[71]

Threshing machines The threshing machine was a fine illustration of technological progress in capitalist agriculture. Its introduction had decisive effects on the life of the rural worker. Now that the traditional flail was no longer required for threshing, an important winter occupation was lost. Threshing was performed substantially faster, and threshers found themselves obsolete as a group. The same amount of work could be completed by fewer workers in much less time. The threshing machine reinforced the seasonal character of agriculture and left rural workers without employment. It also considerably increased the intensity of labour. The task had to proceed with unprecedented speed and co-ordination between workers. The sheaves were forked up, handed across and fed into the machine. Other workers removed the straw, stacking it with forks onto a cart to be trundled away, while yet another group filled the grain into sacks and ferried off the loads. A mechanic ran the engine and ensured that threshing proceeded smoothly. The various groups had to phase their work together, and their individual members were expected to act as a team. The process placed a heavy strain on muscle power, stamina and faculties of reaction.

Set breaks proved necessary when physical exhaustion led to too many accidents. For the same reason, alcohol was eventually forbidden. Previously it had been the custom in agriculture to use it as a stimulus. It was quite normal for the working day to last twelve or sixteen hours. In general, it was determined by the period of daylight, otherwise the threshing would fall below standard. The working day was sometimes protracted by means of artificial lighting. When the day's labours were done, workers often slept where they were in the straw, as a long walk home would have shortened their respite.

Seasonal labour Unlike modern industry, the agrarian economy has always been influenced to a particular degree by seasonal labour. Since large-scale enterprise demanded concentration, certain highly marketable crops either dominated or monopolized the pattern of cultivation. All these crops involved a productive cycle of their own in which the harvest, be it of grain, root vegetables, sugar cane, cotton, tea, tobacco or fruit, played a key role. As a crop ripened, it had to be brought in as quickly as possible. That required a large supply of available labour which could no longer be obtained from the immediate locality, so that workers had to be recruited from elsewhere. Migrant labour began to flow across regional and national boundaries, especially in overpopulated Central Europe. Swedes and Danes flocked to the granaries of northern Germany, workers from western Germany signed contracts in Holland, while Dutch workers sold their labour in north-west Germany. Labourers migrated from Luxembourg to south-west Germany and from northern Italy to Bavaria and Austria. Workers from Russian Poland, Lithuania and Masuria found seasonal employment in Germany's north-eastern grain fields. In Germany itself, the districts of Eichsfeld, Warthebruch and Silesia were major reservoirs of this seasonal labour supply.

Word of jobs and money spread. Workers in overpopulated areas set off for foreign parts. They would meet at major junctions, wait at railway stations for offers of employment, or roam

---

71 Rehbein, Franz: *Gesinde und Gesindel*. Berlin, 1955, pp. 256–60.

120 "Flax Weeding in Flanders."
Painting by Emile Claus, 1887. Rural
women were a large force in agrarian
wage labour, primarily performing the
routine cultivation of diverse crops.

121 English reapers, 1880. Cereals had to be gathered in as fast as possible as the weather permitted. The big grain farms then required large numbers of labourers who could not all be supplied locally. This provoked regional and international migration among rural workers.

122 Steam locomobile, *c.* 1914. Progress in the capitalist agrarian economy could be measured in terms of the technology borrowed from modern industry. Steam power was a key factor. It shortened tasks and released labour. Agricultural work patterns became even more seasonal.

123 Migrant workers set off for Saxony. Photo by Haeckel Brothers, Berlin, 1909. The harvest of root crops in Saxony lured rural workers from all over Europe who hired themselves out for pulling up the sugar beet and processing it. Recruitment and transportation were efficiently organized.

124 Rural women travelling to the fields. Photo by Louis Held, *c.* 1905. Like their urban proletarian sisters, these rural labourers carried a double burden in earning the means of subsistence. Apart from their vital contribution to the household economy and family maintenance, they had to take part in the farm work on their landlord's estate.

from village to village. Actual markets grew up where individuals or groups of workers could ply their labour. Prospective partners negotiated wages and food, sealing their contract with a hand-shake or earnest money.

As the seasonal demand for labour grew and the migrant flocks swelled in number, new patterns of organization were required. The gang system was already taking shape in England in the 18th century. A gang consisted of anything between 10 and 50 men and women with a gangmaster at their head. He was a rural worker himself, and he recruited his gang for a set period of labour. He negotiated wages with the estate-owner or tenant farmer, and his own income depended on the gang's performance. Once the work was finished, he would move on to the next farm with his workers.

Similar systems emerged in Central Europe in the latter half of the 19th century. To recruit seasonal labour, officials would disperse into the overpopulated rural regions, occupy a table in the village inn and set about winning over workers. The officials were paid head money. The biggest demand was for reapers to work in the grain-growing areas and for root-croppers to work the Saxon fields. The group of enlisted workers took their orders from a foreman who was also the liaison officer between the group and each new contractor. He was held responsible for the group and his wage was, likewise, determined by their performance.

The foreman also had to ensure that no one in the group went astray. Special identity cards with a police stamp were issued to migrant labourers to guarantee adequate control.

In this manner, wage labourers broadened their horizons, compared notes and encountered advanced capitalist agriculture. But their work was not continuous. The workers returned to the dependent relations which governed small, family peasant-holdings, where their labour was superfluous.

Reapers in barracks Special forms of shelter were required to accommodate the throngs of vagrant labour mobilized by the seasonal character of the capitalist farm economy. At first, seasonal workers slept in barns and empty byres. This rarely led to conflict, as the workers were more interested in high wages than comfort, while the estate-owners were eager to keep their costs as low as possible. It was not until liberal critics began to protest against the inadequate hygiene and the "immoral conditions" of seasonal hirelings that estate-owners began building homes for them. Different kinds of mass accommodation emerged in the various regions of Germany, but they were all bracketed together under the name "reapers' barracks". They were a new but characteristic feature of the village physiognomy and governed the distinctive relationship between work and free time among seasonal labourers.

Reapers worked in pairs who stayed together for the purpose of harvesting: the man cut the corn, and the woman bound the sheaves together. They were sometimes married, and sometimes

125 Cotton picker, *c.* 1900. Large numbers of seasonal workers were taken on during the harvest, especially in regions with large estates, latifundias and plantations.

IN THE COTTON PICKERY.

they formed a team for one summer. Often whole families would turn up with their children. All of them lived in the "barracks", a term which derived less from the structure of the building than from its purpose. The idea was to offer temporary shelter at low cost to an appropriate number of workers. Most normal functions of housing were ignored. Every worker had a spartan bed. As there was central feeding one fire to cook over was sufficient. The few personal possessions which workers brought along were stowed under the bed, although later on lockers were also fitted.

The labourers not only worked together as a team, but also lived communally in their "barracks" and the immediate environment. They ate and slept together, washed themselves and their clothes at a pump outside the door, repaired their tools and celebrated in company, and discussed problems with their fellows. Their community spirit was enhanced by shared interests, shared working and living conditions and a shared experience away from home. Released from the narrow-minded fetters of their birthplace, they developed a convivial existence relatively free of coercion. The native villagers usually regarded their lifestyle as strange and exotic, if not enviable, which is why the reapers were a magnet, especially for rural youth.

Food, drink and tobacco   Food was the main item in the rural labourer's family budget. In Central Europe, for instance, these families spent over two-thirds of their total income on this one essential. The only way that they could satisfy this demand was to preserve traditional forms of private provision and make careful use of food-stuffs. Rural workers of various types supplemented their wages by keeping cattle, gardening and obtaining produce from their employers. They owned pigs, perhaps some poultry, and occasionally a cow or goat. They received fodder in return for their labour. This gave their food supply a relatively firm basis.

Workers who were integrated into their employer's property usually received meals. Board was part of their wage and negotiated as a clause in the contract. Labourers rated their employers according to their generosity in this respect. Farms which offered poor food acquired a bad reputation and had trouble finding enough workers. It was not rare for a contracted worker to desert on the grounds of inadequate board. The rural labourers' diet consisted largely of the produce which they had grown themselves: potatoes in eastern Germany, milk and cheese among herders, beef for cowboys and gauchos, although the staple in this case was beans.

The semi-luxuries were beyond most workers' reach. Tobacco was smoked in European countries. It could be stored for long periods. Rural workers usually smoked a pipe, saving a cigar for special occasions. Chewing tobacco was also a widespread practice, as it meant the substance could be taken at work. Although rural labourers could not afford many extras of this kind, they were familiar with the delights of alcohol in many forms. In the regions east of the river Elbe, they were especially fond of the home-made potato schnapps which their employers used to sell or donate. It made people tipsy and convivial. Apart from helping to "drown sorrows", it was commonly held to banish physical weariness and satisfy the hunger. Merry bouts of intoxication were sparked off by wage settlements, the end of a job, annual fairs, holidays and celebrations.

The country worker's clothes   One of the most immediate differences between rural workers and town dwellers was their apparel. They did not wear peasant costumes, but neither did they don the fashionable attire of the cities. Their appearance bore the marks of thrift and practicality. A rural worker wore working clothes, and kept them on all the time, as there was nothing to divide the sphere of work from the sphere of free time. In many European countries, they possessed special clothes for Sundays and festivals which revealed signs of urban influence, but after they had served their purpose they were quickly taken off again. In other regions, however, no distinction was made. If working clothes were clean and mended, that was adequate, although there was a tendency to choose newer clothing and possibly add a kerchief or a scarf.

Home-produced clothes were also worn, subject to regional variation. Herdsmen wore wool, leather and skins. The arable proletariat donned woollen fabrics and above all linen. Rural labouring families would process wool, flax and skins, particularly in the winter months, to earn some extra money and to provide the family itself with clothes. As the 19th century drew to a close, in Central Europe this home-made wear declined without disappearing altogether. The urban rag trade produced more cheaply. Flax and wool grew rare, while cotton clothing, which was more resilient to wear and tear, gained international popularity.

126 Mealtime on the estate, *c.* 1900. Single labourers usually obtained their meals from the landlord. Board was part of their wages. Families tied to the estate preferred to cater for themselves in order to dispose more freely of their income.

Colonies and Coolies

Since the 15th century, European commercial capital had been seeking to conquer the world. Arms were used in the quest for luxuries such as pepper, cinnamon, jewels, gold and silver, which the wealthy coveted in parading their fortune and which were urgently needed for exchange in the expanding network of trade. Plundering, piratical trading, forced labour in the colonies and the slave trade were the earliest forms of colonial exploitation. As Europe industrialized, raw materials and markets for industrial commodities became more important. Now, productive capital flowed into the colonies, too, hoping to extract super-profits from the cheap labour. Capital was exported, and along with it capitalist relations. The proletariat acquired brothers and rivals of all races on all continents.

In the earliest stages of capitalism, Africa had been "a hunting reserve for trade in blackskins"[72], but now the emphasis shifted to exploiting African wage labourers in their own country. The import of European commodities into the colonies had damaged the traditional relationship between agriculture and cottage industry and was beginning, as in India, to erode the subsistence of the traditional crafts. Under colonial conditions, raw materials required for the "mother countries" were mined and then exported straight away, rather than being processed in the same place, so that pre-capitalist forms of exploitation co-existed with capitalist forms. The evolution of wage labour in the colonial countries was linked with slavery and forced labour. Colonial exploitation determined the working conditions, patterns of recruitment and living conditions of the emergent working class. It followed a number of paths: either small-scale commodity production in the villages was preserved and incorporated into the web of money and commodity exchange, or else profit was made from forcing peasants to adopt monocultures and raising taxes. In most cases, however, millions of peasants were obliged to flee the land which European immigrants had seized for their plantations. All these factors promoted the growth of wage labour, for the peasants who had been driven off the land had to hire themselves to the white settlers as rural workers on their plantations or sell their labour for wages in the mines and factories.

This economic dependence was backed up by colonial laws and administration, armed forces, and a system of racial discrimination. Compared with their fellows in Europe, the wage labourers created in this manner were largely deprived of rights: there were no legal limits to the working day, conditions were hard and unrelieved by advanced technology, pay was low, there was a distinct lack of opportunities for education and training,

127 Huge numbers of slaves were imported into the United States to work the plantations. They were auctioned like cattle. Richmond, Virginia, was a busy market-place (1856).

workers were powerless in the face of brutality and corruption among overseers and supervisory staff, food and clothing were inadequate, housing was bad, disability often came early and there were no social provisions, female and child labour were widespread and the mortality rate was high.

Wage labour was recruited by means of a wide range of enforced enlistments, some of which were camouflaged by "employment contracts". In some, especially African, countries, there was "debt slavery", which meant that people were compelled to work to pay off tax. The authorities in the service of the capitalist motherlands forcibly enlisted workers for projects of key importance to the colonial economy and export of goods, such as building roads, bridges and railways. From 1906 onwards, railway construction was stepped up in Africa, leading to particularly inhumane forms of forced labour, as the high death rate among African workers illustrated. On the northern route in Cameroon it reached 50 per cent, and on the railroad from Matindi to Leopoldville they reckoned one dead man for every sleeper laid.

The situation of workers in the colonial countries was similar in many basic ways to that of their fellows in the advanced industrial nations of Europe and North America, but the process of proletarianization assumed a more draconian shape than it had done in Europe during the period of primitive accumulation. The rights and living standards of the colonial peoples were as low as the proletarian status could possibly allow. Indian, Chinese and Malayan coolies came to symbolize poverty and social contempt. The civilizatory trends inherent in capitalism bore their fruits primarily in the colonizing countries, while in the colonies the traditional cultures were destroyed with nothing substantial to replace them. In Europe and North America it sometimes seemed as though the proletariat and the bourgeoisie were members of different nations. Here they actually were. Industrial capitalism imposed an alien culture and rule.

Colonial exploitation soon led to workers' protests, such as those which affected several African countries and India during the 1880s. The first Indian general strike took place in 1913. Community support groups of an ethnic or religious nature were the embryos of labour organizations. In Latin America, too, peasants driven from their land constituted a huge army from which rural workers were recruited for the plantations and cattle farms and wage labourers for the mines.

Migrant labour in South Africa's mines After diamonds and gold were discovered in South Africa, the British monopolies began to expand from 1877 onwards. Cecil Rhodes's British South Africa Company secured the monopoly on these underground riches, extending its field of interest in 1889 to embrace

72 Marx, Karl: "Das Kapital." First vol. In: MECW. Vol. 23, p. 779.

128 The American Indians put up steady armed resistance to the settlers who simply took away their land. Their greatest victory came at Little Big Horn in 1876 against Custer's troops.

CUSTER KILLED.

DISASTROUS DEFEAT OF THE AMERICAN TROOPS BY THE INDIANS.

SLAUGHTER OF OUR BEST AND BRAVEST.

GRANT'S INDIAN POLICY COME TO FRUIT.

A WHOLE FAMILY OF HEROES SWEPT AWAY.

THREE HUNDRED AND FIFTEEN AMERICAN SOLDIERS KILLED AND THIRTY-ONE WOUNDED.

SALT LAKE, U. T., July 5.—The correspondent of the Helena (Mon.) *Herald* writes from Still water, Mon., under date of July 2, as follows:

Muggins Taylor, a scout for General Gibbon, arrived here last night direct from Little Horn River and reports that General Custer found the Indian camp of 2,000 lodges on the Little Horn and immediately attacked it.

He charged the thickest portion of the camp with five companies. Nothing is k... n of the operations of this detachment, except their course as traced by the dead. Major Reno commanded the other seven companies and attacked the lower portion of the camp.

129 Forced recruitment in the surrounding villages, extensive exploitation and inhuman conditions for workers enabled the Germans to construct railways through their African colony of Cameroon.

Die Arbeiten zur Vollendung der Tanganjiaka-Bahn in Deutsch-Ost-Afrika.
Die Bahn, ca. 1250 klm lang, ermöglicht von Daressalam bis Tanganjiaka in 36 Stunden zu reisen, wozu man früher viele Wochen brauchte.

130 Indian weavers. Capital relations destroyed the historical fabric of craft and agrarian production in India. As the native crafts died out, millions lost their livelihood and their roots.

131 The British colonialists crushed Indian risings with cruel repression. In 1857 the satirical magazine *Punch* called for justice.

the land of the Mashona and Matabele. This new colony, which was eventually to become Southern Rhodesia, was established after the resistance of these peoples had been cruelly defeated. A proletariat was created in Southern Africa by driving the native population out of their homes and herding them into reservations with unfertile soil. Having been robbed of their livelihoods, they were obliged to sell their labour on the farms of white settlers or to sign on for a period in the mines. Migrant labour became the principal form of waged work.

The colonial authorities encouraged the growth of a labour army by raising taxes, so that peasants were compelled to accept wage labour on the basis of employment contracts lasting anything from one month to three years. A complex recruiting apparatus took advantage of the peasants' extreme circumstances and their ignorance of colonial laws. The Pass Laws introduced in 1895 made it compulsory for every African to carry an identity card with proof of employment. Anyone caught without this card could be labelled a "vagabond" and handed over to any European for a job. About 100,000 African workers were down the South African mines around 1899. Working conditions were tough and payment was often arbitrary. Wages were not fixed until 1897. More and more miners were migrants from neighbouring countries: Nyasaland, Portuguese East Africa from 1902, Transvaal, Basutoland and Bechuanaland. The colonial authorities in those lands had a financial involvement. German colonial officials in South-West Africa, for example, were paid 410 marks for every worker they sent to South Africa.

The lot of the South African mineworkers was hard on two counts: not only were they prey for the severely exploitative methods of the mining companies, but they were also cut off from their families, who were barely managing to survive on unfertile soil. The strict Pass and Labour Laws forbade their wives and children to visit them, and there was heavy punishment for anyone who left the site before termination of contract. The Natives Act passed in 1911 stipulated that anyone who abandoned a job should pay a fine of £10 sterling or spend two months in prison. They lived in desolate colonies of huts, divided up according to tribe, and were exposed to the arbitrary brutality of overseers. Beating and whipping were part of the normal treatment. There was no limit on the working day, no extra money for Sundays, no insurance. If a worker met with a fatal accident, his family was sent £19 sterling (a dead white worker was worth £500). Workers had no chance to better themselves. When they began a new contract, they had to start on the lowest wages again. 1913 witnessed the first big strike by miners protesting against starvation wages and lack of prevention of accidents.

The fate of the Indian coolie India had been under British colonial administration since 1853 and offered a growing market for British industrial products. At the same time, capital export and railway construction provided an impetus to industrialization, breaking up the traditional crafts and stimulating the growth of wage labour.

The first railway line (Bombay to Thana) and the first telegraph wire went into operation in 1853. Peasants whose village communities had disintegrated sought work in the textile and jute factories. In 1879 there were 43,000 workers employed in 56 textile mills, 20,000 workers at 20 jute factories, and another 20,000 workers down 20 mines. In the early nineties, the overall number of wage labourers working for factories, mines and the railway had risen to about 800,000. Uprooted families drifted to the towns and earned their daily upkeep by taking occasional waged work as day labourers, porters, or rickshaw coolies until they managed to find a factory job, where they had to work 12 to 14 hours a day with no social protection under the severest working conditions. Women and children were no exceptions. A law limiting child labour was not introduced until 1881, and women's work was regulated in 1891. Low wages drove workers into the slums, where entire families lived in overfilled rooms with no sanitation and often no water for drinking. Jobs were acquired via an agent, who demanded a fat commission. In many cases he was also a landlord and trader, so that coolies were obliged to rent his primitive accommodation in return for an exorbitant sum and to pay his high prices for food. The outcome was starvation and epidemic disease. In the year 1895, 53 million Indians died of hunger. Epidemics of plague and cholera at the turn of the century cost millions of lives. As this century dawned, the strike movement grew, with workers voicing opposition to their starvation wages. Meanwhile, more and more workers were joining the anti-colonial resistance.

Latin American peones From 1870 onwards, the integration of Latin America into the international economy accelerated. Monopolies (mostly British to begin with, but increasingly American from the turn of the century) soon acquired a dominant position in the state and economy as a result of their capital investments. These focused above all on agricultural monocultures, monoproduction (such as cattle breeding) and mining. It was during this period that a national bourgeoisie in the major Latin American countries, largely derived from the landowning class, embarked on their own process of industrialization.

And so the working class of Latin America grew. Impoverished peasants entered the plantations and cattle farms as rural workers or took jobs down the mines. Another section of the working class, associated with modern industry, gradually formed from the 1880s onwards. Disappropriated Indian peasants constituted a sizeable proportion of wage labour in the mines and plantations. Wage labour and feudal exploitation were combined in the peonage system which governed the lives of many rural workers, but was also found to some degree in industry and mining (in the textile mills of Brazil and the nitrate mines of Chile). The owners treated their peones and their families as serfs rather than wage labourers. They were paid almost exclusively in kind, or else were given a small plot of land for the family to till. The owner supplied building materials or accommodation, which belonged to him, however poor the hut. The working day was unlimited. The miners' fate proved particularly hard, for strict norms, lack of safety measures and primitive equipment took their toll of health and life.

Latin American workers put up more defiant resistance to these living conditions from the beginning of the 20th century. Mass strikes by proletarians, such as the miners' strike in Cananea, Mexico, in 1906 and a strike by Bolivian miners that same year, ended in bloodbaths. The disenfranchised rural workers of Mexico, above all indios, formed a large contingent of the movement of peasants and partisans led by Francisco Villa and Emiliano Zapata in the 1910 Revolution. A general strike was called in Argentina in 1909 after demonstrating workers were shot down on 1 May. Latin America's young working class began to organize. Anarchist trade unions and socialist workers' parties were founded to take up the battle for better living conditions and political rights.

132 Advertisements for colonial commodities such as coffee, tea, cocoa and tropical fruits functioned as a back-up for colonial policy in all the leading capitalist countries. Direct importers tried to corner the market.

The Force of Rule

As capitalism developed, the bourgeoisie created a comprehensive system of institutions to sustain their own political, social and cultural dominance and the oppression of the proletariat. They included the judiciary, police, army, schools, Church and press, and their task was to proclaim, propagate and interpret bourgeois achievements, and ultimately to protect them. In this way, the bourgeoisie managed to extend their potential for economic influence into structures of politics and culture.

In the 18th and early 19th centuries, commercial capitalists, merchants, speculators on the stock exchange, manufactory owners, craftsmen and engineers, even resourceful skilled workers, had acquired money, fortune and property through a mixture of luck, ambition and marriage. They did not only own the machines and ever-expanding plant, but all means of production. As a result, they had the power to purchase the skills and talents, gifts and energies of other people, making use of these for their own interests and benefiting from the value.

The ruling circles interwove economic coercion with political and cultural institutions in order to preserve their private sovereignty over the potential accomplishments of others, constantly consolidating and improving their position and fashioning patterns of permanency. Bourgeois efforts to socialize proletarians in the spirit of bourgeois aims and strategies became more and more intense. Proletarian individuality was to be a product of bourgeois values and ideas. From the cradle to the grave, from the school bench to the club, from labour at the factory to the establishments of leisure, a dense network of rules and institutions sought to integrate the workers into bourgeois culture and bind them to capitalist society in order to strengthen the established economic and social structures.

A Competitive Labour Market

The industrial mode of production could only prevail by breaking radically with the feudal forms and methods of finding and providing work, which were based on estate. The slave of Antiquity, the bondsman and guild craftsman of the feudal age, all lived against a framework which guaranteed security within a set community. Although their circumstances were often wretched enough, the village and family in which they lived and worked offered a certain opportunity for subsistence. The advent of capitalism destroyed these traditional links completely. A great mass of people had been prised away from their soil and robbed of any property basis they had, so that they were forced to seek their salvation in a totally new world. Capitalist society threw up a new institution, the labour market, where people without roots or property met the owners of the means of production in the shape of tools, machines and raw materials. This market regulated the exchange of living labour—the productive forces—and money. As the individual's labour power assumed the form of a commodity, there was a semblance of justice about the exchange. After all, "living labour" was a specific commodity with a value which was visibly expressed in its price, as with any other commodity. The quantity of jobs and available labourers, supply and demand, now determined how high the price for that commodity was going to be. Other factors which kept the labour market flexible and governed the conditions for realizing the value of productive human abilities included the social, political and cultural situation, the concrete balance of power between capital and labour and the competition or unity and solidarity between bourgeois industrialists as well as between workers themselves. An appropriate legal form for wage labour was devised with the employment contract.

From handshake to labour exchange In the early days, individual workers felt hostility towards the free labour market, for they were still unsure of their new social status and inexperienced in using the rights and liberties it entailed. The liberal bourgeois, who thought in individualistic terms, saw this market as a guarantee of social betterment, a testing ground for the fittest.

By the end of the century, the bourgeoisie were confronted by an organized working class which, in most European countries, was collectively disciplined, and in some places, such as Britain, had managed to extend its rights. Meanwhile, the spontaneous individual regulation of a nation's creative potential, characteristic of the "Manchester" period and its principle of "laissez-faire", was also nearing its end on the labour market. Labour exchanges and employment agencies were assuming the functions once fulfilled by taverns, stations and even shelters for the homeless. Conditions for the realization of the productive forces were now being negotiated collectively and set down by contract within the framework of a company or trade.

For the majority of workers, finding a job was no longer quite so like being hired as a mercenary. The centres of industry and focal points of economic prosperity required a regulated labour market. The employment contract was no longer struck outside the factory gates and sealed with a handshake. Oral agreement gave way to the written document.

Coercion at work When Richard Arkwright, the British factory-owner who invented the spinning frame, analyzed his workers' activity, he found them unmethodical and unqualified. He criticized them strongly for their shoddy work habits, which were inadequate to the demands and standards of industrial labour. Most factory-owners complained about the behaviour and manner of their workers. They agreed almost unanimously that this was no way to make profit in the long run. They would have to breed a new producer with qualities that matched the requirements of industry. Wage labourers were subsequently subjected to heavy pressure to perform their work regularly, diligently and conscientiously. Economic incentives replaced non-economic coercion.

The laws defining the freedom of contract assumed that the parties concerned were the capitalist and the individual worker. The state prohibited associations and agreements between the labourers. Until the sixties, the British master and servant laws threatened prison for workers who broke contract. The employment contract was concluded on the basis of a pure market re-

133 The Pyramid of Oppression: the new capitalist class society was de- nounced in many forms.

134 The railway engineer and ship-builder Isambard Kingdom Brunel was a typical specimen of a 19th-century generation of entrepreneurs: bold, determined, ambitious, always on the look-out for opportunities which he seized. Before directing construction of the big steamship *Great Eastern* he managed railway building projects in Italy, India and Australia. Photo by Robert Howlett, *c.* 1857.

135 A New York job centre, *c.* 1910.

136 Job hunters in Hamburg, *c.* 1900.

137 Waiting room for the unskilled at Berlin's employment agency. Organized channels of job allocation emerged towards the end of the century. Labour exchanges collected the requirements of a particular company, trade or town and passed appropriate information on to job seekers. These agencies were set up by trade unions and other labour-movement organizations, local authorities, employers' federations, and urban institutions. They were eventually to develop into the standard employment offices.

138 Poster publicizing an employment agency in Dresden, *c.*1900.

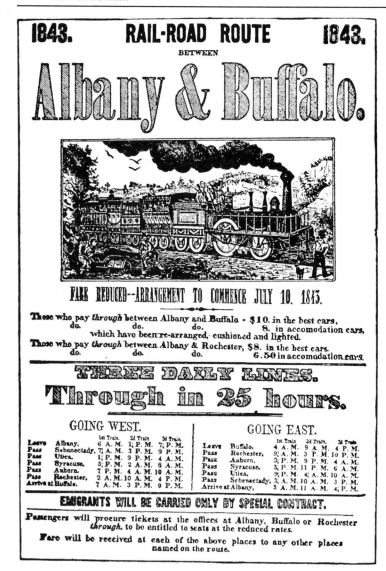

139 "Emigrants will be carried only by special contract" warns this railway company, which conveyed its passengers from the Hudson River to the eastern end of Lake Erie in 25 hours. Emigration to the "New World" offered a chance to find work or make an independent living.

lationship according to the underlying principle of the cash nexus, the length of its term was considered just as important as forms of remuneration.

Discipline always boiled down to the threat of dismissal and loss of livelihood. The general insecurity of proletarian life formed the framework for all coercive measures. The descent into social misery loomed constantly. An existence on the margins of poverty made the worker both acquiescent and rebellious. On the one hand, he stood to lose his income, but on the other his wages hardly paid for the bare essentials. The worker had his back to the wall. Adaptiveness was one possible individual response. To both individuals and groups of workers, spontaneous protest and personal rebellion seemed the most obvious way of resisting.

The economic pressure exerted by the labour market was complemented by internal factory statutes. The labour market distributed productive abilities to specific points of production, while these factory rules regulated disciplined co-operation at work over and above the demands of technology. They established a social structure in the factory, defined the powers of supervisors and overseers, and determined who was authorized to issue instructions.

Apart from this, the rules laid down a general code of conduct, listed valid causes for dismissal and stipulated set periods of notice. They prescribed the penalties for offences, bad time-keeping, failure to observe working hours and breaks, leaving a post without permission, sub-standard work and the destruction of tools. Once the organized labour movement had established a certain influence, employers were under pressure to adopt an old craft tradition and make provision for assistance in cases of sickness, accident and death. The factory regulations outlined a model career for the factory worker from taking a job until quitting the labour process.

Divide and rule Workers lived in constant fear of losing their jobs overnight and no longer being able to feed a family. This gave employers the opportunity to use competition between workers in order to strengthen their own rule. Recurrent economic collapse only intensified the tactic. The uncertainties of working-class life made rivals of labourers in the "fight to survive".

Although production technology and organization had already created an advanced division of labour based on training, experience and natural skills, employers did not merely exploit the rivalry between skilled, semi-skilled and unskilled workers. They also made use of national prejudices and specific differences incurred by age or gender.

Wage structures were a prime tool in stimulating competition between the workers. Hourly rates, piece rates and bonuses of various kinds were applied to compensate individuals or groups for their work record. The piece rate drove a wedge into the working class because it created a state of affairs whereby individual incomes within one and the same factory varied substantially. Different rates were paid for different phases of the production process. On the one hand, higher wages for better work, coupled with opportunities to ascend the company ladder, unleashed repeated examples of individual initiative on the part of the workers, but at the same time the device provoked envy and suspicion.

Capital flooded into areas where labour was cheaper, shifting industries to the newly-won colonies, hiring a predominance of Chinese coolies to build the American railroads and foreign labour from Poland to mine the coal in Lorraine and the Ruhr.

Employers took particular advantage of ethnic differences in order to pre-empt common forms of struggle among the workers. They also discriminated between the religions, age groups and sexes to construct a workplace hierarchy which always bowed to the owner's will. Finally, an employer could keep his own workers in order by appealing to their sense of loyalty in the face of competition between capitalists. A firm threatened with bankruptcy meant unemployment, poverty, a starving family. Workers could hardly demand higher wages or improved conditions from a company which the other capitalists were forcing to the wall.

140 A ''souvenir'' of the lock-out at Vogel & Schlegel in Dresden, 1906. Workers demonstrate their determination and unity outside the barred doors of their firm. Lock-outs were a particularly vicious form of coercion in labour struggles. The employers simply terminated all contracts and the workers found themselves on the street with no entítlements.

The Workhouse

The best way to study the change in methods of educating and oppressing the populace is surely to look at the history of the workhouse. In 16th-century England it was already playing an important role in taming the roving poor. A law passed in 1576 made it compulsory for every parish to open one. It was not long before a sizeable proportion of centralized production was focused on the prisons, poorhouses, workhouses and orphanages. There were similar institutions in other European countries where the homeless poor and apprehended paupers lived and worked.

From the Enclosures begun under Henry VIII of England until the period of the Bourgeois Democratic Revolution in 1848, property-owners and governments across Europe had been demanding drastic measures against mass begging and vagabondage. Everybody was supposed to work, and anyone who did not do so willingly should be compelled to it by society. The aim of the workhouse was to discipline these people and educate them for work. The people who gathered here were uprooted, disabled, sick or old. There were children, too. All of them had simply been idling away the days, but now the workhouse inflicted them with tasks which had the advantage of producing saleable results.

The workhouses were supported in their function by national and local government. Money was no longer distributed as alms, but spent on setting up hosiery workshops and cloth manufactories. For the state and the entrepreneurs, workhouses were attractive from both the economic and the cultural point of view; they held the seeds of industrial development and schooled their inmates in working at a trade. Enterprising employers would take out a lease on a prison or workhouse, fit it out for spinning hemp or linen, and integrate masses of workers into the system of capitalist exploitation. Even orphans, the sick, blind, deaf and dumb, and deranged souls were expected to earn their own keep in these institutions.

England, having invented the workhouse, reformed it in 1834 with a Poor Law which paid tribute to contemporary conditions. Almost two million people were locked up in these strongholds performing socially useful work. Basically, the reforms were aimed at withdrawing public money from the poorhouse and workhouse. The workhouse was to become a final resort where borderline cases would have a chance to prove themselves. Working and living conditions were to be so unpleasant that a protracted stay would mean sheer Hell for the inmate, and labour in a factory, on the railways or in the countryside would seem preferable. By forcing people to work, these institutions had drawn on human productivity, but without developing it further. Force did not really create any motivation to work, and since the Industrial Revolution began the capitalist economy had come to depend increasingly on internalized forms of the compulsion to work, conscious diligence and a willingness to invest energy. Workers learnt and acquired that pronounced economic sense noted by Benjamin Franklin in freely chosen industrial employment. As mercantile production and manufacture declined, the workhouse and other similar institutions lost their real economic and social significance. They were no longer profitable.

The law is the law Clear laws were needed to regulate the complicated, interwoven processes taking place in the economy, politics and cultural life. Bodies were required to impose and protect those laws. Justice could no longer hinge on the whims or favours of an individual ruler. Equal rights for all were constructed on the basis of a standard legal code. It was the task of the judiciary, police and penal authorities to guarantee this civilizatory accomplishment.

The bobby or constable, *gendarme*, *Schutzmann* and sheriff were part of the urban picture. They were the guardians of the law, symbolic incarnations of state power and authority. All these figures, the judge in his robe and wig and the uniformed policeman with his sable or truncheon, on horseback or on foot, commanded respect. The best thing was to avoid them altogether. The local constable in particular, often wearing the moustache or whiskers of his kaiser, king or president, appeared to be a rock of peace and order with no class affiliation. He often came from a proletarian or petty-bourgeois family, carrying out his "duties" on behalf of his superiors as an officer on the beat, a prison warder or a fireman. He was just as loyal when directing the traffic or protecting his head of state as he was when evicting proletarians from their homes, breaking up meetings and pummelling strikers. He became a mascot for the "culture of ruling" in the 19th century.

But although his office and his uniform gave him the confidence and dignity he needed as a pillar of state, cartoonists, writers and folk singers made him a target of their mirth. He was also the butt of working-class jokes.

A world full of clauses The self-reliant individual, whose integrity was guaranteed by the inviolability of his property, was now the sanctified hub of bourgeois cultural values. The new society had something to defend which had never existed before to this extent and with this particular social feature: private ownership of the means of production, the commodities produced and the accumulated wealth, money in the bank and in bourgeois pockets, land, department stores, shops, restaurants and hotels. It all had to be protected from hungry, covetous people who were making growing demands in louder and more forcible tones. The streets of Manchester, Paris, Berlin and Chicago were filling daily with swelling crowds who created social wealth by their own labour and yet enjoyed few of its fruits as a result of their social status. But the very sight of these people in their working clothes,

Die Lösung der sozialen Frage

(Zeichnung von Th. Th. Heine)

„Sie haben völlige Freiheit, mein Lieber, Sie können nach rechts oder nach links gehen, ganz wie Sie wollen."

141 "The solution to the Social Question." Cartoon by Thomas Theodor Heine in *Simplicissimus*, 1898/99. The ruling class offered the workers two alternatives: factory or prison.

J. S. ELLIOTT, Manager. J. M. GARDNER, Engineer.

WEST RIDING POLICE ON DUTY AT HOUGHTON MAIN COLLIERY,
DURING STRIKE, OCT. 8TH, 1893.

142 West Riding Police during a strike in 1893. The police intervened to protect the employers and their property. American workers even had to contend with private police forces and combat units hired by the bosses.

143 Striking miners in the Ruhr, 1912, reading a government decree at the pit gates. It empowered guardians of the law to shoot wherever they felt it necessary.

144 Prussian policemen, 1910. In the 19th century the constable symbolized the authoritarian state.

145 The lumpen proletariat led an existence without roots, and their forms of protest matched. In February 1892 the poor and unemployed of east and south-east Berlin formed a mob and went on the rampage, looting shops and spending a whole day making merry with liquor and other booty. To avoid this happening again, police officers were issued with firearms as well as the conventional sable.

146 Soldiers guard the factories. "A Paris strike in 1898." Drawing by Théophile Alexandre Steinlen. Whenever the police proved inadequate to the task, soldiers were sent in to preserve bourgeois order. Here in Paris the army occupied factories during the strike.

their casual jackets and collarless attire, signalled danger to the bourgeois, aroused his need for protection and security. The right to private property was an inviolable right granted to everyone.

It was not enough simply to guide the workers down a path of virtue. They had to be kept in constant fear of breaking or infringing the law. The world they lived in was full of prohibitions. Often the bourgeois in his carriage or car, with his top hat and tails, even looked as though he owned justice. He had made the laws. The worker was outside this "decent society". Not being able to pay the rent, asking to be chalked up on the grocer's slate of debts, paying the supervisor a fine for a damaged tool were all everyday occurrences. After several pregnancies his wife ended up on a backstreet table, risking not only her life, but also years in prison. Many a girl was forced by sheer poverty to "go on the street". And a harmless pub brawl could erupt into unforeseeable trouble.

And yet capitalist society and culture are inextricably associated with the Bill of Rights, *Code Napoléon* and *Bürgerliches Gesetzbuch*. Law and order were the right words to express the conditions which the new society needed in order to develop as it should. Workers learnt to move within the confines of bourgeois justice, acknowledging this law and order and using it for themselves. Individual forms of resistance were not effective in the long term as reactions to cynical parades of wealth.

Solitary confinement Anyone who did violate bourgeois law was destined, not for the pillory, the debtor's tower, wheel or executioner's block, but for "modern" prisons or bourgeois death machines like the guillotine and the electric chair. The penalties for breaching the public peace, stealing someone else's property, abortion, or smashing a neighbour's skull were becoming increasingly varied. The customary methods of punishment and repression included deportation, penal camps, the *bagno*, prison with or without labour, the workhouse and other such institutions. Some of these methods had been borrowed from history and updated, but others were new. The antiquated system of feudal justice and punishment disintegrated completely with industrialization. The countries which had advanced furthest in fashioning a capitalist society, such as Britain and the Netherlands, devised a modern prison system. The *maison de force* in Ghent, built between 1772 and 1775, was a typical example.

In accordance with bourgeois thinking, the prisoner was regarded as a person, whose treatment depended on individual type. The aim was not revenge, but to punish the individual with his or her personal responsibility for a personal guilt. From now on, prison was to mean a warning, improvement, reform and education. The ideas of bourgeois humanism were thus in harmony with a desire to extract value from human labour by means of capital. The standard form of imprisonment was to be solitary confinement, particularly in British prisons. Trends in the United States illustrate how greatly the enforced improvement by way of punishment varied. The Philadelphia Prison Society founded in 1776 had a prison built in 1790 where strict solitary confinement was observed day and night, uninterrupted even by work. Other penitentiaries, such as Auburn in New York State, which opened in 1823, allowed prisoners to work together in absolute silence, only to be isolated in cells again at night.

Similar establishments were built everywhere during the 19th century: Pentonville near London opened in 1840, Bruchsal in Baden, Germany, in 1848, Moabit in Berlin in 1849.

As far as the prisoner was concerned, solitary confinement was a more intense form of personal oppression accompanied by great psychological torment, but at the same time, this individual approach to penalty opened up the first opportunities for measures to resocialize criminals. The various forms of punishment—solitary confinement, group confinement, conditional discharge, removal to the colonies—were designed to lead them back into the fold, where they would conduct normal, law-abiding lives as members of bourgeois society. Britain and Ireland experimented with reforms, combining a sentence aimed at restoring the convict's moral balance with gradual, practical rehabilitation.

The humanitarian intentions of liberal reformers were thwarted by everyday reality. When a worker had been confronted with the bourgeois courts and penal institutions, he was usually released from prison as a mental and physical wreck. Solitary confinement, withdrawal of permission to work and other forms of bullying provoked rampant psychological disturbance, and problems with social orientation and adaptation. Besides, once a worker had a criminal record he was ostracized. Whether his prison term had only lasted a few months or several years, it remained a stigma all his life. Hardly anyone would offer him a job, former friends and colleagues kept their distance, and the landlord would have given notice to quit. This social marginalization was the start of the downward slope: charity, a shelter for the homeless, alcohol, prostitution and another prison sentence. Once a person was caught in the vicious circle it was very difficult to break out again.

Ruthless violence Whether the bourgeoisie had recently seized power or arrived at it in gentle compromise with the nobility, they had no intention of letting the proletariat limit or even question it. Every workers' protest was observed with suspicion. Workers had no right to vote or were severely restricted by legal measures. The guardians of individual freedom banned associations of workers, hired detectives to spy on trade unions campaigning for better working conditions, or banished politically uncomfortable characters for undefined periods to far-off Si-

147 Central prison in Wronke, 1895.

148 Reformed prisons were the subject of heated debates in the 19th century, and many travellers actually visited them, subsequently recording their impressions. Philadelphia's modern Eastern Penitentiary served as a model for many European establishments. Charles Dickens described it in his *American Notes*: "Standing at the central point, and looking down these dreary passages, the dull repose and quiet that prevails, is awful. Occasionally, there is a drowsy sound from some lone weaver's shuttle, or shoemaker's last, but it is stifled by the thick walls and heavy dungeon-door, and only serves to make the general stillness more profound. Over the head and face of every prisoner who comes into this melancholy house, a black hood is drawn; and in this dark shroud, an emblem of the curtain dropped between him and the living world, he is led to the cell from which he never again comes forth, until his whole term of imprisonment has expired. He never hears of wife or children; home or friends; the life or death of any single creature . . . He is a man buried alive; to be dug out in the slow round of years; and in the meantime dead to everything but torturing anxieties and horrible despair." Separate system in Pentonville Prison, 1862.

beria. Top-security prisons, a chain round the neck or leg, even the executioner awaited workers or intellectuals who took part in revolutionary activities or organized onslaughts on the bourgeois social system.

Throughout the entire 19th century, working-class rebellion was drowned in blood, whether it was peaceful or violent. This cruel and brutal use of power was intended to frighten the workers and make them break off their campaigns. It began with the Peterloo massacre in August 1819, when the cavalry, fresh from victory at Waterloo, mowed down a peaceful demonstration for workers' suffrage at St. Peter's Fields in Manchester. In 1831 and 1834, the rebellious silk-weavers of Lyons and their sympathizers throughout the country suffered defeat at the hands of the military. When Ernest Renan, the French cultural historian, in 1848 spent a brief period in prison after his arrest by the June insurrectionists in Paris, he informed his friends in astonishment that the workers had treated him with decency, consideration and honesty. Any bloody excesses were the work of General Cavaignac's soldiers, who were sent in to restore "law and order". Others were to experience similar merciless violence: the communards of Paris in 1871, trade unionists in the United States, and 150,000 Russian workers demonstrating peacefully in Petersburg on Bloody Sunday in January 1905, when over a thousand of them perished.

149 Inspecting wreaths, 1912. The watchful eye of the police was everywhere, especially when the working class organized any political events. The constable suspiciously scrutinized the wording on the sash before workers were allowed to lay their wreaths at a monument to revolutionaries who fell on the Berlin barricades in March 1848.

150 Banishment and deportation were especially severe forms of punishment. Britain shipped convicts to Australia, France imprisoned them on distant islands. Tsarist Russia set up large penal camps in Siberia and on Sachalin. Political prisoners were forced to live and work alongside criminals under inhuman conditions. Anton Chekhov commissioned this photograph in 1890. The original caption reads: Newly-arrived convicts in Due Prison are chained to barrows or cast in fetters.

Proletarians and the Army

In pre-capitalist feudal society, soldiers had generally been mercenaries maintained by a court as a separate estate which had few links with the social community. Now the gulf between the army and the people was gradually bridged. The transition had begun in the standing armies of absolute feudal monarchs. These became permanent institutions with roots in the structures and relations of society and firm social links. Indeed, they were often part of a society's cultural image. In the wake of this, people's attitudes to the army changed. Previously, the only indications of an army's presence had been billeting or requisitions. During the 19th century, most European states introduced laws on compulsory military service, which became the right and duty of every male citizen, a station in his individual destiny. As the relative size of the rural population diminished in the 19th century, the great armies of the European continent recruited more and more soldiers from among the proletariat.

After their compulsory schooling, many young workers from Lyons, Munich, Brno or Petersburg in the days before the First World War spent several years in the army. In retrospect they often considered it an honour to have served under the national flag. The army showed them that they were part of a great whole: their country. A young private was no longer a Silesian miner or a docker from Le Havre. He was a German or French soldier now defending his nation and homeland against any possible enemy. School had taught him about patriotism, and now the army made it a daily reality.

One generation after the next of French, German and Russian workers were churned through the military school. Service was hard. Unconditional obedience, rehearsed on the drill grounds, was to make them fit for any military adventures which the ruling classes might choose to embark upon. However, the workers also learnt to apply this military order and discipline for themselves and to operate and maintain the latest war equipment. Holding a weapon, like holding any other tool, was one of the tasks of life. Compulsory service imposed forms of individual conduct that were intended to protect bourgeois power and influence, but at the same time workers developed skills which could enable them to destroy the existing structure of rule with the help of military methods and to defend the new society which would rise in its place.

Your country needs you In 1793 the French Minister of War, Engineering Officer Lazare Nicolas Carnot, who held that office for the next two years, presented the National Assembly with draft legislation that would summon every healthy, single man aged 18 to 25 to bear arms, order married men in the same age group into the armoury workshops, and place males aged 26 to 40 who were capable of fighting on a reserve list for the eventuality of war.

The revolution of the third estate transformed the military. Serving in a national army to protect one's country was not only considered a duty, but a right. The law compelled every citizen who received call-up papers to report at an army office for military education and training. This *levée en masse* was built on bourgeois democratic foundations. Compulsory service was gradually introduced throughout Europe, with the exception of Britain.

There was nothing new about it. The ancient Assyrians had a levy system, and Prussia began regular recruitment, especially from peasant circles, in 1733. Every regiment was based in a county, known as a *Kanton*, where it kept a record of young men and then summoned them to military service. Nevertheless, the concept of compulsory service which was born of the 1789 French Revolution heralded a radical change in army structure and in the army's role in society and citizens' attitudes towards it. Henceforth everyone, regardless of estate or social rank, was under the same obligation to play an active part in defending the state, in protecting the country and its social achievements.

In this way, a nation's defence capability was determined by the skills and attitudes of its people, their personal military qualifications and their political and moral convictions. This concept of the citizens' army soon gained acceptance, especially as the early years of the 19th century witnessed many battles where it proved its military efficiency. Bourgeois reformers in Prussia looked to this new constitutional basis for inspiration and, following the French example, placed every male citizen under an obligation to defend the state.

The social, political and cultural tensions created by industrialization were so great that the army was sometimes expected to perform the task of imposing rule and ensuring power. Revolutions or demands for national independence of other peoples had to be put down by military means, or else turned into attacks on third parties. Political structures had to be defended from enemies both without and within. New markets, spheres of interest and colonies had to be conquered. All this called for a disciplined army that would obey every order, and men capable of fighting who could be mobilized quickly and would not shrink from turning their guns on their own people, their brothers.

"School of the nation" When the Prussian army defeated the combined troops of Austria and Saxony in Bohemia in 1866, the Austrians spread a rumour across Europe that the Battle of Sadová (Königgrätz) had been won by Prussian schoolteachers. Prussia's officers were quick to protest. They claimed indignantly that the schools were being praised beyond their merits. For years they had been complaining that their young recruits were not only in poor physical trim, but also patchy in their patriotism. And now the schoolmasters of Prussia were to take the credit for making soldiers brave and true out of the children of workers and peasants. Chief-of-Staff Helmuth von Moltke and his officers insisted that the real school of the nation was the army.

In contrast to other European states, Prussia took a rigorous view of compulsory service. One year's recruits after the next

151 Drilling soldiers, 1885.

152 The older men of the Reserve. Soldiers were expected to set off for the trenches with flowers and a forced smile. Photo of 1914.

went through the military mill for several years of tough training. After three years on active service, they were transferred to the home forces, and from the age of 40 they served in the home guard. Under this system the number of trained soldiers rose annually. Prussian officers used to boast of how they turned these sons of peasants and workers into "decent human beings". They deserved acknowledgement for their work on the parade ground. They drilled the army rules into their soldiers until they became instinctive behaviour. The recruits themselves came to adopt the military philosophy. After two or three years of service, a soldier showed unconditional discipline and absolute obedience. He was ready to sacrifice himself, appreciated the need for order and acquiescence, felt a strong sense of unit identity and had a clear-sighted understanding of military hierarchies.

In 1874, Helmuth von Moltke was able to counter the Austrian calumny in the German *Reichstag*: "It is not the schoolmasters who have won our battles, but those educators, that profession, which has now been raising the nation for almost sixty years to physical fitness, mental alertness, order and punctuality, loyalty and obedience, love of our country, and manliness."[73]

An alternative to poverty   When Theodore Roosevelt founded the Rough Riders, the special cavalry regiment which supported America's war against Cuba, the future President was not simply rounding up adventurers. Among the volunteers were cowboys and many urban workers.

Proletarian existence left many sections of the working class with few opportunities to change and improve their situation. A military profession seemed like an attractive alternative to a life often spent in poverty and misfortune. The army was happy to exploit these sentiments and responded with suitable offers. A longer-serving or professional soldier was guaranteed adequate provision in return for moderate work, and in most countries the end of active service brought a pension or a job in the civil service.

But it was not only the expected provision that made the army such an interesting prospect. In the latter half of the century, military equipment was being thoroughly modernized. Arms technology and naval expansion advanced apace. They were a great temptation to anyone with a technical bent. The navy and artillery, and later the air force, needed capable youngsters who could operate this complicated military equipment properly. Many sons of the working class were proud to join the navy or enter service with pioneers and other special troops. The training would give them a better chance in their future careers, and encourage higher social esteem among their friends and workmates.

153 Grammar-school boys in Berlin demonstrating for war bonds during the First World War. The children were used to military manners, with school drilling, "patriotic" text books, war toys, parades and military festivals to mould their ideas at an early age.

73 Helmuth von Moltke on 16 February 1874 in the German *Reichstag*. Quoted from: Höhn, Reinhard: *Sozialismus und Heer*. Vol. 2. Bad Homburg, 1959, p. 70f.

154 Government orphanage in Rummelsburg near Berlin. Military uniform and spirit permeated every sphere of life, even the daily routine of orphans in state homes. Photo by Titzenthaler, 1902.

155 "Making Men of Civilians." Cartoon, 1885. The army was the "school of the nation". Many officers saw military service as the forge which tempered real men. "... and remember. You came here as civilians, and you will leave as human beings!"

Militarizing public life In most European countries, the army and its members had become a permanent feature of social and cultural life. Serving among its ranks appeared to be a national duty, and dying among its ranks was regarded as a personal honour. The uniform and the men who wore it were models. The military was an intriguing incarnation of state power, national greatness and true strength. A man who had not served was inferior. The uniform distinguished him from the masses and increased his own sense of worth. The soldier was celebrated for his bright coat and glittering gun.

In the Imperial *Reich* of Germany, public life was flooded by military phenomena more than anywhere else. In 1906, a Köpenick shoemaker named Wilhelm Voigt dressed up in a captain's uniform and managed to persuade a group of soldiers to follow his orders and occupy the local town hall. He did not find it difficult to lay his hands on the money chest, for his rank and uniform opened every door, proof to all of his authority. He could rely on the behavioural logic of the people around him, who re-garded anyone below the rank of Second Lieutenant as sub-human.

Only a few years earlier, France had discovered how many military tentacles now reached into social and cultural life. The nation divided into two camps in the debate about the Jewish officer Alfred Dreyfus, who was alleged to have committed treason. Anti-Semitism was on the rampage. It was also suddenly very apparent that the army exerted a tremendous influence on public life in France and on the thoughts and emotions of every class. Nobody had forgotten that General Boulanger had almost established a military dictatorship in the late eighties.

Although Europe was relatively peaceful in the second half of the 19th century, the army maintained a presence in everyday life. The culture and lifestyle of every social class was affected by the image and activity of the armed forces. Enthusiasm for the navy prompted a fashion for sailors' collars, which began in Britain and soon spread to the Continent. A sailor dress or suit became the Sunday pride and joy of many working-class children, too. Kiel Week, which was a famous event beyond the German borders, always boosted the naval propaganda. It attracted visitors by their thousands from every region.

The civil service also adopted the military style. Government institutions such as the post office, railways and forestry were organized along military lines with uniforms and ranks.

Army idioms proliferated in common parlance. Children played with tin soldiers and wooden rifles. As former professional soldiers and non-commissioned officers often ended their careers in the education and transport sectors and tax or customs offices, they encouraged this militarization of daily life. In France and Germany, associations of old soldiers and marksmen throughout the towns and countryside propagated the military spirit and soldierly conduct. The public atmosphere was stimulated by special occasions to commemorate wars or victories and celebrate the birthdays of monarchs. Right up until the outbreak of the First World War, many social spheres were characterized by the military tone.

Military discipline There was a wide range of regulations and disciplinary measures to drum the necessary submissiveness into a 19th-century soldier. The aims were obedience and unquestioning adherence to orders. The German Social Democrats lampooned this behaviour as blind obedience. In barracks and on training grounds, where soldiers were drilled and polished, military views and objectives were often imposed forcibly. Even in the latter half of the 19th century, the British navy and the Union Army in the northern states of America were famous for their brutal methods of securing obedience. British sailors used to be flogged or keelhauled, and during the Civil War American soldiers were still being strapped to the block, whipped and pilloried. Russians in the tsar's forces continued to be flogged in the 20th century.

Superiors resorted to these severe castigations when their customary training methods failed. Daily exercises in subjugation and rehearsals of military conduct were performed to "turn a man into a soldier". The first thing a young recruit discovered was that anything not expressly permitted was forbidden, that he could not decide for himself when to move and when to stand still, and that he had to read every movement required of him from the lips or eyes of his superiors. Individuality had to be broken, shattered, eroded, extinguished, melted away before it could be recast in a new form, enabling a thousand soldiers to respond and obey as one man. Squares and pelotones were done away with, and column tactics were rarely used in wars after 1860, but troops were never allowed to lose their spirit of cohesion. On the contrary, group thinking acquired a new significance. Drilling was geared towards cultivating a sense of comradeship, and the best way was evidently to impose a degree of sameness on all the soldiers in a unit.

The most effective method for making decent soldiers out of all those individual sons of workers and peasants was to make them carry out the same movement in the same instant as thousands of others, subject them to the same hardships and harassment, and not leave them the slightest opportunity to break out of the pattern.

The best advice to a recruit was to stay inconspicuous. This was the cardinal principle in the life of a simple soldier, and in no way did it contradict what was expected of him. By adapting to the conditions, the man was consciously or unconsciously reproducing the army's functional modus. He did not want to be conspicuous because he did not want to attract punishment or harassment; nor was he supposed to be conspicuous, because an absence of conspicuous individuals was the first proof that military training was effective. Political activities had therefore to be renounced at the camp gates. Spreading socialist ideas in the barracks was liable to severe penalties. Anyone who ignored the rules was harassed, transferred or locked up for a long time. Sometimes politically active workers were called up for a dose of military repression.

A soldier's life "You seldom hear of officers who refuse to tolerate any ill-treatment of their men on principle; unfortunately I never met any officer of this type. At that time I had serious thoughts about deserting. Is that surprising? I did not want to commit suicide, for I loved my young life too much, and my tormentors meant too little to me. What about speaking up? Oh, we were told often enough: 'Anyone who complains can be sure his three years will be one long misery; he won't have far to go to the fortress!' So I became like most of the others: thick-skinned, poker-faced, hard-boiled. By the end of it I felt something was missing if I did not hear my daily ration of 'bastard', 'dirty peasant' and 'smelly'. . . One thing I decided straight away: nobody should talk to me ever again about the German soldier's sophisti-

cated sense of honour. I have never heard a worse lie. Quite the reverse, a man's natural sense of honour is systematically stunted and killed by that unworthy kind of treatment."[74]

74 Rehbein, Franz: *Das Leben eines Landarbeiters*. Ed. by Paul Göhre. Jena, 1911, p. 177.

156 "The Iron Cross." Drawing by Heinrich Zille. A piece of lead is all this proletarian has to remind her of her husband.

157 Turkish soldiers retreat during
the Balkan War in 1912.

158 Scottish soldiers captured by the
Germans, 1917.

159 Battle-weary Germans during a
cession in hostilities on the Western
Front, 1917.

160 Fallen Italian soldiers after the Battle of Ciridale, 1917.

Church Social Policy
and Welfare

From the point of view of capital and the bourgeois state, personal liberty, objectified relations and cash payment implied that workers should use their wages to look after themselves and their families. All the uncertain factors in a wage labourer's life were risks that every individual had to be prepared to take.

Poverty, unemployment, homelessness, and periods of unemployability due to sickness, old age or disability did not become a problem for the ruling classes—or a "social question", as they put it—until the rising population and spread of the proletariat began to encroach on public life in a manner which could not be ignored, threatening to disrupt the social peace and provoking the working class to engage in political activity.

After the revolutionary events of 1830 and 1848/49, the state, the employers and the clergy of all industrial nations attentively observed the growth of the proletariat, their increasingly independent lifestyle and the emergence of a labour movement. After all, workers were the owners of the commodity "labour", and as such an indispensable component of industrial production. There would be no prosperity without them, or if their labour was inadequate. Apart from that, they were citizens of a country, subjects of a territorial overlord, members of a nation, and potential defenders of their homeland. And the majority were Christians, parishioners in one or another of the great denominational flocks. So it was that the Church, employers and governments of all European countries reacted, with greater or lesser degrees of sensitivity, to chronic deficiencies in working and living conditions and to political trends among proletarians. These were countered by social reorientation in the Churches, charitable initiatives on the part of private capitalists, government legislation on protection of labour, insurance against accident, old age, sickness and disability, and industrial settlements.

In the long term, the common aim of the ruling classes was to integrate the working class securely into the existing social and economic order and to commit the workers to the survival of capitalist society.

The welfare tradition Until the 19th century, the religious communities and parishes had alleviated the plight of many who were hungry, homeless, sick or old and unsupported, crippled, orphaned or abandoned as babies. For centuries, Christian charity had been one of the great cultural achievements of the Church, saving people from extreme circumstances, helping, consoling and protecting. Catholics, and later Protestants, assumed responsibilities, supplementing or replacing the assistance offered by families and local communities. In the 19th century, however, as a result of industrialization and changing patterns of work, family life and settlement, there was such a prolif-

eration of needy individuals and new situations of distress that the traditional forms of Christian charity could no longer cope with. In response, the Churches began at first to address more of their work to pastoral care and moral, religious education for the faithful, who had been unsettled by all these social transformations. But they were fairly quick to offer practical assistance for the changing circumstances and needs of working people in the big towns. On the one hand were charitable institutions founded directly by the ecclesiastical authorities, and on the other mutual aid associations formed by Christian workers. Catholic priests like Albert de Mun and La Tour du Pin in France, and Bishop Ketteler or the Protestant Johann Hinrich Wichern in Germany were pioneers in this field. The Home Mission founded by Wichern in 1848 assumed a broad range of tasks which illustrate how many human problems this Church social work was attempting to tackle.

By the turn of the century this Mission was running crèches, nursery schools, centres for the supervision of schoolchildren after lessons, clinics for poor children, rehabilitation centres for down-and-outs, and institutions for the mentally ill and for epileptics. It set up associations for apprentices, journeymen and other young men, for young women and servant girls, and for moderation and morality. It opened sanatoria for alcoholics, refuges for prostitutes, care centres for tramps, camps for workers and soup kitchens. It offered facilities for emigrants, sailors, railway workers, migrant beet harvesters and convicts. It provided volunteers to nurse soldiers and perform wartime social work.

161 Inside the Mormon church in Salt Lake City, 1893. It seated 8,000 people.

162 The boys' room in the "Rough House", a Christian education institution founded by the Protestant reformer Johann Hinrich Wichern in Hamburg in 1832. It illustrates one of the "educational" methods designed to preserve children and young people from pauperism.

And it trained people to work with the poor, the sick, prisoners and children.

It organized lectures and wrote articles commenting on social problems, such as child and female labour and the housing shortage.

These needy social groups and similar patterns of individual distress requiring alleviation were present in all the cities and industrial conurbations. As social provisions were still almost non-existent, this kind of welfare remained the prerogative of the Churches even in the 19th century. The Christian social movements initiated by the two main denominations also pursued charitable and "spiritually uplifting" goals. In Austria, Belgium, France and Italy, Catholic clubs sprouted for peasants, craftsmen, journeymen and workers. The Protestant Church began setting up Christian workers' associations in Britain and Germany from the middle of the century, and broader organizations followed towards the end of it.

In 1882 a miner of Gelsenkirchen, Ruhr, called Fischer founded a Protestant working men's club which functioned as a model in both the form and content of its activity for other similar associations. Their common objective was to strengthen the Christian faith and general knowledge of workers, but they also offered their members support in cases of sickness or death.

These Protestant workers' clubs were interspersed by petty-bourgeois strata, and they were a meeting-point for a group with a sense of identity rather than organizations to defend workers' interests. Politically they were always guided by Church directives. They dreamt of a peaceful solution to the conflicts between workers and employers, and argued for loyalty to kaiser and country. They were emphatic opponents of left-wing trends within the working class.

The story was similar in the labour movement which grew up under Catholic influence. Scattered workers' support associations and socially-orientated Christian societies had been founded around the middle of the century. Shortly before Bismarck's law against socialists was repealed, there were 168 workers' associations and 51 miners' associations of this kind in Germany alone, and they had a total membership of about 40,000. The inspiration behind all these clubs was that self-help and mutual assistance should grow out of Christian love, because charity from other classes smacked of pre-capitalist alms-giving, which many people found obnoxious.

Good deeds in Christ's name The most popular religious organization in the late 19th century to be set up for the purposes of conversion and support was the Salvation Army, which almost every proletarian came across at some time in life. It was founded in London in 1878 by the former Methodist preacher William Booth, and within only a few years it had established a foothold, mostly in the large towns and densely populated areas of advanced industrial countries. The exceptions were Austria, Spain and Russia.

The Salvation Army worked independently of the established Churches. Indeed, its uncommonly militant methods often brought it into conflict with these or with the state. At the turn of the century, its newspapers and pamphlets were published in 25

163 The teacher and the preacher with a class of German elementary pupils, 1908. The clergyman gave religious instruction, which was an important part of the school syllabus.

164 A chapel for miners in Freiberg, Saxony: prayer was still part of the working environment. Photo by Karl A. Reymann, 1913.

165 Confirmation, 1905. Entry into adulthood was symbolized by confirmation or communion, even for many working-class children.

166 The first refuge for servants in Vienna, 1891.

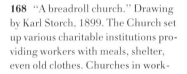

Das erste Dienstboten-Asylhaus in Wien.

167 A meeting-room for women in a Berlin hostel, before 1910. More and more establishments were necessary to regulate the growing problem of homelessness and unemployment.

Private and state authorities attempted to counter the plight which hit unemployed, homeless women particularly hard.

168 "A breadroll church." Drawing by Karl Storch, 1899. The Church set up various charitable institutions providing workers with meals, shelter, even old clothes. Churches in working-class parishes of Berlin sometimes offered poor man's coffee (malt extract) and rolls along with the service.

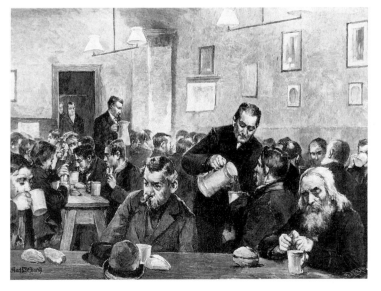

languages. These "soldiers of Christ", dressed in uniform, carried the Gospels to the "popular masses sunken in sin and misery" wherever they found them. Singing and preaching, they rattled their collecting tins from street to street across the cities. They went into pubs, dance halls and other "bastions of Satan" urging transgressors to atone and have faith. They were particularly concerned about drunkards, fallen women, the homeless and other broken spirits, and singing hymns was by no means their only occupation. Many who were unemployed, ill, disabled or destitute owed their survival to the Salvation Army's welfare institutions, its shelters and soup kitchens. By collecting clothes and money they alleviated the direst needs, and unfortunately also eased the conscience of the donator.

The Army's weapons were unsuitable for achieving its ultimate moral ideal, which was that the work and profits of all should eliminate working-class poverty, need and insecurity.

Preserving the people's religion   Pope Leo XIII published his Encyclical Letter *Rerum Novarum* in 1891. This was an attempt at the supreme level to resolve the Worker Question in a Christian sense. In foregoing years, prominent Catholic clergymen such as Bishop Ketteler, Albert de Mun, Bishop Hermillo and Cardinal Manning had voiced their support for trade-union activities undertaken by the working class. It was obvious to these men that mere charity was insufficient, and welfare alone could not resolve the great social problems. They realized more clearly than their fellow-believers that Catholicism needed a social doctrine. If the Catholic Church wanted to preserve its power and influence, it would have to adopt a stance on the secularized social relations in capitalist countries and on the social effects of industrialization.

In 1878 the Encyclical Letter *Quod Apostilici muneris* had already vehemently defended the right of private property against the teachings of socialism and communism, and *Rerum Novarum* took up where this left off. The Pope emphatically rejected communist ideals of any kind as they contradicted, in his view, the basic natural rights of property and inviolability of individual freedom and of the family. Although he did admit that isolated workers were defenceless against the anti-social spirit of the wealthy and against the pressures of ruthless competition, he argued that class struggle could not provide a solution. Instead, the social classes should complement one another, regarding each other with respect and meeting in love. He quoted the teachings of St. Thomas Aquinas to explain the just application of wealth: "Whoever has been generously supplied by God with either corporal and external goods or those of the spirit, possesses them for this purpose—to apply them equally to his own perfection and, in his role as a steward of divine providence, to the benefit of others."[75] Social equality and justice, he continued, could not be achieved by changing the relations of property; true social community must grow out of love for one's brother and neighbour. In

anticipation of the Church's new status, the Pope drew attention to the state's particular responsibility in considering the interests of "the small and the weak". He, too, encouraged the professional associations and organizations to persevere in their efforts to alleviate the greatest distress and thereby contribute towards overcoming the differences between the two main classes in capitalist society.

If you want culture you must learn it   Bourgeois liberals and Christians with an open mind for social problems worked together to improve proletarian education. They criticized the poor education levels prevalent among workers and believed that adult education opportunities would offer a solution to growing poverty, for it would make workers better equipped to fight for a livelihood.

Sunday schools for adults and "fraternal societies" which ran lectures for workers were formed in Britain and the United States around 1800. They were followed by the mechanics' institutes and, around 1850, by the workers' colleges, in which Christian socialists also played a part.

From 1870 onwards Oxford and Cambridge attempted to disseminate education among the people by opening lecture series to broad sections of the population under the university extension scheme.

During the British settlements movement, university academics went to live in working-class districts and slums, where they performed educational and social work. Toynbee Hall in East London was founded in 1883 and became an organizational focus for bourgeois education projects. In 1899 Ruskin College in Oxford began offering two-year residential courses to workers. The influential Workers' Educational Association was founded in 1903.

The story was similar in Germany. Liberal bourgeois politicians began setting up clubs for workers' education in the forties. By the sixties, more and more of these institutions were rejecting the bourgeois influence, and the middle classes responded in 1871 by founding a Society for the Dissemination of Popular Education. Before the First World War broke out the organization was responsible for 7,000 local clubs, 4,000 public libraries and 1,200 mobile libraries. Another body which helped to co-ordinate workers' education from the bourgeois perspective was the Centre for Workers' and Welfare Institutions, which was set up in 1895.

A further bourgeois form of adult education was the people's university. It originated in the Danish movement for "popular renewal" which began in the 1840s at the initiative of Bishop Grundtvig. Its aims were comprehensive reforms of educational opportunities for the common population. Education should be relevant to everyday life and community-orientated. The ideas spread into other Scandinavian countries, where a number of people's universities were established, particularly for peasant children, and thence to Germany, where similar institutions were founded on a residential basis, first for young people in rural areas, and later for their urban contemporaries. Courses lasted two to six months and offered general and occupational knowledge.

The capitalist patriarch The French factory-owner Léon Harzel, nicknamed "the good father of Val des Sois", set up a number of social institutions for workers in his company. For some years he was closely associated with the club activities. To encourage independence among his workers, he helped them to found co-operatives. Unions representing more than one trade were allowed to operate in his factories, where the first factory councils were called into existence. Benevolent funds were available to aid families in distress. In Germany, Alfred Krupp granted his workers annual leave, special working conditions and company housing in order to preserve a regular workforce.

When capitalists made private concessions of a social nature to their workers, their motives were usually political or economic. The German factory-owner Stumm-Halberg stated this clearly when he introduced his own company provisions: "I hope in this manner to ensure that you remain insensitive to the temptations of Social Democracy long after I am dead . . . Preserve your old unshakeable loyalty to our noble monarch for all time. Do not swerve from Christian love and true awe of God . . . and then your good fortunes will continue insofar as mortal powers may dispose."[76]

It was not simply that company welfare for workers depended entirely on the will of the boss. He also assumed the right to control the way his workers thought and acted outside the factory gates. Stumm hated trade unions of every hue and forbade his employees to join associations. In 1890 he insisted that workers at the ironworks in Neunkirchen should inform him of their marriage plans. In fact, the factory rules made it compulsory. He energetically opposed workers' committees and would not even tolerate liberal journals such as *Hilfe*. Workers who frequented inns where this magazine was displayed could expect to collect their cards without notice.

Every man for himself: the American angle The bourgeoisie in the United States were more inclined to agree with Henry Ford and his managers: "We do not believe in paternalism. When first we raised the wages to five dollars a day, we had to exercise some supervision over the living of the men because so many of them, being foreign born, did not raise their

169 Cartoon from *Der Wahre Jacob*, 1905. Insurance funds, accident cover, old age and disability pensions, pension funds and employer's housing were designed to fetter workers to the capitalists' plans for social wealth, and discourage them from social, cultural and political strategies of their own. The aim was to "gild the proletarian's chains", preventing social revolution by introducing minor reforms.

170 "The friendly Politicians." Welfare for workers: if proletarians wanted to utilize social wealth for their own development, they would have to take matters into their own hands. Drawing from *Der Wahre Jacob*, 1890.

75 *Rerum Novarum*. Encyclical letter published by the Catholic Truth Society. London, 1983, p. 13.
76 Carl Ferdinand Freiherr von Stumm-Halberg in 1889 in an address to his workers. Quoted from: Schraepler, R.: *Quellen zur Geschichte der sozialen Frage in Deutschland*. Vol. 2: *1871–Gegenwart*. Göttingen, 1957, p. 93.

171 A local insurance office in Berlin. Germany introduced national insurance in 1883 as part of state social policy. German workers gained a degree of economic security and better conditions. The German system functioned as a model in many European countries.

standards of living in accord with their higher incomes. That we entirely gave up when the need had passed.

"We feel that a man ought to have savings enough to tide him over any crisis, but there are times when illness wipes out the savings, and then we arrange for loans. We have legal and real-estate departments and stand ready, in fact, to render any reasonable service that is asked for.

"We hold that it is part of our industrial duty—that is, part of our service that supports the wage motive—to help people to help themselves. We believe that what is called being charitable is a particularly mean form of self-glorification—mean because, while it pretends to aid, it really hurts. The giver to charity gets a certain cheap satisfaction out of being regarded as a kind and generous man. This would be harmless enough in itself were it not that the recipients of charity are usually destroyed—for once you give a man something for nothing, you set him trying to get someone else to give him something for nothing.

"Charity creates non-producers, and there is no difference at all between a rich drone and a poor drone. Both are burdens on production. It will take easily a generation to wipe out the effects of the dole upon the peoples of Europe."[77]

State social policy: the German model The bourgeoisie in Germany were economically successful, but they lacked a unifying political approach. Their economic strength was not con-verted into a confident political thrust based on liberal bourgeois principles. The middle classes were either conservative and paternalistic, or else they attached liberal convictions to the "free play of economic forces". Krupp and Stumm-Halberg tied their workers to patriarchal apron strings, but others preferred the motto "Laissez-faire, laissez-aller". Meanwhile, the Worker Question was left increasingly in the hands of the government. Chancellor Bismarck devised a two-pronged strategy with regard to the working class, and the Prussian German state pursued it rigorously.

The aim was to counter the workers' insubordination, and especially their political strength. The first priority was to put an end to the "machinations" of the Social Democratic labour movement which were posing a threat to the state and society. Plans to ban the workers' party were initially drawn up in 1875/76, and after two attempts to assassinate Kaiser William I the law against socialists was passed. Bismarck's speech in defence of this new act indicated the intentions of government social policy, which was to back up the ban on Social Democratic activity with broad social legislation along the lines of "sugarloaf and whip". The social measures were announced by the kaiser in 1881 and introduced in three stages: in 1883 a law was passed on insurance against sickness. Workers and employers were to share the costs equally.

A law passed in 1884 laid down that, in the case of industrial accident, the bosses were to finance insurance payments themselves. The third provision came in 1889, with laws on retirement and disability pensions. Here, again, workers and owners would share the financial burden, with the government assisting both parties.

"In my view, one major reason for the success which the Social Democratic leaders have enjoyed with those future goals which they have not yet explained clearly anywhere is that the state has not engaged in enough state socialism; it has left a vacuum at a point where it should be active, and this is being filled by agitators who are meddling in the state's business."[78] This plea in the German *Reichstag* on 15 March 1884 for more state socialism came from the Chancellor of the *Reich*, Prince Otto von Bismarck. He was defending the draft legislation on accident insurance for workers.

This law proposed by Bismarck as a "complement to the law on socialism"[79] was a step in the Chancellor's efforts to make the working class more amenable to the existing state and draw them away from the revolutionary Social Democrats. He was always sensitive to issues of power, and was responding to the threat posed by the growing strength of the working class.

It was characteristic of Bismarck that he personally envisaged a form of social insurance which would be financed by the state and the employers, for as soon as the workers had to contribute to the fund they would experience the measure as an attack on their meagre wages, and the effects could be quite the opposite from those intended by the Chancellor.

However, Bismarck lacked both the parliamentary support and the money he needed to put his social policy ideas into practice. Nevertheless, he clung all his life to the hope that one day workers would be entitled to government pensions and would therefore shun any revolutionary involvement like the plague. When the *Reichstag* came to debate the pension laws in 1889, Bismarck told the members: "I believe that if you can perform this benevolent deed by creating over half a million modest pensioners across the *Reich*, you . . . will also be teaching the man on the street to regard the *Reich* as a charitable institution."[80]

August Bebel, the parliamentary representative of the Social Democrats, had already stated a position during the initial discussion of the draft legislation which reflected the workers' view of state provisions in the field of social policy. He recalled that Bismarck had promised during discussion of the law against socialists "to ensure some positive measures in the workers' interests and thereby to combat Social Democracy. Gentlemen, we are delighted, for that proves that it was we who initiated this draft legislation, and that will not make such a very unfavourable impression on the German workers, I assure you. And if, in the further course of your activity, you propose a few dozen similar laws, that will not harm us either. Indeed, we shall examine the drafts soberly and objectively, and, once we are convinced that they really can fulfil the promises that have been given, we shall also vote for them."[81] Bebel went on to point out tongue-in-cheek that the present draft could be considerably improved as a weapon against the Social Democrats, as the bourgeois state had only produced legal regulations to cater for a fraction of the social measures which the workers were demanding.

---

77 Ford, Henry: *Today and Tomorrow*. In collaboration with Samuel Crowther. London, 1926, p. 159 and p. 179.

78 Bismarck, Otto von: *Gedanken und Erinnerungen, Reden und Briefe*. Berlin, 1942, p. 370.

79 *Ibid.*, p. 362.

80 Speech in the *Reichstag* on 18 May 1889. Quoted from: Born, Karl E.: *Von der Reichsgründung bis zum Ersten Weltkrieg*. Munich, 1981, p. 146.

81 Bebel, August: "Rede im Deutschen Reichstag zum Gesetzentwurf über die Unfallversicherung der Arbeiter (4. April 1881)," in: Bebel, August: *Ausgewählte Reden und Schriften*. Vol. 2, 1st half volume. Berlin, 1978, p. 137f.

ÉVÉNEMENTS DE LYON,

Barrière de la Croix-rousse 21 et 22 Novembre 1831.

Se vend à la Croix-rousse rue du Chariot d'Or N. 6 chez Murigneux et à Lyon chez Chateau Imprimeur en taille douce C. rue Mercière N. 42.

172 Government troops attack the barricades built by Lyons silk-weavers on 21 and 22 November 1831. The first armed working-class rising was crushed after costly battles. Contemporary engraving.

Workers' Protest and Class Struggle

"He, who before was the money-owner, now strides in front as capitalist; the possessor of labour-power follows as his labourer. The one with an air of importance, smirking, intent on business; the other, timid and holding back, like one who is bringing his own hide to market and has nothing to expect but—a hiding."[82] This was Karl Marx's slightly sarcastic portrayal of the two main actors in the capitalist mode of production. The prospects for the first were profit, a powerful position in the state, and the delights of a social status and earthly goods; for the second they were labour under conditions made by those who reaped the profit, state discipline, and wages which permitted little more than a regular return to work. The bourgeois class, which made profit or lived by it, did not have the same social position or the same interests as the working class, which created the profit or remained unemployed.

Hard work, thrift, education and high morals only enabled a handful of workers to raise their living conditions above the average of their category. If the workers wanted wages, conditions or rights at work or in the state which threatened to diminish profits or curtail powers over the labour force, then they had to have recourse to resistance and struggle.

In the early days of industrial capitalism, workers tried to halt their proletarianization by means of revolts, protests, machine-breaking, forms of non-co-operation such as go-slows or absence, or emigration to other regions or countries. As the modern proletariat emerged, they needed to tackle social conflicts with different means.

Owning capital brought power which workers could only counter by organizing their numerical strength. The limited forms of association between journeymen based on the former guilds were replaced by trade unions. The workers who joined them were not all from the same place or factory, and thus they put an end to the competition which had always made them undercut one another, in favour of a common cause against the capitalist. Strikes for higher wages and shorter working hours were the main forms of their struggle. By the end of the century, workers in all the advanced industrial countries had won the right to join trade unions and to strike, although governments and autocratic capitalists continued to challenge that right repeatedly. Between 1789 and 1848, workers on the Continent still followed predominantly bourgeois politicians in the fight against feudalism, but in the thirties Chartism gave birth in Britain to an independent proletarian political movement. By the First World War the working class had formed its own political parties in all the industrial nations. These campaigned for workers' interests in the day-to-day battle to protect and improve rights and conditions as well as in the long-term struggle for a socialist society. They won suffrage for the working class and entered parliament to exert a certain influence on legislation. They set up a First and Second International under the common slogan published in the *Communist Manifesto*: "Proletarians of all countries, unite!" Clubs and mutual aid societies which ranged in concern from consumers' co-operative societies via social assistance to education and sport strengthened workers' confidence and won support for the labour movement.

Marxism, which interpreted the social conflicts between workers and capitalists as a class struggle and offered strategies to resolve it, gained influence. Whoever sought to combat or change the labour movement at the end of the century had to take on the Marxist challenge.

---

82 Marx, Karl: *Capital*. Vol. 1. Moscow, 1971, p. 172.

The labour movement evolved its own culture of organization and struggle which enabled it to defend workers' interests in a sustained, disciplined and methodical manner with the tools of scientific analysis, and to extend its concerns to more and more spheres of life.

Clashes between the proletarians and the privileged classes could be extremely bitter, as shown by the plebeian currents in the French Revolution after 1789, the working-class uprisings in Lyons in 1831 and 1834, the uprising of Silesian weavers in 1844, the revolutions of 1848/49, the Paris Commune of 1871 and the Russian Revolution of 1905.

On the one hand, the workers were quelled by brutal repression, but on the other, governments and capitalists were prompted to draw conclusions about their relationship with the working class and try to defuse or prevent conflicts. If workers threatened private ownership of capital and enjoyment of its fruits, there was no mercy. On this front the ruling classes became increasingly resolute and united. By the end of the century, in the developed countries, they had come to terms, hesitantly, unwillingly, often only tactically, conditionally, and never without reservations and revocations, with working-class suffrage, the right of association for workers, protective labour legislation and a standard working day. This defined legal channels through which social conflicts could be processed and in effect acknowledged certain working-class interests. The quest mounted for other ways to influence the masses and a mass press was born.

By the First World War the labour movement had become a real force to be reckoned with, particularly in terms of its mass character and its level of organization. It represented working-class interests so effectively that a general strike for political purposes was considered possible and there was serious discussion about whether to use it to end capitalist rule. Socialist workers did not see their organizations merely as instruments to defend their everyday interests, but as means to achieve a new society. In fact, the organizations themselves were regarded as the core of that new world.

At the same time, however, the economic and political rulers were forced to find new ways of dealing with the proletariat so that they could settle conflicts before force was applied. In 1875, Karl Marx had already warned the German Social Democrats not to mistake contractual relations between the proletariat and bourgeoisie for socialism.

A new stage of the class struggle dawned in a society which was organized to a fine degree and full of conflicts. Socialists all believed that this would be the highest and last stage of capitalism. The reformists among them hoped that the highly organized state of society would further workers' interests to such an extent that class struggle would be superfluous. The centrists expected that it would at least provide a new dimension to social conflicts and so cause the old order to collapse. The left-wingers wanted the working class to speed this process up with a united onslaught on political power.

From the Luddites to the Second International

The roots of the labour movement stretch back to the beginnings of capitalist society. The embryonic working class adopted forms of resistance in keeping with its various stages of development as a pre-proletariat, manufacturing proletariat and industrial proletariat. They ranged from spontaneous refusal to work, via local strike committees, to the formation of national and international organizations based on their trade unions or socialist parties.

Apart from supporting the bourgeois movements during the Early Bourgeois Revolution in Germany in 1525, the English Revolution from 1640 to 1649, and the French Revolution of 1789, the early proletariat voiced some anti-capitalist demands of their own. They first played an active role as an independent force in the Chartist movement in Britain (1832 to 1848) and during the weavers' uprisings in Lyons (1831 and 1834) and Silesia (1844). The spread of industrial labour swelled the ranks of the proletariat, and during the period of machine-breaking the workers discovered that technical progress could no longer be halted, let alone revoked. Their poverty was not actually caused by the means of production, the machinery and factories; it was the way these were used that was driving them to starvation. While Icarists and others painted glorious visions of the future, utopian

models of society were not going to stop capitalism. Even in America, God's own country, there were growing rumours that things were following the European pattern, and the wonderfully named sects that intended to build a new world on that continent were overtaken by the times.

Day-to-day proletarian resistance created many forms of struggle and organizations. After all, the trade unions and socialist parties had a mass membership. Many took their political inspiration from the *Communist Manifesto* drawn up by Karl Marx and Friedrich Engels. The First International founded by working men in 1864 encouraged the growth of national labour organizations, but it fell apart in the dispute about the forms of resistance. Marxism, British trade unionism and Russian Bakuninism could not be reconciled. The Second International, founded in 1889, was an umbrella organization for trade-union federations and working-class parties. This was the most advanced form of political organization created by the international labour movement before the outbreak of the First World War.

Luddites and the first working-class rising When craftsmen and homeworkers driven to despair by the oppressive conditions of cottage industry took to breaking machinery, it was no more than a defensive reaction. The bloody uprisings in Silesia and Lyons gave an unintentional boost to the process of proletarianization. The capitalists opted for concentrated production in factories, and soon strikes became the principal form of class struggle.

Britain had been obliged to pass laws protecting textile machinery and stocking frames in 1782 and 1788 in response to attacks by impoverished weavers and hosiers. From 1811, when more modern textile equipment was being introduced in Britain, a secret military organization of stocking-weavers known as the Luddites sustained a campaign of risings and attacks. Enoch[83] was the Biblical name they gave to their great hammers, which they used to shatter machines, raid businesses, extort money and threaten the bourgeoisie. They were not daunted by the death penalty introduced in 1812, which was applied in several cases. The movement, under the legendary leadership of "General Ludd", who was never caught and probably never even existed, petered out around 1817, and yet the bourgeois society of England was rigid with fear once more in 1829, when workers destroyed steam looms and burnt entire factories to the ground during hunger rioting.

The first independent mass action to be undertaken by the proletariat was the insurgency by Lyons textile workers in November 1831. This "first working-class rising"[84] made it clear to all Europe "that the workers are no longer willing to bow to an order in which bourgeois property exercises unlimited control over their labour and their lives"[85].

The silk-weavers' uprising began as a peaceful march by journeymen and their masters on 21 November 1831. They emerged from their slums and headed for the centre of Lyons. The town council and the factory-owners had promised to grant them a minimum wage. Now they were asking for this to be set down in a contract, and so they went peacefully and in disciplined unity to see the men whom they had actually helped to power in the revolution of 1830.

Their desperate plight was expressed in their slogan "Live working or die fighting!" The National Guard and battle troops blocked their path and shot into the crowd with no advance warning. This incident provoked an uprising which installed the workers as masters of their town, albeit only briefly.

The defeat of this proletarian rebellion had consequences, both for the French labour movement, which subsequently en-

Böhmische Weber zerstören Maschinen.

173 Weavers in cottage industry could not compete with factories full of machinery. Like the Silesian weavers in 1844, impoverished Bohemian weavers in their despair wrecked machinery and other installations during the Revolution of 1848/49. Illustration by Otto E. Lau.

83 According to the Bible a direct descendant of Adam and Eve, a son of Cain. Cf. The Bible, Moses; I, 5, 18.

84 Cf. Engels, Friedrich: "Die Entwicklung des Sozialismus von der Utopie zur Wissenschaft," in: Marx, Karl, and Friedrich Engels: *Werke*. Ed. by Institut für Marxismus-Leninismus beim ZK der SED. Vol. 19. Berlin, 1956–68, p. 207.

85 *Die internationale Arbeiterbewegung. Fragen der Geschichte und Theorie.* In 7 vols. Vol. 1: *Die Entstehung des Proletariats und seine Entwicklung zur revolutionären Klasse.* Moscow, 1980, p. 319.

countered bitter opposition to any independent activity it conducted, and for conservative forces across Europe, who had been given food for thought. The revolts were a more urgent warning than ever before to be wary of the proletariat, and sensitivity was deepest in Prussia, where domestic policy became more intransigent towards liberal forces of every shade. Indeed, the bourgeoisie themselves were so alarmed by their own national experience of rebellion and uprisings that they reached a degree of "understanding" with the landed nobility. This laid the groundwork for a state social policy which was adopted in practice after the Silesian weavers' uprising in 1844.

Closing the bourgeois ranks On 8 December 1831 the bourgeois *Journal des Débats* published the following article, which urged the middle classes to close ranks against the proletariat: "Like every other society, our society of commerce and industry has its Achilles' heel: the workers. There can be no factory without workers, and yet a population of workers which is ever growing and always needy leaves society no peace . . . The barbarians who threaten society . . . are dwelling in the suburbs of our factory towns . . . They suffer poverty. Why should they not aspire to better circumstances? . . . How should they resist the temptation to launch an attack on the bourgeoisie? They are stronger, more numerous . . . The middle classes must become fully aware of the state of affairs . . . The middle classes would be deceived should they let themselves be persuaded by any demagogic principles to concede weapons and rights in their folly to their enemies, should they admit proletarians to flood the National Guard and the local authorities, should they grant them access to the electoral laws and everything which constitutes the state . . . We are not talking here about republics or monarchies, but about saving society."[86]

Chartism in Britain As the Industrial Revolution entered its final stage in Britain, a broad popular movement came to replace the Luddite risings. William Lovett drafted his *People's Charter* in 1838, prompted by the Reform Bill of 1832 and the economic crisis of 1837. Chartism began as a suffrage campaign, uniting petty-bourgeois radicals, artisans and factory workers. In the forties it assumed the character of a proletarian political organization, becoming, as Engels noted, the first working-class party of the day. Legally organized strikes, statutes which anyone could acquire, and public agitation marked a departure from clandestine groups functioning underground. The League of Communists founded in London in 1847 stated this quite clearly in its manifesto. In organizational structure, this international league drew on the experience of England's Chartists. Membership was based in local branches, these were grouped into districts under regional then national leaderships, and Congress was the supreme body. This fundamental structure was to govern all future working-class organizations. During the European revolutions

of 1848/49 the first labour representatives were elected to national legislative assemblies. For the workers, this meant a new stage in their activity. Politically speaking, the distinctions between the proletariat and petty-bourgeois radicals were not yet clearly defined. When the democratic movements and risings in which proletarians had often assumed leadership were eventually quashed, the labour movement had to draw new breath and replenish its forces from fresh economic and political struggles. The focus of the revolutionary proletarian movements also shifted within their national frameworks.

Germany's first national working-class party After France and England, it was Germany's turn to serve as a model to other labour movements, a function which it fulfilled for a long time.

German workers started to organize in the sixties. They already had experience of self-support in a wide variety of forms: occupational associations, education clubs, savings societies, retail co-operatives, productive associations, and funds for solidarity, strike, disability, widows, accidents, benefit, marriage and even funerals. Thus workers had attempted to relieve the plight of social insecurity. Ideas about organization had reached a level which made them receptive to the modern concept of organized labour. In 1863 Ferdinand Lassalle founded the first nationwide socialist working-class party, the *Allgemeiner Deutscher Arbeiterverein* (General Workers' Association of Germany), in Leipzig.

The First and Second Internationals In September 1864 workers meeting in St. Martin's Hall, London, decided to set up the International Working Men's Association (IWA). Karl Marx wrote the Inaugural Address, which was the foundation document of this First International. The Association focused its activity on drawing together the individuals, trade unions, co-operatives, education associations and working-class parties which affiliated to it, and encouraging their ideological and political independence. It collected money for strikes in Britain, Belgium, Switzerland and Germany. The IWA also helped to keep out blackleg labour during strikes. It supported the Paris Commune and succeeded in isolating Bakunin's anarchists. It raised the demand for an eight-hour working day. The IWA's foundation stimulated the development of mass parties with international links. Its general rules amounted to a proletarian Declaration of Human Rights:
Considering
That the emancipation of the working classes must be conquered by the working classes themselves; that the struggle for the emancipation of the working classes means not a struggle for

---

86 Quoted from: Tarlé, Eugen: "Der Lyoner Arbeiteraufstand," in: *Marx-Engels-Archiv*. Vol. 2. Ed. by D. Ryazanov. Frankfurt am Main, 1927, p. 93.

class privileges and monopolies, but for equal rights and duties, and the abolition of all class-rule;

That the economic subjection of the man of labour to the monopolizer of the means of labour, that is, the sources of life, lies at the bottom of servitude in all its forms, of all social misery, mental degradation, and political dependence;

That the economical emancipation of the working classes is therefore the great end to which every political movement ought to be subordinate as a means;

That all efforts aiming at that great end have hitherto failed from the want of solidarity between the manifold divisions of labour in each country, and from the absence of a fraternal bond of union between the working classes of different countries;

That the emancipation of labour is neither a local nor a national, but a social problem, embracing all countries in which modern society exists, and depending for its solution on the concurrence, practical and theoretical, of the most advanced countries;

That the present revival of the working classes in the most industrious countries of Europe, while it raises a new hope, gives solemn warning against a relapse into the old errors, and calls for the immediate combination of the still disconnected movements;

For These Reasons—

The International Working Men's Association has been founded.
It declares:

That all societies and individuals adhering to it will acknowledge truth, justice, and morality, as the basis of their conduct towards each other and towards all men, without regard to colour, creed, or nationality;

That it acknowledges *no rights without duties, no duties without rights.*"[87]

In 1872 the IWA transferred headquarters to New York, and then in 1876 it was dissolved. The Second International was founded in July 1889, at a workers' congress to commemorate the 100th anniversary of the French Revolution. By this time workers had established national labour federations and socialist parties all over Europe. The Second International demanded the workers' right to take control of production and society. It co-ordinated the campaigns of national labour movements against a backcloth of broad theoretical work. A leadership committee, the International Socialist Bureau, was set up in 1900 to this end. 896 delegates from 23 countries attended the Congress of 1910. It was the Second International which adopted 1 May as a day of action and celebration for workers everywhere. Leading figures in the organization included Victor Adler, August Bebel, Jules Guesde, Camille Huysmans, Karl Kautsky, Jean Jaurès, Paul Lafargue, Rosa Luxemburg, Georgi Valentinovich Plekhanov, Paul Singer, Victor Serwy, Édouard Vaillant, Émile Vandervelde and Clara Zetkin.

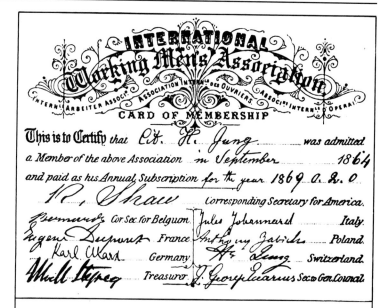

174 The front and back of a membership card issued by the IWA in 1869. The text is taken from the Inaugural Address, the Association's political manifesto.

175 The emblem of the First International with the motto "Equality, Liberty, Fraternity" and the joined hands, the main symbol of the labour movement prior to 1914. This sketch is from the Czech section.

---

87 Marx, Karl: "Allgemeine Statuten und Verwaltungs-Verordnungen der Internationalen Arbeiterassoziation," in: MECW. Vol. 17, p. 440f.

176 The delegates to the Basle Congress of the First International (6–11 September 1869). The Congress stressed the demand for social ownership of the land and acknowledged an alliance with the peasants. The meeting witnessed heated arguments between Marxists, Proudhonists and Bakuninists.

Proletarians of all trades, unite! This slogan appeared in the newspaper *Echo de la Fabrique* during the second uprising in Lyons in 1834. It summoned workers of every occupation to join forces against the bourgeoisie, and expressed a desire for workers to bury the differences caused by varying conditions, wages, structures of dependence and traditional prejudice.

The fabric of trade-union organization was governed by national traditions, political class struggles and economic patterns. The big companies of Britain and Germany, with their authoritarian management, centralized leadership and methodical principles called for labour associations that were just as well organized. Theodor Yorck, a German labour official, declared in 1872 that working-class organizations must combine the unshakeable hierarchy of the Church with the efficiency of factory division of labour and all the advantages of a united army.[88]

France presented a different picture; there were many more small enterprises. Capital concentration was advancing more slowly. Industry was spread throughout the country. The dense pockets of labour created by British and German companies were not so pronounced. As a result, the labour movement was initially a federation of predominantly local concerns with syndicalist trends. It was difficult merging the local associations into one. The printers were the first to set up a national trade union in 1861, followed in 1879 by the hatters. Others followed suit, but the federal structure was widely preserved. Revolutionary and reformist tendencies indulged in public, often violent combat. The ban on associations was lifted in 1884, permitting the foundation of a national trade-union federation in Lyons in 1886. In 1892 local "syndicats" merged to form a Fédération des Bourses du Travail, a parallel form of organization. The first of these "stock exchanges" for labour had been set up in Paris in 1887 and acted as a kind of cartel. Attempts to unite the national bodies began in the nineties, and the Confédération Générale du Travail (CGT) was created in 1895. This adopted a binding Constitution in 1902, and funds were pooled in 1910. It was the first united, nationwide trade-union organization in France.

Forms of resistance The labour movement drew on many traditional forms of resistance from below, adapting them to new conditions. Workers in every country showed how inventive they could be by attempting to develop innovative methods in defending their interests. They ranged from the work-to-rule and boycott to the general strike and political revolution.

A movement had to select methods which matched the economic situation and took account of its ups and downs. Defensive means prevailed in times of crisis. In more prosperous periods trade unionists went on the offensive. How the factory-

LA FRANC-MAÇONNERIE & LA COMMUNE.

177 This copper engraving by Moloch (real name B. Colomb) combines the symbolic figures of France and Liberty to express the unity between France and the Paris Commune.

178 The Paris Commune enjoyed international solidarity. 30,000 British workers demonstrated in Hyde Park on 16 April 1871.

88 Cf. "Protokoll über den 3. Congress der social-demokratischen Arbeiterpartei. Abgehalten zu Mainz am 7., 8., 9., 10. und 11. September 1872." Brunswick, no date, p. 14.

179 Workers publicized their demands on demonstrations, where they also paraded their strength. 30,000 dockers and as many workers of other trades went on strike in London from 12 August to 14 September 1889. Long columns of marchers pressed home the point.

180 Unemployment was a heavy blow to workers and their families. This jobless march on 30 May 1909 demanded the right to work for all citizens, regardless of background, skin colour or sex.

owners resisted would then determine their counter-response. In the United States, the bosses hired trigger-happy private policemen, so the workers armed and fired back. But forms of resistance were also influenced by the conventions of different countries, regions and trades. Skilled English mechanics, for example, were quicker to forge firm organizational links than American railway workers. The earliest generations of workers opposed factory discipline by refusing to turn up for work on Mondays and deliberately working slowly. No sooner had they overcome the indirect payments of the truck system than workers began striking against reduced wages and, eventually, for higher wages. There was more to this industrial action than struggle. The workers made merry, drank, spent the evening dancing and listened to entertaining and spurring songs. It was not only in Germany that strike funds grew out of the social funds which journeymen had once collected for the purposes of both solidarity and celebration. When political demonstrations were banned, workers responded by organizing Sunday walks together. Once workers had experienced a taste of solidarity through their organization, they stayed loyal to the concept and were ready to embark on greater campaigns. Often soup from the strike kitchen and common beer in the pub did more to strengthen unity than speeches and appeals.

Resisting also meant using methods which the law did not yet guarantee. Strikes were often banned. Workers wanted by the

181 "Before the strike." Painting by Mihály Munkácsy, 1885. Striking was always a tough decision for workers. The pros and cons were considered in lively discussion.

182 Labour struggles in the United States were sometimes very militant. Armed workers on strike at the Baltimore and Ohio Railway in 1877 pulled drivers and firemen from the trains.

authorities had to be smuggled out of the country. It took self-sacrificial courage even to distribute forbidden leaflets or hoist the red flag above a tall chimney. Scrawling graffiti, designed to encourage the workers or expose their employers, on factory gates and owners' houses called for audacity and imagination.

Women without rights in bourgeois society Proletarian women in capitalist society suffered discrimination on two counts, as members of the propertyless class and as women, for in 19th-century law the women of the industrial nations were regarded as minors. American women had won civil rights, but politically they, too, were unrecognized. In Germany, Britain and Scandinavia a number of legal concessions had been made (in property law, for example), but women were still not considered responsible subjects and were spoken for by the "head of the family". Women did not count as citizens. The situation in France, and other countries influenced by the *Code Civil*, was particularly backward. Women, along with all their possessions, were still "enslaved" by men, who were entitled to appropriate their wages and deny them permission to enter employment.[89]

In the early days, when bourgeois society began to assert itself, women had already protested against this discrimination. Neither the democratic Constitution which emerged from the American Wars of Independence nor the bourgeois revolution in France granted full human rights to women. At first, the sagacious and far-reaching ideas about sex equality formulated by Condorcet, Mary Wollstonecraft, Theodor Gottlieb Hippel, Claire Lácombe and Olympe de Gouges towards the end of the 18th century made only a weak impact on the feminist movements of various countries. The cardinal challenge to patriarchal society was soon to take the form of a demand for unmarried bourgeois women to be admitted to the world of education and professions. Campaigners for women's rights believed that the key to a self-determined, emancipated existence lay in the right to vote and stand for election. Hence the suffragettes became the symbol of the bourgeois women's movement in the late 19th century. Lack of time was enough to prevent working women from joining their militant demonstrations and protracted meetings, even though they, too, had a fundamental interest in the right of suffrage. Eventually, organizations of working women and various European working-class parties were to voice emphatic support for this demand. Whereas bourgeois women had to fight bitterly throughout the 19th century for their right to work, developments in capitalism had already transformed the context. Wage labour by proletarian women was an economic fact, and it was simply no longer feasible to question their "right" to employment. Working women did not have to worry about whether they were allowed to work: they had to work. Their employment had brought a certain degree of equality with the men of their class,

183 After the turn of the century labour struggles became more versatile and mobilized broader masses. Local general strikes, as in Charleroi in 1912, became an effective tool in achieving demands.

89 Cf. Bebel, August: *Die Frau und der Sozialismus.* Stuttgart, 1910, pp. 280ff.

184 Russian Revolution, 1905: Cossacks were sent in against working-class women as they defended their striking menfolk.

who also laboured for a wage and were exploited in the same manner. When they did express a political commitment, they did not yet make a priority of asserting individual female aspirations as part of a conscious strategy for emancipation, but were more concerned with their rights as workers. For this reason, the bourgeois women's associations could not seriously be expected to represent the interests of their proletarian sisters, even when they paid tribute to their "exploitation and suffering" and stepped up their own philanthropic activities.

Working women in economic and political struggle The common woman had always taken a serious view of her personal responsibility for the physical wellbeing of her relatives, demonstrating as much in her tireless work for the family household. Even when she resorted to elementary forms of public protest, such as tax rebellions and food riots, she was fighting for family survival.

"The mothers, daughters and wives of the sansculottes participated with vehemence in the revolutionary events, at risk to their lives, and completely true to the old model of women's role in the traditional resistance and hungry unrest of the 18th century."[90] They were inspired by hopes for a better life for themselves and their children. Women played an impressive public role in the early economic struggles of the British labour movement. Chartist accounts describe women fighting shoulder to shoulder with men on the streets, and joining in the discussions and drinking at the pub. The British situation, however, was exceptional. Male and female workers had experienced fifty years of industrialization before the rise of Chartism, but on the Continent and in North America, women were only just beginning to enter wage labour.

For women, joining the army of industrial wage labour did not simply mean contributing more to the family budget. This first-hand encounter with capitalism turned workers' wives into proletarians. Like their menfolk, they now had to fight in order to sell their labour under more favourable conditions. Moreover, women were obliged to voice demands aimed at enabling them to carry out their duties as mothers and housewives. That meant taking up the gauntlet for tolerable working conditions, a shorter working day, higher wages and equal pay for equal work, employment protection, maternity provisions, and insurance against sickness and unemployment. The logical consequence of all this was that women had to join trade unions. Organizing female wage labour has been hindered throughout history by both objective and subjective factors. Women in capitalist industry constituted a reserve army of labour which competed severely with the men for wages and jobs. Male family breadwinners who were obliged to earn as much as possible and without interruption felt that they were being degraded in their own occupations, threatened in their livelihoods and personally humiliated. They saw women's labour as evidence that they were failing in their role as the financial pillar—and hence undisputed head—of the family. German workers were not the only ones who found it fairly hard to accept the historical inevitability of female wage labour. Although not all of them went so far as to bar women from factories, like the Lassalleans, it was nevertheless a lengthy process before male proletarians of all nations recognized the cultural progress actually implicit in women's employment and felt able to conduct joint economic and political class struggles with women.

In the latter half of the 19th century, even politically active workers tended to visualize that a "good working-class wife and mother who stays at home, lives off her husband's wages, cares for him, brightens his spirits, and raises children to be not merely godly but also class-conscious, an ideal which, even in Britain, could not possibly be achieved until much later, and then only among a labour aristocracy. But the effect of this was that before long many women only knew the labour movement from dances and Christmas parties or from the influence which a strike exercised on the kitchen saucepan. In Britain (and America), organized workers adopted the bourgeois view of women earlier and more comprehensively than elsewhere. At any event, from 1850 onwards women had been marginalized by the British labour movement, and the trade unions in particular waxed quite lyrical with their proletarian counterpart to the bourgeois vision of domestic bliss."[91] It was certainly rare for married proletarian women in this period to take a full-time job outside the home. Many, however, were engaged in homeworking or domestic

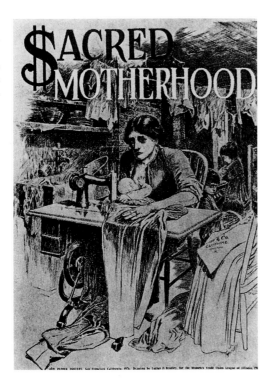

185 This poster by the Women's Trade Union League of Illinois shows a homeworker in 1907. Women's unions fought for working conditions which would enable women to carry out their domestic duties.

services. Maternal duty and family life dominated the lives of working-class women, their personal development, and even their upbringing. Children were sufficient to keep a woman at home for most of the time while her husband gained social experience at the factory, at political rallies, in associations or at the pub.

Managing the family budget was an inescapable lifetime chore which exerted a prime influence on a woman's daily experience, governed her behaviour and also limited her intellectual horizons.

These restrictions made women less receptive to matters which were not confined to their own four walls. Their husbands' political activity often made them suspicious or frightened, as it meant nothing to them but a threat to the upkeep of their dependents. Many working-class women sought guidance and consolation in religion.

Family considerations always diminished a working woman's choice of employment, not only the nature of her job, but also the time and energy she could invest in it.

Women in employment found it exceedingly difficult to assert their rights, as their jobs were geared entirely to family concerns, their labour was often accidental in content and frequently interrupted, and they were scattered between small outfits in the service sector and their homes, where many worked for the textiles industry. Women (most of them single) pursuing the traditional female trades under industrial conditions were the first to discover their proletarian identity, join labour organizations and observe a code of solidarity, but even they did not find it easy to act with far-sighted discipline.

The spontaneous outbursts of earlier days had sometimes produced immediate results for the outraged female participants. Personal commitment to trade-union struggles, on the other hand, meant making sacrifices for more distant goals, while immediate survival was in jeopardy. As a rule, women tended to see the risks involved in their struggles rather than the political dimensions.

International organizations of proletarian women During the last third of the 19th century, working women in all the major industrial countries formed trade unions and entered the structures of the male labour movement.

Women working in industries in the United States started to form independent trade associations from 1870. After 1880, male unions accepted female members. When the Knights of

90 *Listen der Ohnmacht. Zur Sozialgeschichte weiblicher Widerstandsformen.* Ed. by Claudia Honegger and Bettina Heintz. Frankfurt am Main, 1981, p. 13 (Preface: "Zum Strukturwandel weiblicher Widerstandsformen im 19. Jahrhundert").
91 *Ibid.*, p. 13 f.

186 Social Democratic women meet
in Berlin, 1891.

Labor, a big working-class organization, admitted female industrial workers, an important step was taken towards recognition of their equality. By this time every branch of the Granger Association for farmers and rural workers had women among its membership.[92]

In 1898 there were 826,735 women working in factories and 250,380 in workshops in Britain, and 116,016 (about ten per cent) belonged to labour organizations. 25 male trade unions were admitting female members. Almost all the women in the textiles industry were organized jointly with men. Another 13 trade unions had an exclusively female membership.[93] In 1901 France had 75 mixed unions and 36 solely female. There were independent women's organizations for flower-makers, seamstresses, laundresses, tie-workers, embroideresses, home helps, typesetters, bookfolders and typists. Box-makers, tobacco workers, brush-makers, dye workers, and producers of chocolate, glass, gloves, jewellery, umbrellas and paper bags formed joint organizations for both sexes.[94]

In 1893 2,700 out of 9,600 women working for the Belgian textiles industry in Ghent had joined the men's union.[95] In Austria, tobacco workers and the seamstresses and laundresses of Vienna set up trade unions for women, while women in the other trades organized alongside men.[96] In Germany, reactionary laws prohibited women in many regions from founding their own associations, so that the females of the proletarian class played a more active part in the trade unions and political work of the males. After the Berlin Conference of Trade Unions in 1890 women were admitted to these labour organizations. Trade unionism spread quickly among women from 1895, and from 1892 to 1899 the number of female members soared from 4,355 to 19,280.[97]

In many countries, such as Austria, Switzerland, Denmark and Belgium, the working-class women's movement had close links with the working-class socialist parties. The relationship between the Social Democrats in Germany and groupings of working women was particularly intense. It was the German Social Democrat August Bebel who wrote *Die Frau und der Sozialismus* (Women under Socialism), the book which proletarian women of all countries, and even their bourgeois sisters, turned to for intellectual orientation in their quest for emancipation. It was first published in 1879, and by the First World War it had appeared in 14 languages. Germany's organizations of proletarian women were more consistent than any others in applying the book's

187 Bebel's *Women under Socialism*, a library copy of the 50th edition in 1910. By this time the work had appeared in fourteen languages.

92 Cf. *Handbuch der Frauenbewegung*. Ed. by Helene Lange and Gertrud Bäumer. 1st part: *Die Geschichte der Frauenbewegung in den Kulturländern*. Berlin, 1901, p. 471.

93 *Ibid.*, p. 272.

94 *Ibid.*, p. 387.

95 *Ibid.*, p. 400.

96 *Ibid.*, p. 185.

97 *Ibid.*, p. 119.

188 Demonstration for women's suf-
frage in Berlin on 19 March 1911.
Photo by Otto Haeckel. Austria,
Denmark, Switzerland and Germany
were marking the first International
Women's Day.

underlying political principle, which was that the "Woman Question" should be linked to the working-class struggle for liberation, in the international arena.

The first International Conference of Socialist Women was held in Stuttgart in 1907. There were 58 delegates from 15 countries, including Holland, Belgium, France, Italy, Britain, Sweden, Russia and the United States of America. They delivered reports on the socialist women's movements in their countries and discussed the campaign for women's suffrage, which was considered an important issue for rallying working-class women. The

Conference agreed to set up an office to co-ordinate international activity. It was to be located in Germany, and Clara Zetkin was appointed to lead this International Women's Secretariat. The Social Democratic women's magazine *Die Gleichheit*, of which she was editor, was to act as the journal of the Secretariat.

The second International Conference of Socialist Women in Copenhagen in 1910 decided that an International Women's Day should be marked each year as a focus for the suffrage campaign. It was observed for the first time in Austria, Denmark, Switzerland and Germany on 19 March 1911.

The Struggle for Social Security

Pre-industrial forms of social provision for the working population, from the duties of the parish, via guild traditions, to organic family bonds, were falling apart. A cash contract had replaced the common table, village or house. The conditions of sale for labour were subject to change, and everywhere there were certain national factors at play. How workers in a particular country managed to win basic social security, and in what form, depended on the methods which capital and labour chose to iron out their conflicts, on the strength of the trade unions and the extent of government controls.

In Germany many of the guild rules were continued and old systems of insurance preserved. Some factory-owners tried to adapt these conventional provisions to the new conditions by setting up works associations and recognizing the journeymen's social funds and compulsory self-help (benefit funds, co-operatives). Workers, too, were so concerned about their insecure livelihoods that they formed their own self-support organizations, including funds for disability, widows and funerals. The trade unions which grew out of these bodies carried on exercising those functions. When state and commercial insurance policies were later introduced, they affected more than the size of trade-union membership. Workers were no longer motivated to join merely by fear of unemployment or illness, in order to claim their entitlements. This meant that trade-union objectives altered. Around the turn of the century, they were able to focus completely on campaigns against wage reductions, for higher wages and standard working hours.

In the United States, the picture was quite different. Capitalism there was born without a context of tradition. This enabled the bourgeoisie to develop more freely, and they had but three enemies: Indians, who laid claims to territory, big landowners, who exploited slaves, and national labour organizations of varying sizes. They succeeded in crushing any attempts by immigrant workers, most of them German, to continue the guild traditions of social provision. The pressure was so strong that the majority of North American workers failed, even later, to organize. That is why they never managed to achieve any system of

national insurance, and were to a large extent dependent on their own resources when it came to establishing some kind of social security. That is doubtless one reason why the lifestyle of American workers is so different from that in Europe. Average wages in America were considerably higher, for in all vicissitude the main financial cover against unemployment, sickness, disability and old age was supplied from private savings, private insurance, family assistance and even public charity.

Australia, on the other hand, remained a British colony for many years, acting as a vast prison for the mother country's criminals, vagabonds and rebels. Although deportation was abolished in 1840, the old fabric of laws and social mechanisms survived. The prison system, somewhat generalized and liberalized, served as a basis for Australia's social insurance. Only in 1901, when the six colonies were declared states in the Australian federation and the continent received the new status of a dominion, were European forms of national insurance introduced gradually on the basis of the British legal system.

By 1914 there were three fundamental types of social insurance, which resulted from different cultural traditions, trade-union struggles of varying impact, petitions, inquiries, parliamentary debates, strikes and demonstrations. These were the European, American and Australian models of insurance cover against disability, old age and accident, with provision for widows and orphans. In those days there was no comparable protection against unemployment.

Outmoded security The aim of the guild statutes drawn up by the European craftsmen of yore was to ensure the livelihood and upkeep of members. The guilds kept competition at bay, protected the journeymen from poverty and provided social assistance. They imposed limits on the numbers of journeymen with one master and made it an offence to lure a man away from his master. Wages, working hours and boarding were settled. The frail and the sick, and any members who had been maimed by accident, received subsidies or loans, sometimes even weekly benefits and payment in kind. Parents, godparents or children were

189 When Hamburg dockers went on strike in 1896 their cards were stamped daily. Print by E. Limmer. An organized worker was entitled to receive strike benefit if he had paid his union dues regularly and took part in strike action every day.

190 As life became more precarious, more and more European peasants and workers were driven across the ocean. New arrivals had to register. This drawing from the *Illustrated Newspaper* shows German immigrants in 1866.

191 Strike money is ceremonially meted out in Preston, England, 1853. Strict regulations within proletarian support organizations provided a degree of security during industrial action. Contemporary wood engraving.

192 The tailors of Germany, like other trades, founded their own funds or insurance societies to provide cover during unemployment.

responsible for maintenance during the non-productive stages of life.

The journeymen set up their own social network after tussles with the masters. They kept funds to assist their "brothers" in cases of unemployment, illness or accident. They collected an admittance levy, fines, fees and dues. They also undertook the task of finding jobs, allocating accommodation and drawing up rotas to watch over the sick. Invalids had to beg. All journeymen were under an obligation to attend funerals. Trade unionists in the Berlin breweries adopted funeral rules reminiscent of this tradition as late as 1885. Every member was required to turn up in a dark suit with a tall hat and a wreath, sporting the association's symbol with a bow. The ceremony itself observed strict rites. The brewery workers paid the costs by taking a collection, and everyone had to contribute.[98]

"Competition is for the people a system of extermination"

The universal transition to wage labour extinguished these old forms of insurance and made the purveyors of labour rivals among themselves. It was now vital for workers to extend mutual solidarity and campaign jointly for jobs, decent wages and binding social provisions.

Louis Blanc described this new state of affairs, which gave birth to trade-union struggle, in 1839: "Is the poor man a member or an enemy of society? . . . Can he till the land on his own account? No; because the right of the first occupier has become right of property. Can he pluck the fruits which the will of God has ripened in the path of man? No; because like the soil the fruits have been appropriated. Can he resort to hunting or fishing? No; because they constitute rights which the government supports. Can he take the water of an enclosed well? No; because the proprietor of the enclosure is, by virtue of the law of inheritance, proprietor of the spring. Can he, dying with hunger and thirst, stretch out his hand to the pity of his fellow men? No; because there are laws against mendicancy. Can he, exhausted with fatigue, and without shelter, fall asleep on the pavement of the street? No; because there are laws against vagrancy . . . The conclusion from this is very easy. *Secure* work to the poor . . . Is competition the way to secure work to the poor? But to put the question in this shape is to solve it. What is competition with respect to labour? It is labour put up for auction. A speculator requires a workman. Three present themselves.

How much for your labour?

Three francs; I have a wife and children.

Good; and you?

Two francs and a half; I have no children, but I have a wife.

Indeed; and you?

Two francs will content me; I am single.

You, then, are preferred.

It is done; the bargain is struck. But what becomes of the two rejected workmen? They will die quietly of hunger, it is to be hoped . . . Should a fourth workman arrive sufficiently robust to fast one day out of two, the scale of reduction would descend to the lowest point; and, lo! another pariah; perchance another recruit for the galleys!"[99]

Defenceless workers

The German Land Laws of 1794 made parishes responsible for the poor. The community was obliged to feed and provide for citizens who were unable to earn their own income and had no relatives to support them. There were no benefit rights. Assistance was restricted to the bare means for survival and a free funeral. By accepting this aid, citizens became legal minors.

As the Industrial Revolution spread across Europe, towns and villages alike bore uglier scars of growing misery. With so many craftsmen being drawn into the proletariat in Germany, as in other countries, the funds kept by journeymen and parishes were less and less able to cope with. And yet the army of needy cases kept swelling. Besides, there were new types of social distress to tackle. Machines operating without safety measures and open transmission belts led to accidents which resembled war injuries. Occupational disease, accident and disability soared. Poor light, bad air and poisonous fumes on the shop floor spawned unknown industrial illnesses. But when factory workers fell sick, their bosses handed them their cards. Unemployed journeymen lost their entitlement to sickness benefit. Former rural workers found themselves without shelter or support. The new state of affairs began to look critical for the propertied classes, too. And sickly workers' children bode ill for the factories and armies of the future.

Co-operative self-help

Middle-class individuals who were sympathetic to the lower strata first argued for "association" during the Industrial Revolution. Community self-help was to cure an ailing society. Impoverished craftsmen, traders and peasants could overcome the crisis of competition by setting up co-operatives to issue loans, provide jobs, buy in produce and set up stores. They would thus be spared the fate of the proletarian.

According to this view, the best way for workers to counter financial hardship and inadequate security was by setting up retail co-operatives. The Rochdale Pioneers' Society, inspired by Robert Owen, set an example to many in the European countries. Their activity was publicized above all by the letters, travels and articles of George Jacob Holyoake.[100] This co-operative was originally founded by 20 poor flannel-weavers of Yorkshire and Lan-

---

98 Cf. *25 Jahre Organisation der Berliner Brauereiarbeiter. Entstehung, Entwicklung und Wirken des Brauereiarbeiter-Verbandes in Berlin.* Presented by Wilhelm Richter. Berlin, 1911, p. 19f.
99 Blanc, Louis: *The Organization of Labour.* London, 1848, pp. 27–29.
100 Holyoake, George Jacob: *The History of the Rochdale Pioneers.* London, 1893.

193 The little shop grew into a big enterprise. The original Rochdale Pioneers, photographed here in 1860, were seen as the founding fathers of the co-operative movement in Europe.

194 "The first co-operative store in Rochdale." Contemporary drawing by Thomas Wakeman.

195 Retail co-operatives sprang up all over Europe. Many workers believed they would provide lasting guarantees for working-class customers. The societies had to compete with private traders. The Stuttgart society used its coach as a mobile shop, *c.* 1910.

cashire in October 1844. They opened a jointly-owned store selling groceries and clothes. They had plans to build houses, assist each other in "improving their domestic and social condition", cultivate land, and even establish a settlement of their own with a Temperance Hotel. On the official day of opening they were more or less the only customers and only took a dozen and a half shillings, but 20 years later the Society had many branches numbering 6,000 heads of households among their members. Their wealth amounted to millions. Many later co-operatives could not keep their heads above water. This was not the way to guarantee social security for all. And yet the co-operative ideal did not die: it made a great contribution to the theory and practice of solidarity.

From workers' funds to national insurance Workers saw their support funds as an independent and embryonic form of the insurance system that they would one day administer for themselves. Alongside these kitties were the works funds set up by factory-owners. Other companies took over the system of social funds run by journeymen. There were also various health associations, private insurance firms and savings societies. After the turn of the century the co-operative stores became consumer organizations, managed along purely economic lines and politically neutral. Socialist co-operatives helped workers to purchase goods and rent homes, but offered no assistance to sick people in dire straits or to invalids. This called for a universal system of national insurance. In Germany it evolved out of existing funds and government welfare for the poor.

In the sixties and seventies, the workers' funds had given birth to far more comprehensive organizations to defend class interests, notably trade unions and political groupings. Their basic demands for financial security won them more and more supporters. The German bourgeoisie responded with two very different political measures: a ban on all Social Democratic organizations by the law against socialists in 1878, and three stages of social legislation from 1883 to 1889. As a social guarantee for workers, these insurance laws were an historic innovation. The only other countries to adopt similar laws prior to 1914 were France (1910), Luxembourg (1911), Roumania (1912), the Netherlands and Sweden (1913). Britain borrowed some elements from Germany's national insurance system without totally relinquishing the existing form of civil provision.

A victory for the labour movement The main credit for Germany's adoption of the most advanced insurance system for workers before the First World War was due to the labour movement. The German Social Democrat leader August Bebel in particular had realized that, while the law against socialists was designed to eliminate the working-class party politically, the insurance legislation was intended to destroy the social basis for the German labour movement. In an astute evaluation of the economic and political differences between the capitalists and the big landowners, Bebel gave a speech in the *Reichstag* stressing the role of working-class pressure and the parliamentary force of their party in obtaining these social policy concessions.

He was acting on the advice which Friedrich Engels had sent him in a letter dated 24 November 1879. The "questions on which Social Democratic representatives can escape this negation are very narrowly restricted. They include all those questions where the relationship of the worker to the capitalist is a direct factor: factory legislation, standard working day, liability, wages paid in goods etc. Then at best improvements in the purely bourgeois sense which constitute a positive advance: standard coins and measures, liberties, greater personal freedom etc. . . . In all the other economic questions such as protective tariffs, nationalization of the railways, assurance companies etc., Social Democratic representatives must always be adamant about the decisive criterion, which is not to approve anything which strengthens the government's power over the people."[101]

196 Proletarians were completely at the mercy of their landlords in such basic matters as shelter and housing. It took them a long time to organize solutions of their own. In 1871, when workers took power in Paris, they decreed rent rebates and strengthened the legal rights of tenants. The announcement was issued on 29 March 1871.

RÉPUBLIQUE FRANÇAISE

N° 41   LIBERTÉ — ÉGALITÉ — FRATERNITÉ   N° 41

COMMUNE DE PARIS

LA COMMUNE DE PARIS,

Considérant que le travail, l'industrie et le commerce ont supporté toutes les charges de la guerre, qu'il est juste que la propriété fasse au pays sa part de sacrifices,

DÉCRÈTE :

Art. 1er. Remise générale est faite aux locataires des termes d'octobre 1870, janvier et avril 1871.

Art. 2. Toutes les sommes payées par les locataires pendant ces neuf mois seront imputables sur les termes à venir.

Art. 3. Il est fait également remise des sommes dues pour les locataires en garni.

Art. 4. Tous les baux sont résiliables, à la volonté des locataires, pendant une durée de six mois, à partir du présent décret.

Art. 5. Tous congés donnés seront, sur la demande des locataires, prorogés de trois mois.

(Un décret spécial réglera la question des intérêts hypothécaires.)

Hôtel-de-ville de Paris, le 29 mars 1871.

LA COMMUNE DE PARIS.

The Fight for a "Normal Day"

When industrialization began, capital, in "its blind unrestrainable passion"[102] for surplus labour, had pushed the daily expenditure of labour power to the bounds of possibility with a working day of 14 to 16 hours and more. British workers were the first to be affected, and they soon launched a counter-movement which went beyond individual resistance. This proved to be a factor, just as it did later in other countries, in certain legal restrictions being imposed on the working day for women and children in the first half of the 19th century. But even this British factory legislation was originally introduced to confront an exceptional situation: certain excesses of exploitation in the textile mills.

Even at this early stage, however, the length of the working day in the various productive sectors clearly depended on the resistance put up by the workers concerned. This led to the obvious conclusion that the amount of labour time demanded by the capitalist was generally the outcome of class struggle: "The creation of a normal working-day is, therefore, the product of a protracted civil war, more or less dissembled, between the capitalist class and the working class."[103]

At the Geneva Congress in September 1866, the International Working Men's Association had adopted as a resolution one of the points in Karl Marx's instructions to delegates, proposing that "8 hours work as the legal limit of the working day"[104] should be a general demand for workers in all countries. Although Marx urged the Brussels Congress of the International in 1868 to "draw practical conclusions from this resolution"[105], the fledg-

ling national labour movements were not really in a position to achieve this very far-reaching goal. The fight for a binding limit on the working day did not become a realistic objective and strong motive force for the labour movements until the end of the century. In fact, it was this new orientation which lifted the workers' economic struggles for improved working and living conditions onto the plane of national and international political struggle.

One key to this development was that large sections of the working class were acquiring a new awareness of the value of non-working time. It was not only necessary "to restore health and physical energies", but also as an opportunity for "intellectual development, sociable intercourse, social and political action"[106].

101 "Friedrich Engels to August Bebel in Leipzig. 24 November 1879," in: Marx, Karl, and Friedrich Engels: *Werke*. Ed. by Institut für Marxismus-Leninismus beim ZK der SED. Vol. 34. Berlin, 1956–68, p. 423f.
102 Marx, Karl: *Capital*. Vol. 1. Moscow, 1971, p. 252.
103 *Ibid.*, p. 283.
104 Marx, Karl: "Instructions for the Delegates of the Provisional General Council. The different questions," in: Marx, Karl, and Friedrich Engels: *Selected Works*. Vol. 2. Moscow, 1969, p. 79.
105 Marx, Karl: "Draft Resolution on a Limited Working Day, proposed to the Brussels Congress by the General Council," in: Marx, Karl, and Friedrich Engels: *Selected Works*. Vol. 2. Moscow, 1969, p. 200.
106 Marx, Karl: "Instructions for the Delegates of the Provisional General Council. The different questions," in: Marx, Karl, and Friedrich Engels: *Selected Works*. Vol. 2. Moscow, 1969, p. 79.

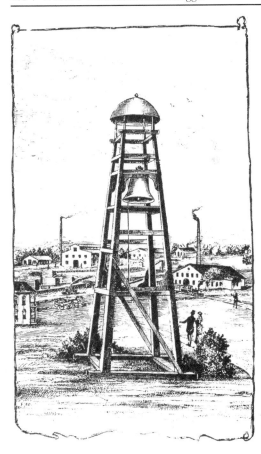

197 A mechanics' bell erected in 1831. At sunrise it summoned workers to the mill. Work ended at sunset. In 1791 American carpenters declared: "It shall be presumed among us that a working day begins at six in the morning and ends at six in the evening every day." In other words, they were already demanding fixed hours.

198 Like the guild statutes of old, this schedule for Massachusetts factory girls in works accommodation dictated the daily pattern from start to finish.

Moreover, successive generations of workers entering the proletariat had been forced to learn that only certain forms of struggle were effective here. Individual responses, such as idleness, slow working, truancy and frequent changes of job, never provided any more than momentary relief. Even when powerful individual unions had won a shorter working day by placing massive pressure on employers in many European countries and in the United States, their efforts had not accomplished any fundamental settlement, although they did foster the trend towards shorter hours. The working class was embarking on a strategy of political economy by demanding a universal legal limit on labour time, over and above which the wage labourer was not prepared to sell his life-time on the labour market. The objective was thus uniquely appropriate for raising consciousness about the common interests of all workers. It was evident to everyone that success hinged on the powerful centralized, national labour organizations and how fit they actually were for combat.

National trade-union movements launched campaigns for the eight-hour day in Canada and the United States (1884) and France (1888), prompting the International Workers' Congress in Paris in 1899 to "organize a big international rally simultaneously" on 1 May 1890 "in every country and every city". The participants were to "demand that the public authorities stipulate a working day of eight hours".[107] The movement won substantial reductions in working hours over the next twenty years. Many European countries introduced legislation on the working day around 1900. A universal eight-hour day, however, was not achieved. Not even the French workers made any headway here when the CGT declared a general strike in 1906. It was an objective which could not be reached until the great revolutions which put an end to the First World War. Soviet Russia was the first European country to introduce the eight-hour day in 1917. And on 23 November 1918 the Council of People's Representatives in Germany issued a Demobilization Order which fixed the industrial working day at eight hours.

Once the eight-hour day had been guaranteed in most industrial countries, the struggle to protect labour turned to other goals. The labour movement was still concerned about the overall question of time, and demanded a shorter working week, annual leave, and a fixed retirement age.

The pre-industrial working day As rural labour depended directly on natural conditions, the burden of labour which fell to a pre-industrial peasant varied substantially from one season to the next. Most work had to be performed in the harvest months of July and August, when humans and animals alike had to cut their rest down to a minimum. In winter, too, there was work to fill every waking hour, for there were cattle to tend, the household

107 "Protokoll des Internationalen Arbeiter-Congresses zu Paris." Nuremberg, 1890.

199 The slogan at the first Labor Day demonstration in New York, as anywhere else, was "Eight Hours to Constitute a Day's Work". The marchers sang their eight-hour song: "Eight hours to work, eight hours to rest, eight hours for what we like doing best."

200 August Spies in his cell. This German-American labour official told the jury from the dock: "But if you think you can extinguish the labour movement by having us hanged . . . then go ahead and hang us! You will be stamping out a spark here, but there, and behind you—and in front of you and everywhere new flames will flare up. It is an underground fire. You cannot extinguish it." August Spies was executed on 11 November 1887.

economy continued producing, and buildings and equipment were in need of repair. And yet labour was far less intense than in summer, with plenty of breaks. More time was allowed for resting, which also kept consumption down as far as possible. Free time for individuals to dispose of as they pleased was unknown in the countryside before the days of industry.

Life was similar in medieval towns and monasteries. Although there were bells and clocks to impose a pattern on the day, which the urban crafts were obliged to observe in the same way as the monks, with their eight hours each of work, prayer and sleep, the length and intensity of labour in pre-capitalist production oscillated greatly. In many trades, the amount of work to do depended on the orders that were taken. Besides, supplies of raw materials were not constant, and there were days when nobody worked at all, either because of the long list of religious festivals, or because of customs like Monday truancy or half Saturdays. As a result, the production process was frequently interrupted and rhythms were irregular.

In the craft economy, moreover, work was geared to a complex series of tasks which called for a "personal" productive rhythm. Machines did not yet dictate the pace, but the master did bring his influence to bear. This gave all artisans a certain freedom to fashion their labour as it suited them, even though certain times had to be respected due to traditional norms, guild regulations and police bye-laws. The very objectives of guild statutes pre-empted a rational calculation of time. Temporal efficiency was not yet a priority, but, rather, ensuring that every member of the guild had enough to eat and live by. As the guild monopoly staved off all competition, time was not used to particular advantage.

"The division between 'work' and 'life' seems to be least pronounced in societies where time is 'task-orientated'. Relationships between people are combined with work. The working day can be longer or shorter according to the task which needs completing, and there is hardly any sense of a conflict between 'work' and 'passing time'."[108]

Ruthless extension of the working day A more efficient use of labour power could already be observed in the manufactories set up by absolutist powers in Europe to satisfy the state's growing demand for equipment and luxury goods. There were religious, political and economic arguments to support the actions of state and private manufacturers: "That mankind in general," wrote one English economist in 1770, "are naturally inclined to ease and indolence, we fatally experience to be true, from the conduct of our manufacturing populace, who do not labour, upon an average, above four days a week, unless provisions happen to be very dear." Pointing to the situation in France, he predicts that: "the cure will not be perfect, till our manufacturing poor are contented to labour six days for the same sum which they now earn in four days."[109] Here lies the secret to the new form of exploitation: as capitalist commodity production spread, the working day

201 This song sheet was printed and distributed for the May Day celebrations in 1895. The lyrics call for an eight-hour day, and they were sung to the well-known tune of the Marseillaise.

was ruthlessly prolonged for masses of toilers. The first to be affected were villagers, whose poverty was already dire as a result of overpopulation: entire communities were impoverished, many peasants had lost their land, while homeworkers and rural artisans had been beaten down by manufactories. Women and children above all were obliged to accept employment under any conditions in the "industries earliest revolutionized by waterpower, steam, and machinery"[110]: spinning and weaving. The state of affairs was similar in other sectors of rural production: distilling, sugar and preserved foods, brickworks, glass-making, and some mines and foundries. Poverty was so extreme that wage labourers were completely at the mercy of the factory-owners. As a consequence, struggles for shorter hours were very rare. Even when the new century dawned, excessive hours remained a feature of these enterprises.

The picture was quite different in the towns. When metalworking and mechanical engineering expanded rapidly and were transferred to factories, and when the electrical and chemical industries were born, there was a sharp rise in the demand for skilled workers with craft qualifications. Workers with the traditional consciousness of the urban crafts entered the factories and confronted the industrial capitalists. Admittedly, the rules and standards generated by the craft economy, such as guild restric-

tions on the intake of apprentices and journeymen, were not effective in this situation.

But it did not take long before these old patterns of self-protection were modified. The demand for a normal working day became the most widely applicable formula for limiting the employers' power and defending jobs and wages.

"Eight hours of work a day are more than enough" The regional shortage of qualified labour was the main reason why a legal limit to the working day was originally achieved outside Europe. Australian workers won the most comprehensive legal agreement of the 19th century. In 1856, Melbourne building workers set up an Eight-Hour League, and their demand had soon been met everywhere. Australia was the first country in the world with a law fixing the working day at eight hours. New Zealand soon followed suit.

But the workers' struggle for a standard working day first began in another former British colony: the states of North

---

108 Thompson, Edward P.: "Time, Work-Discipline and Industrial Capitalism," in: *Past & Present* No. 38, 1967, pp. 56–97.

109 "An essay on trade and commerce." London, 1770, p. 15 and p. 69. Quoted from: Marx, Karl: *Capital.* Vol. 1. Moscow, 1971, p. 262.

110 Marx, Karl: *Capital.* Vol. 1. Moscow, 1971, p. 282.

America. One factor may have been that many aspects of working-class life had been defined by laws ever since the settlers arrived. Rules about wages, clothes, hairstyles, social gatherings and permissible pleasures were designed to restrain the aspirations of skilled workers and moderate their pressure on the bosses. The working day was considered to last quite naturally from dawn till dusk, although there were rules about mealtimes and breaks. This time schedule was preserved after the War of Independence, at least for a while. An average of twelve hours were worked for at least six days a week. But as capitalism developed more freely, the factory-owners stepped up their pressure on the wage labourers. This provoked the first reactions. In 1786, the journeymen printers of Philadelphia organized a turn-out which won them a daily wage of one dollar and a working day of ten hours. Other occupations followed with their own protest actions, but did not meet with such success, although they did coin a slogan which was retained for many years to come by the movement for a ten-hour working day: "Six to six!" (It included two hours for mealtimes.)

The great surge in the North American labour movement in the mid-thirties—with 26 nationwide strikes from 1833 to 1837—achieved the ten-hour day for skilled workers in most states. Ultimately this victory shortened the hours of other workers, too. The average day in the late fifties was eleven to twelve hours. The movement entered a new stage when the northern states won the American Civil War. The abolition of slavery also changed the social status of free wage labourers. From 1865, the mechanic Ira Steward, a Boston trade unionist, led a movement for an eight-hour day. Several hundred Eight-Hour Leagues took up his call for a legal limit on working hours. The All-American Workers' Congress which met in Baltimore from 20 to 25 August 1866 placed the demand at the top of the trade-union agenda. The conference made such a deep impact that Karl Marx proposed including this point in the manifesto of the First International. By 1868 the trade unions had won the vote of eight state parliaments. In practice, however, both private and government employers usually found loopholes in the law when drawing up contracts. A shorter working day meant an appropriate cut in wages, and so Steward's hopes had still not been fulfilled. He pursued a theory of social policy which argued that more free time must lead to new needs and therefore more wages. His wife popularized this idea in a rhyme:

Who cares if it's piece rates or hourly pay?

We'll increase our wages and shorten our day!

Despite these failures, the eight-hour slogan never died. 1878 witnessed the National Congress of the Knights of Labor, and two resolutions adopted by the American Federation of Labor (AFL) in 1884 were to have far-reaching consequences. They called for Labor Day (the first Monday in September) and Moving Day (1 May) to be recognized as public holidays. Moreover, from 1 May 1886 eight hours were to be regarded as the legal standard for a working day among the workers in all countries.

202 The labour movement also used the new medium of the postcard. Workers sent May cards to show that they had taken part in the eight-hour rallies.

203 Progress bears the eight-hour banner and Victory carves a breach in the capitalist fortress. The New Year edition of *Der Wahre Jacob* in 1895 graphically depicts the political and cultural significance of a normal working day.

Ein Neujahrsgeschenk, wie es sich die Arbeiter wünschen.

Wie stolz die Zwingburg sich erhebt, | Es tobt und lärmt die Protzenschaft, | Des Volkes lange Qual und Plag'
Man merkt, wie sie im Grund erbebt. | Doch sieh, wie dort die Bresche klafft. | Wird kürzen der Achtstundentag.

On that day, police in Chicago attacked a rally of workers who were striking for the eight-hour limit. On 4 May a mass meeting was held in Haymarket Square to protest against the police brutality. An unknown person threw a bomb at the police as they advanced yet again.

The bourgeoisie took advantage of the Haymarket tragedy to block the eight-hour movement and launch a nationwide assault on labour organizations using every means at their disposal. Trade-union officials were arrested, and in Chicago four of them were executed.

But it was impossible to keep the movement down forever. In 1886 the AFL Congress decided to concentrate all its resources on introducing the eight-hour day from 1 May 1890. AFL leader Samuel Gompers sent a message to the International Socialist Congress of 1889 in Paris proposing that 1 May 1890 should be a day of international action for legal implementation of the eight-hour day. By the early 20th century, large sections of workers in the United States had virtually accomplished their objective.

Capital interests and the normal day Employers who had purchased a day's labour were eager to ensure a constant high rate of energy input from the labourer, and the principal means which they used to achieve this, at least to begin with, were economic pressure on the wage packet and direct supervision.

As mechanical labour spread and assumed new functions in pacesetting technological sectors of the economy, work organization became more methodical and easier to calculate. One aim was to make maximum use of both technology and human labour by adapting them to each other more closely. Superfluous and inefficient actions, and in particular breaks, had to be discarded from the working day. The employer's interests thus shifted from the length of labour to its intensity. Experiments showed that shortening working hours could actually lead to higher productivity. Concentration improved, downtime was cut, and fewer mistakes were made.

As a result, factory-owners who had raised their productivity/time ratio, thanks to more advanced technology and scientific principles of labour organization, and who had thereby "compressed" labour, were now equally keen to see a legal limit on the working day. This was the only way to kill off companies which compensated for their inefficient technology by excessively prolonging work time.

Once labour sciences were used to compress labour time in this manner, new and greater demands were being made of labour power. Physical strain was coupled with intellectual effort and psychological stress. The reproduction of labour power, therefore, called for new forms and content. A longer period for reproducing labour power could no longer be postponed.

Workers' Leisure
and
Proletarian Culture

Observers saw the emergent proletariat as "this useful class of society . . . which performs the most wearisome, the vilest, the most disgusting functions, which takes, in a word, on its shoulders, all that is disagreeable and servile in life, and procures thus for other classes leisure, serenity of mind and conventional dignity of character". The worker and the person of privilege were "not the same man that first works, and then reposes; but it is because the one works that the other rests"[111]. From the outset, and during the complete evolution of industrial capitalism, the social classes acquired unequal shares of work and leisure, time for rest, relaxation and self-determined activity, for education, science, art and politics. Nevertheless, workers obtained more free time than the toiling strata had ever enjoyed before. Leisure became a right and, with an employment contract, trade-union agreement and legal limit on the working day, it was available daily in a regular rhythm. Work and leisure divided the day into two radically different halves. These were so very dissimilar that Adam Smith regarded non-working time as the freedom and happiness which the labourer sacrificed in production. And in the analysis of the young Marx: "Only outside labour does the labourer feel he is himself, for in labour he is outside himself."[112] The proletariat turned the extent and use of leisure into a social question, a theme for social movements and struggles, a sales outlet for special goods and services which, increasingly, were produced on an industrial scale.

Proletarian leisure began as a brief period for restoring the energy to work. In the eyes of the capitalist employer, this was the most acceptable purpose. After all, on the one hand he required a fit workforce, and on the other he was anxious to fill in gaps in the work process by banishing unproductive activity by workers, such as training, discussion, recreation and pleasure, to the hours after work. For the labourer, too, restoring energy was vital, for earnings depended upon it, and with them access to the necessities of life. As a consequence, there was less and less time after work for producing food and clothes, for raising the children, or for taking an interest in art or science in response to the developing aspirations of the class. And so workers made more and more use of goods and services supplied by the consumer and leisure industries, which thereby exerted a growing influence on their free time.

Leisure meant temporary liberty from the fetters of highly intensive division of labour and work which was usually physically strenuous, as well as from the immediate dictates of capital. In all previous ages, workers had played little, if any part in political developments, or in the science, art and luxuries of higher circles. Proletarian leisure brought the chance to enter these realms, even if it was only as a consumer of limited means. There were various strategies which workers could adopt in making use of their free time. They could relax in order to return refreshed, well-motivated and well-equipped to an above-average performance in the work process. They could try to compensate for the stresses and constraints of production by enjoying their pleasures as deeply as possible. They could indulge in the delights of bourgeois culture and create an illusion of escaping from their proletarian destiny, either for a few hours or, potentially, for good. Or they could take advantage of their detachment from the

---

111 Passages drawn from the economic historians Heinrich von Storch and Simon de Sismondi and quoted by Karl Marx in: *Capital*. Vol. 1. Moscow, 1971, p. 606.
112 Marx, Karl: "Ökonomisch-philosophische Manuskripte," in: Marx, Karl, and Friedrich Engels: *Werke*. Ed. by Institut für Marxismus-Leninismus beim ZK der SED. Berlin, 1956–68, supplementary volume, 1st part, p. 514.

capitalist exploitation process to improve it in the workers' interests or even overcome it through organized class struggle.

The problem confronted by an independent proletarian strategy for leisure, either for individuals structuring their life priorities or for labour organizations planning their cultural activities, was how to combine those elements: industrial fitness, pleasure, access to the latest fruits of bourgeois-dominated culture, and working-class struggle for self-determination.

Frameworks for Leisure

Labour organizations campaigning for legislation on working hours usually cited economic and medical arguments: job security and protection against the immediate exhaustion of labour power. Their demands coincided with ideas elaborated by bourgeois reformers and economists who wanted wage labour to be maintained as cheaply as possible in the interests of capital as a whole.

Although the individual capitalist could reap extra profit by ruthlessly exploiting labour power which he had purchased at a price far below its value, he was basically assuming an overabundance of wage labourers, and, in fact, violating the interests of the bourgeois class in general, who had to make sure that the necessary supply of wage labourers fit for work never waned. The bourgeois state, as the instrument of dominant sectors of capital, offered a vehicle for compromise between working-class demands and capitalist interests. State legislation to limit the working day fixed a daily minimum time for restoring labour power which expressed a convenient average. At the same time the bourgeoisie launched educational campaigns to persuade the workers that their non-working hours really should only be used to restore their energies quickly. In this way, the value of labour power as a commodity was to be kept as low as possible.

Labour-movement struggles to shorten the working day resulted in much more than an economic compromise with the bourgeoisie. Free hours which workers could spend as they chose meant that, apart from preserving their individual capacity for work, they could also devote some time to organizing against the bourgeoisie.

The struggle for leisure time, then, was always politically motivated, too. Moreover, it was associated from the start with a belief that the dignity, social respect and self-confidence of workers depended on their scope for human activity beyond work. For workers to take a receptive interest in the rich world of cultural needs and enjoyment, they required significantly more free time than was necessary for simple reproduction of their labour power: time for living. Leisure time was thus essential for proletarian class culture to develop.

Skilled workers were the first to dispose of this kind of personal scope from around the beginning of the 20th century. From their leisure behaviour it soon became clear that workers were quite capable of appropriating the culture which urban, industrial capitalist culture had to offer and of fashioning a proletarian lifestyle and a culture of their own.

Wealth, leisure, disposable time When workers demanded free time they were carving inroads into a tradition many millennia old whereby the human race had been divided into labouring and leisured classes. Way back in early pre-class societies effort and pleasure had been everyone's lot. Occasional abundance, usually a blessing of nature, distinguished the fat years from the lean.

Things did not change until work became more productive, resulting in a constant surplus. The functions of social government and other elevated activities—science, art, play—were severed from the production of means of existence and became the prerogative of certain social groups. The privileged now decided the fate of the producers, and tended to condemn them to spend all their lives working, permitting them just enough time and produce to remain live and well. Anything in excess of that, the "surplus product", was taken from them and consumed outside their sphere of life and work. Thus the results of their own efforts confronted them as the hostile power of their overlords. The fruits of their labour helped to develop a culture of which they themselves had no part.

Society's "free time", created by the production surplus, was shared by a very small group of people who were able to forge the ideal of activity for its own sake. This found supreme expression in those human beings who were able to live entirely according to their inner principles, and whose existence consisted of nothing but free action, leisure and pleasure. The first proletarians lived long enough ago to encounter those late feudal aristocrats whose social function was to devour wealth with pompous splendour. Their behaviour provoked egalitarian protests that were nourished by the work ethos inherent in Lutheran, Calvinist and Pietist brands of Christianity. Usurers, and later gentlemen of "private" means and coupon cutters, were condemned in similar tones. Utopian Socialists propagated a belief that working people should lay claim to their share of the wealth: whoever toiled should enjoy the rewards. By this logic, the industrial bourgeois, who also worked, was widely regarded with approval, for he made productive use of the riches he had acquired.

In the latter half of the 19th century, labour-movement leaders argued clearly that the higher productivity brought about by industrial labour now enabled society, not merely to continue the "superior activities", but also to concede a period of privately disposable time to all producers. Paul Lafargue made a pithy defence of the proletarian "right to idleness", or, rather, to indi-

204 This etching by Matthias Scheits dates from 1676 and shows peasants after their day's labour is done. The utensils indicate the variety of household tasks to be performed. Communication in the hours of repose takes place within a close circle of neighbours. There is no separate space for leisure away from work and home.

vidual free time which comprised more than a restoration of labour power as a commodity. On the basis of industrial productivity, the labour movement's socialist objective, that every fit person should work to earn pleasure, no longer posed a threat to civilization. The demand heralded a new level of culture no longer characterized by élites who lived on a separate plane. It would permit all workers a degree of leisure and superior activity and a share in social decisions.

The dichotomy of a worker's life   In pre-industrial days work and rest, daily toil, evening repose and festive occasions were intricately woven together. They all took place within the same social location and followed a set pattern. Conduct was governed by the guild, by custom, convention and law, and there was a proper time for everything in a regularly repeated process with a universally accepted meaning. The wage-labour relationship destroyed this unity between work and the remainder of social existence. It divided proletarian life from the start into two diametrically opposed spheres.

On the one hand there was work, which was experienced as stressful, exhausting and alien due to competition on the labour market, coercive factory discipline and pressure which was undisguisedly designed to exploit the energy of the bought labourer. Moreover, division of labour in the factory as a result of mechanical labour replaced product-orientated craft labour and workshop communication. This, too, made work a superficial business, no longer a suitable vehicle wherein to discover the meaning of one's life. This meaning had to be found outside work.

On the other hand there was privately disposable time outside the factory. It would have been premature to talk at this point of free choice about how that time should be spent. Rest had to be the most important element, so that spent energies could be restored to some extent. Initially the remainder of active free time was eaten up entirely by acquiring the basic necessities of life: shelter, food and clothing. This task was also governed by previously unknown constraints, especially the fluctuating state of the market.

But if, at first, there was no freedom of choice worth mentioning, there was at least personal responsibility for making sensible use of a relatively regular monetary income and allocating work-free hours efficiently. Against this background, non-working time evolved as an autonomous sphere of life. Of course, it depended on the work situation in many respects, particularly as it was limited by the length of the working day, and yet the coercions of labour did not apply here. Free time meant that new social links could be forged and, ultimately, leisure and superior activities pursued, albeit within narrow confines and subject to the fact that proletarians themselves often regarded their decisive social contribution, that is, their productive labour, as an unpleasant and superficial precondition for a meaningful life during their non-working hours.

Which workers had free time?   In every country, the distribution of working-class free time was uneven. Rural workers were still not able to dispose independently of any work-free time. Campaigns for a shorter working day and more free time had met with varying success in the different sectors of industry. The time ratio fluctuated even within categories of labour and working-class families.

Married working-class women with paid employment, for example, had no free time at all. Their work-free hours were devoted completely to household chores. Even on Sundays, only women with well-paid husbands could spare a little time to relax during a walk, an excursion or a trip to the cinema. As the family budget hinged primarily on the man's fitness, his rest periods were only curtailed in emergencies. Besides, as the proletariat had followed tradition by ascribing all housework to women, men felt no compulsion to relieve them to any significant degree so that they could also benefit from free time.

Married men, too, enjoyed but a brief portion of free time. After nine to eleven hours a day in the factory, they needed the evening to recover. Only Sundays left them with any real scope. A poll conducted among German workers just after the turn of the century to ascertain their leisure priorities listed "lying in" above everything else.

Young single workers enjoyed the best quota of free time. They often had to help their parents, and the young women had their own household duties to perform, but at 16 most of them were economically independent. Until they started a family they had money and, compared with their married fellows, a relatively large portion of free time. Young people in particular therefore set the tone in working-class leisure behaviour, defining major aspects of form and content.

They had seen from the life their parents led that they would only enjoy the pleasures and delights of individually determined free time until marriage. Whoever wanted anything out of life had to make the best of their youth. Bourgeois observers of working-class youth criticized their craving for pleasure, the girls' love of baubles and sweets, their devotion to dancing, sport and many other distractions, and above all their obstinate predilection for joining social movements.

Germany's first Leisure Congress   In allowing workers to determine their free time for themselves, capital was incurring the risk that they might take advantage to challenge its interests. Free time had to be prolonged because labour was so much more intense, but there were growing signs that the workers' conduct did not conform to the system. The German bourgeoisie, therefore, responded with typical thoroughness by convening a congress which was to draw up a comprehensive programme for regulating workers' free time.

The first Leisure Congress in Germany was held on 25 and 26 April 1892 in the hall of the Berlin Architects' Club. Almost 250

205 At the turn of the century Berlin was the world's biggest tenement. On fine Sundays, working-class and petty-bourgeois families headed for the open air. Carl Koch illustrated this Sunday fellowship in Tempelhof Fields outside Berlin around 1890.

206 Whereas their rural ancestors lived and worked amid nature, urban workers rediscovered it as a scene of leisure. Swimming was both fun and recreation. Young city dwellers were the first to go bathing in the open. Photo of 1905.

207 An entertainment industry was born in response to the leisure needs of all urban strata. One feature were the pleasure gardens with their ever costlier technical attractions. This "Swedish slide" had two cars and tracks.

delegates attended, representing 16 bourgeois charities, ten urban authorities, 38 boards of major companies and several ministries. All of them were affiliated to the Centre for Institutions of Worker Welfare, which had already addressed the matter of "workers' recreation" at its founding conference in 1891. They now turned their attention, on behalf of the workers, to "appropriate applications of Sunday and holiday hours". The discussion focused on cultural policy recommendations to restrict the influence of Social Democracy, strengthen patriotism and promote a lifestyle which would enhance the reproduction of labour power. There was plenty of empirical research on the Worker Question and also various studies of the Social Question for the Congress to consider.

There were two main papers. Professor Franz Hitze, a Catholic theologian, parliamentary member for the Centre Party, and Secretary General of *Arbeiterwohl*, a Catholic industrial society, lectured on "Workers' Recreation in the Family". He argued in favour of a friendly home with a diligent housewife who could cook cheap, tasty meals, make everyone feel comfortable and raise well-bred offspring. He recommended specific leisure activities to encourage recreation and entertainment: edifying literature, family music-making, handwork and needle-work, a small garden or at least some indoor plants, family outings and games, joint visits to church and educational events, and to friends and relations.

The other main paper, on "Workers' Recreation outside the Home", also advised stronger family bonds and harmless, ennobling pleasures. But this speaker, Professor Karl Viktor Böhmert, an economist and committed liberal reformer who edited the magazine *Der Arbeiterfreund*, had a long-term vision of a national community transcending all classes, where social antitheses would balance out. He appealed to the wealthy and educated to counter proletarian immorality, especially dissipation and alcoholism, by setting an example from above. In 1888 he had co-founded the association *Volkswohl* (People's Welfare) in Dresden which had already been making an impact with its ideas of sociability "with the people". Charitable factory-owners and councils were to work in conjunction with welfare organizations to set up people's libraries, people's parks, people's homes, people's cafés, people's theatres, people's evening entertainment, people's games, people's recreation, people's palaces etc.

This *Volkswohl* movement was a lasting factor in bourgeois understanding of the issue, but for all the resources invested it never exerted any significant influence on workers' free time.

The good life All the efforts undertaken by bourgeois welfare organizations to determine how workers should spend their free time were aimed at ensuring that they refreshed their labour power without any detrimental side effects. In other words, they should not drink too much alcohol or indulge in other such excesses, but choose more harmless and ennobling pleasures. They

208 A bioscope show at Melford, Suffolk, 1908. For workers, cinematography was second only to the pub at the turn of the century. Film began as a fairground sensation and developed into mass entertainment and information. In 1914 Emilie Altenloh, a sociologist of the cinema, ascribed this rapid boom to working-class needs: "Rest from work must not make new demands on the individual. As long as involvement with art is not quite play, as long as there is a didactic interest, for example, the simple appetite for spectacle will seek nourishment elsewhere."

should save their money for times of trouble, live as part of the family and breed a future generation of decent workers. And that was all they should do.

This approach was born of a compromise which embraced quite opposite and self-contradictory bourgeois attitudes to the proletariat. On the one hand, leading sections of capital had already realized that "the best workers in the world . . . are those with the most needs"[113]. On the other, however, growing needs and cultural aspirations made reproducing labour power a costlier business. This, in turn, diminished the profits of the great majority of companies which did not have the technology and streamlined methods to do more than merely keep abreast of the higher price of labour. As time went on, capital was doing more to foster the consumer needs of a spawning proletariat in order to reap the economic fruits. But at the same time, working conditions, pay and hours were particularly bad in those sectors which produced consumer goods for workers, and called for a workforce of proletarians without such needs.

Given this conflict of interests, it is hardly surprising that the bourgeoisie were always critical when proletarians sought pleasure, possessions and the good life. Idleness was damned as the mother of sin by a combination of moralizing prejudice and correct observation.

The situation of many proletarians in the latter half of the 19th century was, without a doubt, so negative and uncertain that they thought only of the moment and preferred pleasures which were available without much effort: lethargic repose, intoxication, sexual intercourse. Even better-paid workers lived to a rhythm of weekly payments. Their leisure behaviour was strongly characterized by momentary pleasures which the weekly budget of time and money allowed, and was not governed in the average case by any more far-reaching intentions.

Other factors reinforced this short-term orientation. It was essential to use work-free hours for relaxation and recreation because labour had become so compressed. Contemporary sociologists described the new modes of conduct generated by intensification as increasing apathy on one hand and a passion for entertainment and pleasure on the other. One study published in 1914 interprets these observations as follows: ". . . with this more intensive tension and exploitation of energy . . . the reverse side of the daily coin, repose, had to provide a greater counterweight in lack of purpose, in activity not directed at any aim."[114]

Both bourgeois and proletarian critics of this lifestyle made the same error in explaining why fleeting pleasures were preferred. They assumed that "an ignorant person crushed by the grindstone of daily labour will feel a particular need for variety to whip up all the senses . . ."[115] That was not entirely the case. Pro-

---

113 Schulze-Gävernitz, Gerhart von: *Der Grossbetrieb*. Leipzig, 1892, p. 65.

114 Altenloh, Emilie: *Zur Soziologie des Kino*. Jena, 1914, p. 95.

115 Drucker, Salo: "Das Kinoproblem und unsere politischen Gegner," in: *Die Neue Zeit*. Stuttgart, 32/1914, instalment 23, p. 867.

209 In 1912 over 100,000 fans watched England play Scotland. Football spread from Britain to the other industrial nations of Europe. Soon football matches were one of the workers' favourite spectator pleasures. The passion for betting prevalent among British proletarians did not reach the Continent until later.

210 A Berlin beer palace. Opened by brewers, these buildings became important leisure establishments. Workers, too, held parties and meetings here. They were encouraged to do so by political legislation banning open-air meetings of workers in urban areas.

211 The foreman's Sunday afternoon. Well-paid workers could now afford a small flat with a balcony at the front end of the tenement. Older workers relaxed at their regular pub, in their garden or on a balcony chair among the flower pots.

letarians whose work was physically strenuous and mentally vacuous liked to spend their free time sleeping, resting and performing various tasks with their hands.

The new leisure needs, on the other hand, evolved among urban industrial workers who had to cope with the strains of modern technology and labour organization. Their leisure behaviour was marked by permanent curiosity, an insatiable appetite for new ideas, a love of sensation and a consumptive interest in everything under the sun. Young workers in particular usually experimented with every conceivable delight. They were willing to follow the fashions of the market and public life, and constantly tried to incorporate the customs of the more comfortable strata into their leisure behaviour patterns.

Marketing leisure The pub, the cinema, trivial literature and other industrialized products and services catered for the need to purchase as many practicable and pleasant things as possible at a cheap price during leisure hours. The entertainments and pleasure industries were born alongside the proletariat. They evolved simultaneously with other institutions for the reproduction of urban working masses: inner-city transport, markets, department stores, chain restaurants, beer halls, hospitals and asylums. The range of mass-produced, permanently available consumer goods and services slowly expanded, and leisure wares and establishments were a component part. Industry churned out recreation, relaxation, distraction, education, intellectual stimulation and other forms of edification to cater for mass demand.

Capitalist business acumen was the driving force, spurring on small companies and large-scale industry alike. The quest for profit inspired leisure facilities of every kind, from swimming baths to pubs and theatres, from silent movies with piano accompaniment to swift sex, from a bout of boxing to a river cruise or a barrel-organ recital in the yard. It was the quest for profit, too, which launched all those new products on the market which were aimed at leisure consumption and sold within the leisure sphere: beer, spirits, soft drinks, books, penny dreadfuls, newspapers, four-colour prints, ramblers' canes, song books, garden tools, swimming trunks, postcards, bicycles, footballs, primus stoves, picnic foods, cigarettes, rowing boats, peaked caps, specialized literature etc.

The market was slow to respond to the reproductive needs of workers and the lucrative demand they implied—with the one exception of the distillers, who saw proletarians as a welcome valve for surplus production of spirits. The market had not created these demands, but it did exploit them with imagination and thereby set the pattern for their satisfaction (and hence, to some extent, their future development). The rapid acceptance and spreading popularity of beer, pubs, cinemas and trivial literature can only be explained by the broad gap between the leisure needs which already existed and the inadequate opportunities for satisfying them.

Proletarian leisure culture The division of working-class life into labour time determined by others and free time determined by the individual made the evolution of leisure behaviour a decisive process in the formation of proletarian culture. A relatively independent proletarian leisure culture had emerged by the early 20th century with the following characteristics:

Large sections of workers had acquired a conscious relationship to the manner in which they spent their lives, and increasingly regarded work-free hours as the realm of their individuality, which they were able to fashion according to their own strategies. This was indicated by their growing complaints about lack of time.

One aspect of proletarian lifestyle were the relatively stable leisure customs of varying national flavour. Whereas British workers tended to choose sport, betting, outings and a spectator cul-ture, German proletarians liked the conviviality of associations and educational pursuits.

Workers now had firm venues and institutions as a framework for leisure. In the early 20th century the capitalist market adapted to workers' leisure habits, as did local authorities, the state, the Church, factory-owners and industrial associations. A highly differentiated network of leisure facilities had emerged and continued to take shape over the years to come.

Having won more free time for workers, the labour movement experienced a burst in active membership. It also adopted a conscious approach to proletarian leisure habits, drawing up a cultural programme of its own to cover every aspect. The working-class movement had already laid organizational and institutional foundations for the major leisure activities.

The Working Man's Pub

In the 17th and 18th centuries, the inn was usually the only place for urban manual labourers to meet. While the bourgeois of London, Paris and Vienna sat in the café to do business, talk politics and discuss art and literature, the lower classes continued to gather in the traditional taverns and hostelries. These, too, often performed an economic function, notably as job agencies, and the unemployed could come here to eat and drink on credit.

In the 19th century, the pub was the most important place for urban proletarians in search of company, relaxation and a change of atmosphere. Poor housing conditions in all the capitalist cities were enough to make the *Kneipe*, pub, saloon or *bistro* an indispensable element in working-class districts. They mushroomed in every industrial country. By the turn of the century there were 35 Belgians to every pub. Berlin topped the rat-

212 George Cruikshank drew his London gin distillery with friendly detachment, capturing the open, casual communication between customers who now drank on their feet and soon grew tipsy from the strong liquor. The artist notes with a critical eye that not even women were averse to a tipple and quietened their offspring with gin. One drinker rejects the scolding of his wife, who is on her knees.

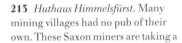

213 *Huthaus Himmelsfürst*. Many mining villages had no pub of their own. These Saxon miners are taking a beer and a schnapps at the pithead before setting off home. Photo by Karl A. Reymann, 1914.

214 Waiter, *c.* 1865. These tertiary-sector workers earned meagre wages in the proletarian and petty-bourgeois taverns.

215 After work in the market halls of Paris, *c.* 1900. French workers stuck to their traditional drink, wine. Hard liquor did make an impact on urban *bistros* and bar-like establishments, but much of the Latin wine culture was preserved, including the round tables.

ings in Germany with one for every 129 inhabitants, followed by Hamburg with one for every 159.

One reason why the pubs attracted so much custom was that they played so many roles. To begin with, they provided daily meals for the young, unmarried workers who had arrived in town and found nothing more than a bed to sleep in. Meagre as their free time was in these early days, they had nowhere to go but the street or the tavern. Here they were protected from the cold, the heat and the rain. Spirits, beer and wine were the first little extras that workers managed to afford beyond elementary necessities. Unlike the "sober" bourgeois drinks of coffee and tea, they encouraged an egalitarian merriment where the distance between strangers sharing the same fate was quickly overcome. Pub contacts and debates created links which burst the confines of factory, family and neighbourhood. For workers, pubs were public houses in the additional sense that they could gather there to pool their knowledge of working conditions, wages, any jobs available, and proletarian life in general. They were, therefore, embryonic sites of proletarian organization. That is why bourgeois educational associations for workers, many of which eventually went their own ways, took up residence here. Workers came to the pub to discuss their trade-union battles, and strike committees installed themselves on the premises. It was the only place where the electoral associations of working-class parties could meet. The party-pub network enabled these organizations to function smoothly. Most forms of proletarian leisure were also linked to the restaurant room: games, sporting contests, competitions, singing, founding celebrations and trade-union dances were held in the same way as weddings, funeral breakfasts and other working-class family events.

Young people hated to miss a dance, and that was where many found their partners. Pubs came to be such an important element in the life of workers that some even set up their own co-operative "schnapps casinos", as in the German Ruhr in the nineties.

By the end of the 19th century, workers in the big cities were using a wide range of specialized catering. Apart from the regular pub, there was the beer hall, the garden pub, the fast-food cafeteria, the dinner-and-dance restaurant and, most important of all, the out-of-town restaurant for outings. Working-class associations would often set up their own facilities at sports grounds or in the allotments where many proletarians spent their weekends gardening.

The drunkard's deterrent Industrialization transformed lifestyles, and working-class pubs changed, too. The way the first generations of proletarians drank had fashioned their attitude to the venue. "Free liquor" had already been consumed throughout the extremely long working day, and initially the prime aim of drinking during brief leisure hours was, similarly, to numb the senses. The tavern was not so much a cheerful refuge from the miseries of production as a stopover point. Whisky, gin and

216 Weavers robbed by machines of their livelihood discuss how to strike back in their austere village tavern. "Consultation." Lithograph from Käthe Kollwitz's cycle "A Weavers' Uprising," 1898.

217 Poster for a Parisian *bistro* by Théophile Alexandre Steinlen. It was gradually becoming acceptable in big towns for young working-class women to visit the pub, although only with a male escort or in groups.

schnapps were the "quickest way" to forget the filthy industrial settlements. The urban gin palaces of Britain, which replaced the old beer houses, were a typical sign of the times. In one week the fourteen biggest palaces in London with their new-fangled counters could serve 270,000 customers.

But while the brewers, vintners and distillers, in collaboration with the restaurant trade, were keen to encourage drinking among the workers for the sake of their profits, it was usually the pub which acted as a deterrent. Drinking took place in a group under the general surveillance of the workers. New moral standards developed in working-class pubs, influenced by the political movement and by proletarian club life. Workers learnt how to take their alcohol and exerted their own control. Although far more free time was being spent in company at the pub in the late 19th century, alcoholism did not rise, but declined in most industrial countries. In those regions where schnapps had been the norm, beer gradually replaced the rapidly intoxicating, high-proof liquids. A new tone in bourgeois criticism of working-class behaviour also suggested that the pub had become a conforming influence in proletarian lifestyle. Workers were rarely accused of consuming too much alcohol, but the time they spent in the pub was regarded with a certain disapproval. The bourgeois reformer Wilhelm Bode, for example, wrote in 1892: "The pub steals not merely from domestic life, but equally from all realms of education, noble, uplifting entertainment, and service to humanity and God."[116]

Pub and family life Urban workers' pubs continued the guild traditions. When journeymen assembled for an evening's drinking, like students, they banned women, and the convivial life of the proletarian pub was also, in most cases, confined to men. Women were excluded generally from public life in the capitalist societies of the period, and besides, proletarian wives had neither the time nor the money to visit the tavern.

Although working-class women still regarded the night at the pub as a man's natural prerogative, they were nonetheless critical. After all, only their husbands could enjoy this opportunity to drown the sorrows of everyday family life. Two comments recorded by Levenstein at the beginning of the 20th century testify to the men's motives: "To be honest I find more pleasure at the pub than at home. If you're at home, the wife just makes a fuss and the husband loses even more heart. You drink the booze at the pub and all the dark hours vanish."[117]—"With a job that grinds you down and a wretched flat surrounded by a horde of children, who can talk about pleasure? Capitalism destroys family life, and that's why I go to the pub."[118]

116 Bode, Wilhelm: *Die deutsche Alkoholfrage*. Leipzig, 1892, p. 43.
117 Levenstein, Adolf: *Die Arbeiterfrage*. Munich, 1912, p. 248.
118 *Ibid.*, p. 264.

218 A Sunday dance for the ordinary residents of Munich. Drawing by A. Langhammer, *c.* 1890. Factory workers, clerks, craftsmen and soldiers danced with serving maids, cleaners, sales girls and factory women. The young women would often spend all their earnings on doing themselves up. After all, the Sunday dance was the only pleasure most of them had—as well as a chance to find a permanent sweetheart.

219 Pubs in working-class districts of the big cities were not just an evening haunt. Single and shift workers came for breakfast. Photo by J. Hamann.

220 Out-of-town and garden restaurants were especially popular with German workers. This one was in Leipzig, *c.* 1913. The family would come here together on a Sunday. German and Bohemian emigrés opened similar beer gardens for the family (as well as saloons based on the traditional beer-drinker's pub) in the towns of North America.

But pub life, too, often posed a direct threat to the vital interests of a working-class family, for there was often a risk that too much of the insufficient family budget would find its way down the wage-earner's gullet, perhaps before payday was over. Even conscious, politically active workers and those not given to excessive drinking spent too much money in the pub. What they saved on beer and wine they gave for newspapers, books and party dues. Besides, political activity put a man's job in jeopardy. Working-class wives devised many stratagems to keep their husbands away from the pub.

"The sole bastion of proletarian political liberty" Cafés, salons and clubs provided the bourgeois class with centres of intellectual life before they were able to turn the institutions of public politics into tools serving their class interests. The pub served a similar function for the proletariat. This was especially true of countries where democracy was poorly developed or where the ruling classes attempted to eliminate every working-class organization through particularly severe coercion.

In Imperial Germany there was an especially striking contradiction between the strength of the labour movement and its scope for political activity. As in other countries, trade unions and political class organizations had been born in the pub, but they were also completely confined to that sphere during the repressive years of the law against socialists. Karl Kautsky commented in 1891: "Under the Law on Socialism, when all workers' associations had been dissolved and yet Social Democracy continued to survive as a united political body, police and public prosecutors sought with busy desperation for the secret organization which was binding all socialist workers together. In their unsuccessful quest they overlooked the fact that every pub frequented by party members was a 'secret league' which propagated unanimous thinking and action, sustaining the links between individual comrades . . ."[119]

The connexion between the pub and politics brought its own problems and prompted opponents of alcohol in the labour movements of several countries to protest. Karl Kautsky replied by pointing out that: "the sole bastion of proletarian political liberty which cannot be taken from him so easily is—the pub. Teetotallers may wrinkle their noses, but that does not alter the fact that under present conditions in Germany the pub is the only place where the lower classes of the people can gather freely and discuss their common concerns. Without a pub, the German proletarian would be deprived not only of a social life, but also of a political life."[120]

Bourgeois propaganda aimed at combating the Social Democrats proved just how right he was. Alfred Krupp, for example, who did not consider his workers capable of understanding politics and formulating their own judgments, warned them against "troublemakers" and gave them this advice: "Pub politics is also very expensive. The money can be better spent in the home.

When you have finished your work, stay among your families, with your parents, wives and children. Find your recreation there, think about the household and the children's upbringing. First and foremost let this and your work be your politics. You will find the hours pass pleasurably . . ."[121]

The Anti-Saloon League The American middle classes gave birth in the 19th century to a temperance movement of many shades which saw alcohol as the root of all social evil. The danger was considered to emanate from the drug itself, not from the consumers, their social situation or social relations as a whole. A complete ban on this addictive poison was supposed to prevent bankruptcy, poverty, proletarianization, slums and criminality.

Once the healthy middle-class society they envisaged proved to be a mirage, as the corporations amassed concentrated economic power and the proletariat continued to grow, these energies were channelled into an influential political organization. Its aim was to close down the urban saloons. The Protestant Churches ran big campaigns to support the Anti-Saloon League in its zealous efforts for a clean, orderly land free of addiction. The saloons were attacked as hotbeds of immorality, meeting points for workers and immigrants, organizational bases for the trade unions and spawning grounds of socialist propaganda. They were declared indecent and un-American.

When John D. Rockefeller and other leading figures of the monopoly bourgeoisie understood that there were great economic and political advantages to be gained from prohibition, the Anti-Saloon League won their assistance and made spectacular headway in restricting proletarian culture and class organization.

119 Kautsky, Karl: "Der Alkoholismus und seine Bekämpfung," in: *Die Neue Zeit.* IX, Vol. 2, 1890/91, p. 108.
120 *Ibid.*, p. 107.
121 Quoted from: Baedeker, Dietrich: *Alfred Krupp und die Entwicklung der Gussstahlfabrik in Essen.* Essen, 1912, p. 165.

The Workman's Club

Apart from pubs, proletarians had access to working men's and trade-union clubs. As the working class grew more organized and powerful, they created their own network of cultural establishments, among them the "people's houses".

They were owned by trade unions, societies, branches of Social Democratic parties, co-operatives or workers' sports associations. It was the first time that workers were building centres for themselves and keeping them in their own possession. They raised the funds by collecting additional contributions at great personal sacrifice, or else purchased shares in a co-operative and contributed their labour during their free time. Several conditions had to be met before a club like this could be founded. It called for a site or else a suitable building or rooms. The starting capital had to be available, and workers were required to manage the venture with the skills of a proper businessman. It all called for knowledge, talent and above all the right pieces of paper.

A working men's club needed halls, rooms for various events, libraries, reading rooms, information offices, secretarial bureaux, a restaurant, administrative space, a skittle alley, a billiard table and accommodation. There were some clubs which were confined to a small hall, conference rooms, a few administrative offices and a guest room, but some trade-union clubs were enormous. These included the *Volkshäuser* in Berlin, Leipzig, Halle, Hamburg, Bremen, Breslau, Dresden, Erfurt and Jena, the *Maison du Peuple* in Brussels, the *Abeidernes Foreninings og Forsamlings' Bygning* opened by the Danish Social Democrats in Copenhagen, the Helvetia in the Swiss town of Biel and the People's House in Prague in a converted feudal palais.

The spiritual fathers of these "people's houses" wanted them to be "the most beautiful buildings in the town . . . as magnificent as their lofty purpose", "scenes of the most noble of life's pleasures". The idea that the working man's club should be "the Church's successor in cultural history and the proletarian advance on the pub", where the proletariat would experience "spiritual and moral uplift", found a broad echo for many years. In reality, however, they could never be "cultural temples" of this kind.[122] But from the outset they were places where the working class conducted social and political struggle, an important organizational focus for education in the class spirit and cultivation of the workers' sense of group identity, and an expression of the cultural and intellectual emancipation of the working class. Once it had been the Church, the princes and the bourgeoisie who displayed their social power through buildings. Now the proletariat began to reflect their social aspirations in grand architecture. Well-known architects such as Horta in Belgium and Taut in Germany produced the designs.

Club history In 1848 a Leipzig workers' association had opened a communal centre *Am Peterschiessgraben* where workers could eat, drink and meet outside working hours and also take lessons in their trade. The association was banned in 1854 and the building had to close down. The organized working class needed more and more locations to gather for political and cultural activity. The proletariat in the big industrial communities were particularly anxious to find such venues. Increasingly they wanted their own premises for branch meetings, protest rallies, sociable get-togethers and labour-organization offices, where they would not be dependent on a pub landlord. If the party or trade union wanted to move away from the pubs and beer halls, to escape detailed police supervision and to counter the ever-present bourgeois leisure market, acquiring premises for their members was the only solution.

In late 1875 the united trade unions of Cappel in Chemnitz took the first step towards a club of their own by setting up a workers' hostel in the *Hotel Weisser Adler*, where workers were also offered help with finding jobs. The first trade-union club was leased in Stuttgart in 1895, and the *Parti Ouvrier Belge* opened its *Maison du Peuple* in Brussels in 1899.

In the following years many people's houses and trade-union clubs were to be built. By 1914 there were 76 of them in Germany. The *Volkshuis*, *Folkets Hus*, *Volkshaus* or (Hungarian) *Nepház* was a versatile mixture of tradition and innovation, of gentlemen's club and proletarian association, of guild life, journeymen's hostel, pub and co-operative.

221 People's houses were working-class fortresses where the labour flag was flown. The old wing of Hamburg People's House, 1914.

---

122 Peus, Heinrich: *Das Volkshaus wie es sein sollte*. Berlin, no date, pp. 13–16.

222 Poster publicizing the opening of the *Maison du Peuple* in Brussels in 1899. In many countries, these people's houses demonstrated the strength of the labour movement and its thirst for culture.

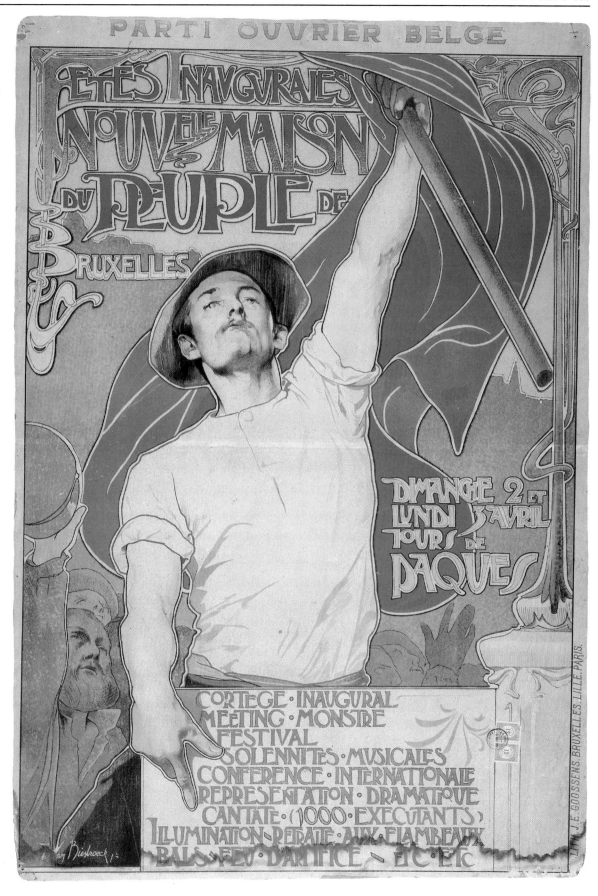

223 The dining room and hall of the People's House in Bernburg, an industrial town in Central Germany. The labour movement offered alternatives to the usual leisure facilities on premises of its own.

Everything under one roof These centres were intended as a base for the entire labour movement in a town. There was great selected variety under one roof: political work, ideological and vocational education, social life, entertainment, dancing, art (active and passive), sport, recreation and a catering service.

A proportion of the workers' political life took place in the centre. Labour-movement leaders spoke at meetings and rallies. It was part of workers' political experience to hear "prominent" comrades and trade unionists at their local club. When the *Volkshaus* in Hamburg was opened in 1906, thousands packed the big hall to listen to August Bebel, who called the trade-union centre a forge of the Hamburg proletariat.

The centres hosted events which made an impact on political life. The building in Copenhagen was the scene of the Congress of German Social Democrats from 29 March to 2 April 1883 and the Second International Socialist Women's Congress in 1910. In 1912 the house in Prague staged the 6th All-Russian Conference of the Social Democratic Workers' Party of Russia (Bolshevik). In the People's Park in Halle on 4 December 1914, officials of the Social Democratic Party from the district of Halle (Saale) voted to support Karl Liebknecht for his one-man parliamentary stand in rejecting war bonds. Solidarity and support campaigns of all kinds were launched from the centres or based there.

Another important field of activity which also took place in the clubs was education, which ranged from once-off lectures to series, longer-term courses and weekend schools. The Workers'

Educational Institute founded in 1907 and, temporarily, the Young Workers' Educational Institute found a home in the Leipzig *Volkshaus*. The basement of Hamburg's trade-union centre was used to educate hundreds of young workers about politics. Education associations and committees and other proletarian organizations assisted workers with further training. Here was a meeting-place for the Workers' Samaritan League, societies devoted to sport and body culture, the Workers' Photography League, the Society of Proletarian Freethinkers, Parents' Leagues and much else besides. Labour secretariats and "workers' welfare" held surgery and counselling sessions and sent out written and material assistance.

Workers met for music-making, choral singing, and amateur dramatics. They made models, played chess, swapped stamps and attended performances of the arts ranging from orchestral concerts and recitals by singers, solo instrumentalists and groups of chamber musicians to literary matinées, discussions and dances. In the people's houses of Finland the most important form of social entertainment was the *iltama*, a working-class festival opened by a musical march and welcome address, with poetry recitals, gymnastics displays, political speeches, working-class songs, singing with audience participation, and then an hour of dancing to round things off. The pattern was typical in other countries, too.

On working-class holidays and festivals, the party, trade unions and other organizations put on May Day celebrations, foundation parties, and even ceremonies for young people who rejected a Church confirmation and parents who objected to Christian baptism. There was entertainment, too, with summer parties, garden parties, children's parties, skat contests with a goose or goat as first prize, New Year celebrations, Christmas exhibitions and balls, and banquets of hare, goose and venison. This range of activity reflected the wide variety of needs experienced by workers and their organizations. Respect for the cultural heritage was coupled with interest in contemporary art, and workers were encouraged to find their own artistic expression in poetry and songs. "Many are the aims which the labouring people hope to achieve in these rooms. This house opens its doors to the hard struggle, serious study, the fine arts, good company and much besides."[123]

123 From the Allegory enacted on Opening Day at Halle's People's Park on 13 July 1907. Quoted from: Piechocki: *Der Volkspark als Kultur- und Bildungsstätte der halleschen Arbeiter (1907–1914)*. Halle, 1968, p. 41.

224 People's House in Prague, *c.* 1912. Wherever the labour movement was powerful enough and legal, it used these centres for organizational purposes.

225 The newspaper room in the People's House at Jena, which was built in 1905.

BOXING MATCH FOR 200 GUINEAS BETWIXT DUTCH SAM AND MEDLEY FOUGHT 31 MAY 1810. ON MOULSEY HURST NEAR HAMPTON

The Concourse of people exceeded any thing we have ever witnessed. The Spectators were computed at ten thousand. At one O'Clock the Champions entered the ring, and Sam had for his second Harry Lee, whilst Joe Ward officiated for Medley. after a severe and bloody contest of 40 Rounds Victory was decided in favour of Sam.

226 Workers first indulged in sport for the money. They had their share of famous champions, even in the early 19th century, but some careers ended in dismal failure. This "severe and bloody contest" between Dutch Sam and Medley went 40 rounds in front of 10,000 spectators.

Workers' Sport

Before the working class conquered sport, it meant nothing more to labouring people than children's games, labour and martial exercise, cult and tradition, or a spectacle for sale. Rarely did they indulge in the play of superfluous energy for the sheer fun of it. The aristocrats invented modern sport when their martial talents ceased to be the social speciality of their estate. As they were no longer required for waging wars, these skills were vaunted in less lethal contests. The young men of the bourgeoisie followed their example, demonstrating the new-found strength of their class in physical exercise. It was only the modern working class who incorporated sport into their lifestyle as a welcome break from the burden of labour, regularly pursued and measured in competition, a passion capable of seizing the masses.

Intensified labour in industrial capitalism meant "the development of each man to his state of maximum efficiency, so that he may be able to do, generally speaking, the highest grade of work for which his natural abilities fit him"[124]. The labour process was stripped of everything which did not enhance this efficiency, and at the same time workers achieved more free time in which they could be their own masters and satisfy their own needs. They turned to sport to compensate for the effects of labour, which constituted "a permanent threat to the mental and physical health of each individual worker" and caused "the muscles of the human organism to atrophy".[125]

Sport resembled labour in that it demanded performance, but was essentially different in that the play of forces was not linked to the creation of a use value: the enjoyment lay in the performance itself. Sport offered workers an opportunity to control their own bodies and energies. Workers who joined a sports club were part of a community with the same goals, and standards defined by the members themselves. Competition did not mean the struggle for survival.

It was British workers who began in the 1870s to flock regularly to sports grounds as spectators. They wanted to witness the athlete, often one of their number, asserting himself in combat, drawing entirely on his own resources and skills. They rewarded him for the expérience with their enthusiasm and respect, and gave money for bets and entrance tickets. They did not tolerate arrogance. When spectators took sides or became loyal supporters, they sensed solidarity and group identity. Betting made matters more exciting, encouraging expertise and also treacherous hopes of good fortune which would wipe away financial worries.

---

124 Taylor, Frederick W.: *The Principles of Scientific Management*. New York, 1911, p. 9.

125 From the Main Paper at the 8th Congress of the Workers' Athletic League held in Stuttgart in 1907, in: *Handbuch des Arbeiter-Turnerbundes*. Leipzig, 1911, p. 50f.

227 There was no distinction between early professional sport and circus, variety, fairs and gambling. This postcard was a publicity gimmick for Mayer's appearances at the Berlin Elysium, a variety and concert hall, in 1902.

Modern professionalism grew out of the boxing, wrestling, weightlifting and running contests held on streets and squares, in rented halls and amusement palaces, where the athletes, managers and spectators staked their money. The privileged classes condemned it, hoping to preserve their exclusive hobbies from proletarian incursions. Professional sport gave some workers a chance to improve their conditions and income.

Whenever workers had the feeling that they were being treated obstructively or with condescension in their sporting activities, they took over the reigns of organization for themselves. They wanted nothing to do with the ruthless ambition or obsequiousness prevalent in bourgeois sports associations or factory clubs run by the employer. Many workers' sports associations combined several purposes at once; here was a chance to take pleasure in one's strength, keep fit for work and for the workers' cause, shun the sphere of bourgeois influence in the company of one's peers, and support the aims of the labour movement. Right from the outset there was a debate in the movement about whether sport distracted workers from the class struggle or led them to it by way of working-class organizations, and this debate continued to rage for many years to come. At any rate, it should never become an obsession. Working-class athletes acquired a corpus of songs which express their view of sport as a key to self-determination: "Und froher Mut zum frischen Wagen/Erwächst uns aus des Sportes Spiel,/Noch heisst es Knechtschaft tragen./Doch, Brüder, alle herbei,/Der Kraftsport macht uns frei."[126] "Valiant cheer to dare afresh/Grows of our sportive play./We are

yet slaves,/But brothers, come,/Sport shall make us free." Freedom lay in sport, sport must be free, and sport must serve liberation.

Fresh and free, strong and true   Workers who wanted organized sport for its own sake went in for gymnastics, track and field athletics, team games, calisthenics, and hiking. These forms of exercise were related to everyday movements and called for less equipment than other sports. That is why horse-riding, fencing, sailing and rowing remained an exclusive preserve for some time to come. From the mid-19th century onwards more workers were joining athletics associations run by the bourgeoisie, where the ideals included democracy and all-round development of body and mind. But over the last thirty years of the century the bourgeois athletics movement gradually became a pillar of chauvinism, militarism and authoritarian rule. Even so, workers retained their membership because these associations had access to better grounds and equipment and offered social benefits in the sporting world and at work.

"But as more and more industrial workers entered the association, an imperceptible rift appeared between the 'better' and 'ordinary' members." In the end, some communities had several sports associations, "one for the upstanding bourgeoisie, the sec-

126 From the song *Ein fester Bund*, in: *Der Arbeiter-Athletenbund Deutschlands, sein Wert und seine Bedeutung. Ein Wort an die kraftsporttreibende Arbeiterschaft.* Magdeburg, no date, p. 52.

228   The full contingent of working-class athletes from the club at Essen-Borbeck turned out for an Open Day, demonstrating their team spirit with group exercises and pyramids. There had been severe obstacles to admitting children and young people. In 1907 the German government still refused Social Democrats the right to teach sports as they were suspected of "insufficient moral integrity". Photo *c.* 1908.

229 The banner of Diesdorf Men's Athletics Association near Magdeburg, Germany. It was founded in 1885 as a front organization for the banned Social Democrats. Most of its members were stonemasons and mechanical engineers. Here is a particularly direct example of the links between workers' sport and the political movement.

Arbeiter = Radfahrer = Bund
= «Solidarität.» =

Kampf dem Feind!
Deutscher Rad- und Motorfahrerverband .
«CONCORDIA» Siß Bamberg.

Allheil! Concorden auf's stählerne Roß
Ohn' Zaudern und Zagen gestiegen!
Wutschäumender Radler feindlichen Troß
In trußiger Fehd' zu bekriegen.

230/231 Like their political counterparts, proletarian and bourgeois cyclists were sworn enemies. The newspaper published by Solidarity reproduced these two postcards on 15 September 1911 along with the following commentary: "On the one hand, three merry companions, their lights shining forwards and driving the black spirits away; on the other hand, a pathetic figure wearing the black-and-white colours holds the stick that struck the hated 'red' rider to the ground. The cycling association sponsored by the Centre Party thus illustrates poignantly that it cannot halt the advance of the 'reds' with intellectual weapons and that it regards a sound thrashing, so frequently recommended in the Centre press, as its sole salvation in the face of this rising tide. Their motto is: Take up the rod for God, king and country."

232 Solidarity, the Workers' Cycling Association, printed this postcard around 1900. The banner indicates that working-class cyclists saw themselves as part of an international movement.

ond for the middle classes, and the third for the workers' estate"[127]. At Whitsun 1893 delegates from 51 associations met to found the Workers' Athletic League of Germany, the first national proletarian sports organization. The Free Athletes of Saxony declared the purpose of this independent body: "Let us pay allegiance no longer to reactionaries; let us vie instead alongside the class to which we ourselves belong, fresh, cheerful and free among its ranks!"[128]

In their own associations, workers demonstrated to themselves and others what they could accomplish under their own steam. Their membership soared many times faster than that of their bourgeois rivals, in spite of retaliation for tendentious politics (in 1912 200 of the associations affiliated to the League were being represented in court by over 100 solicitors), in spite of authorities who barred their entry to public sports facilities, and in spite of their meagre finances. By 1913 membership topped 190,000. Copies of the newspaper sold by the ten thousand. The League provided insurance against accident or death, published booklets and ran courses to educate its members, supplied equipment, clothes, hats, posters and badges. It was a motto of the League that "the core of organization is a well-founded kitty"[129]. The associations involved women, ran social events and outings to the country, staged contests which were often imposing spectacles of mass skill, and displayed their arts at labour-movement festivals.

Most working-class athletes rejected the idea of prizes, competition and individual record-breaking. They did not entirely approve of specializing in single sports. They regarded professional sport as an abuse of the athlete. Their daily lives provided enough one-side specialization, pressure to perform, competition and sale of energy; sport had to be different.

Cycling to, from and after work The bicycle was to the worker what the horse, and later the motor car, was to the man (or woman) of means. From the nineties, when bikes acquired two wheels of the same size and Dunlop tyres of compressed air, the worker dismounted from Shanks' pony and took to pedals.

Britain set the tone again. In 1896 there were an estimated million cyclists in the country, and industry was churning out 200,000 bicycles a year. The United States invested "huge capital", and 450,000 bikes are reckoned to have been produced by 1895.

A person on a bike moved many times faster than a person on foot, and that meant access to a far greater environment. Cheaper housing could be rented in the suburbs, and longer distances could be travelled to work, opening up the choice of jobs. The bicycle brought a new sense of freedom to move anywhere at any time. Cycling became a hobby and a sport which promoted health and courage, with trips to the countryside, trick cycling and racing. Spectators who lined the streets or tracks were attracted by the contest, the betting, and the sheer speed which could be achieved by technical control and human power.

In 1888, when workers earned eight to ten marks a week, a penny-farthing cost 500 marks. But even the mass-produced bicycles were not exactly cheap. Proud owners were preoccupied with the choice of models, the technical details, maintenance, maps, and conduct on the highway—a dangerous place with bad-tempered dogs and no rules to guide traffic. They found help and people with the same concerns in cycling associations.

Workers set up their own cycling associations in many industrial countries, including France, Switzerland, the Netherlands, Denmark, Austria and even Russia, for much the same reasons as they set up their own athletics associations. The biggest of all was the Solidarity Workers' Cycling League in Germany, founded in 1896. By 1914 there were 150,000 members, and its newspaper had a circulation of 169,000. It sold bicycles and all the accessories down to clothing and sashes, insured members, even against accidents during cleaning operations, ran a savings society and social events and was a breeding ground for Social Democracy. In fact, it provided the "red cavalry" which carried leaflets and news and spread the word in dangerous situations.

233 Friedrich Ludwig Jahn, the "father" of the athletics movement in Germany, is depicted on this glass (c. 1910) holding the emblem of the Workers' Athletics League. The letters FFST stand for "fresh, free, strong and true". Working-class sport was a convivial affair. The club canteen was the place to make arrangements, air opinions and quench a healthy thirst.

127 Frey, Karl: *Streitschrift für Mitglieder des Arbeiterturnerbundes.* Leipzig, 1907, p.41.
128 From the "Appeal to the Free Athletes of Saxony" of November 1892. Quoted from: Schulze, E.: *Ein Weckruf an alle Arbeiter, die der freien Turnervereinigung noch nicht angehören.* Wurzen, 1893, p.6.
129 *Handbuch des Arbeiter-Turnerbundes.* Leipzig, 1911, p.370.

Cycling workers proved indispensable to the Social Democratic press, for time was of the essence in competition with the bourgeois newspapers.

Football Until the 18th century, playing ball with hands and feet had been a popular game, which towns and boroughs played against each other. When industrial capitalism provoked such a dramatic rise of the proletariat, however, only the higher strata continued to play. Modern football evolved in Britain, encouraged by several factors. It began among the schoolboys and students of superior circles. Clergymen then set off for working-class districts with a ball and a Bible to improve morals. Finally, an advanced railway network brought the players and spectators together.

When the offside rules were modified in the seventies, individual dribbling gave way to passing among team members. Physical commitment, stamina, fast reaction, division of labour and teamwork now brought the kind of success hitherto reserved for industrial production. This was the point at which workers discovered the taste and then the money for the game, joining teams and crowding round the playing fields. Now it was the working class above all who reclaimed football, while the upper strata stood disconcerted on the sidelines. A milestone came in 1883, when Blackburn Olympic, a team of Lancashire factory workers, beat the Old Etonians, the aristocrats of football, 2–1 in the FA Cup Final. The rule of privilege was broken.

Beginning in the industrial countries of Europe, where the British example made an impact, tens of thousands became football players and hundreds of thousands became weekly fans. The spectators watched as the players did battle for 90 minutes. Individual talent, team spirit and daring decided the result. Noisy shouting seemed to influence the proceedings, too. School playing fields and exercise grounds were now inadequate and stadiums were built. Floodlights were erected as early as 1873. FIFA, the international football federation, was founded in 1904, and players' trousers were permitted to stop above the knee. By 1892 players and team officials were allowed to bet along with the public. The bookmakers gave way to the pool.

Football was becoming a profitable business. Fair play took a dent as a result, and injuries were more frequent. In 1902, at the match between Scotland and England, a barrier collapsed killing 25 people and injuring 340, but after a half-hour delay the organizers called for play to resume.

The proponents of football argued that it kept workers from squandering money and drinking; opponents pointed to the overflowing pubs and clubs around the football grounds.

Professional sport gave the worker a chance to climb the social ladder, or at least to escape the monotonous factory rhythm and improve his working conditions. But even if he did manage to boost his earnings thanks to his monopoly of a special talent, and to win respect and perhaps buy a pub or a shop, in his habits,

234 Football became the workers' favourite sport. These contemporary montages illustrate two matches: Newton Heath (later Manchester United) versus Derby County in December 1892 and Woolwich Arsenal versus Newcastle United in September 1893.

mentality and roots he stayed close to his class. He was skilled in a proletarian art. He may no longer be working like a worker, but the experts on the terraces watched his performance all the more closely. If he showed commitment, they would forgive his blunders.

Clubs which workers had founded in their own housing districts preserved particularly close links with the working class, who maintained control over team affairs and made use of the local ground and headquarters. Manchester United, for example, was set up in 1878 by workers from the railway yards, and Schalke 04 by miners. Most of the youngsters at Schalke earned 1.28 marks a shift, but a pair of football boots cost at least 9 marks, a football 6 marks and a pair of shorts 1 mark. The club members and fans were a sworn community defying their rivals under bourgeois management.

Rambling   Hiking across the countryside had always been the journeyman's lot, but the mass of workers did not discover the joys of the sport until the closing years of the 19th century, when they set out to explore their surroundings by rail, by bicycle and, above all, on foot. They were broadening their horizons in search of physical and mental relaxation by leaving the coercion and traces of their industrial labour behind them. Here was a new consumer class for restaurants, transport, souvenirs, canes, maps and postcards.

Initially time and money were short, so that workers had to be content with rambles in their local surroundings. The Friends of Nature was an organization founded in 1895 as a workers' tourist association, providing a framework for mutual support and advice on what to look for and where to find it. From 1905 it spread from Vienna to Munich, Zurich, Bern, Lucerne, Berlin, Paris, and London. The founders wanted to draw workers "out of the confines of their homes, out of the factory and pub fumes into nature, bringing them health, beauty and pleasure. They must be given the opportunity to free their bodies and spirits from the dis-

mal, desolate monotony of everyday existence."[130] The aims were to open workers' minds to different landscapes and people, to preserve nature and enhance community spirit. The Friends publicized planned routes, arranged expeditions at a tolerable price, opened hostels, organized lectures, ran social events and invited like-minded members to share their hobbies. They disliked tobacco, alcohol and pubs.

Many workers developed a passion for hiking. They wanted to dispense with cash commodities and services for a while, and they sensed a glimmer of freedom after a week of hammering and concrete slabs when they stepped out side by side into a natural world of sunshine, singing old songs which echoed through the trees.[131] The spiritual fathers of the organization went so far as to ascribe a philosophical significance to the experience of nature. The workers, they said, found hope here, new ideas, and "recognize the underlying laws of development, seeing clearly how all things move eternally onwards, upwards, into the heights, driven by the indestructible logic of nature"[132]. This natural analogy fostered optimism among Social Democrats that the liberation of the working class would pursue the same inevitable course as nature.

Hikes and rambles were part of the working-class leisure programme. The social life of the labour-movement organizations would not have been the same without those expeditions into the natural environment on Sundays, during periods of unemployment, on political occasions such as 1 May, or during a party congress.

---

130 The words of Georg Schmiedl, one of the early initiators. Quoted from: Schügerl, Gerald: *80 Jahre Naturfreunde Österreich*. Vienna, 1975, p. 35.

131 Images culled from the song *Wann wir schreiten Seit an Seit* written by Hermann Claudius and Michael Engbert for the Free Youth of Hamburg-Altona in 1916.

132 Wilhelm Bölsche in the preface to: Grottewitz, Curt: *Sonntage eines grossstädtischen Arbeiters in der Natur*. Berlin, 1906, p. 4.

235 Stuttgart branch of Free Youth on an outing in the Swabian mountains in 1911. Country walks were a vital element in the life of young people in the labour movement. Sundays were spent in the open air and devoted to sport, the performing arts, festivities and general relaxation.

Reading

Writing, reading and printing were techniques which had been denied to the working masses, with few exceptions, for centuries. They passed on news by word of mouth, learnt empirically by following examples, sealed contracts with a promise or handshake, were summoned to joint action by orators, pieced history together from hearsay, relied on symbols for their philosophy and, if they wanted anything written or read, turned to the professionals.

In 1770 about 15 per cent of the Central European population over the age of six were literate. By 1900 this figure had risen to around 90 per cent, and the reason for this was the evolution of the working class. In all industrial countries proletarians had to be able to read and write. The proletariat was thus the first toiling class to make use of literature and to exert an influence on it.

Alphabets meant that information could be disseminated without loss and retrieved at any time. Printing meant that a text could be reproduced many times over and distributed far afield. The rotary press in 1846 and linotype in 1884 provided a technology fast enough and cheap enough for mass communication. The workers' free time may have been short and thriftily allocated, but literature crept in through the pores.

Workers needed literature in the broadest sense of the word to keep abreast of the far-flung and complex developments which determined their lives in the socialized world of capitalism. Empirical learning had to be supplemented, because industrial production called for the same scientific technology to be applied everywhere in precisely the same manner. Duplicated advertisements for entertainments, political events or commercial offers had to be available for masses of workers. Even if workers wanted to ensure nothing more than their customary rights, they needed written contracts. Their organizations needed to distribute information reliably, quickly and on a mass scale to guarantee the effects of united action in the long term.

Again and again workers were confronted with the written word. They read their contracts, the factory rules and their own production records, culled data from newspapers and posters, drew general knowledge and moral advice from brochures, perused political leaflets and pamphlets, relaxed with a novel, consulted specialist texts, and penned their own applications and letters. The potential effects of literature were a bone of contention among the social classes. There were those among the ruling circles who believed that literate workers might be "the blind tools of travelling performers of the meanest kind who addle the senses, religious fanatics and visionaries, rabble-rousers and seducers of the people in political affairs, especially in turbulent times . . ."[133]. Others hoped that literature would make labourers fit and willing to work, and foster social peace.

---

133 "Über die Lesevereine in Deutschland," in: *Deutsche Vierteljahresschrift.* No place, 1839, p. 401.

236 A page from Wilhelm Weitling's *Guarantees of Harmony and Freedom* (3rd edition, 1849), which illustrates the revolutionary fighting spirit of the communist labour movement in the thirties and forties and its key slogans: Liberty, Equality, Community, and Duty, Rights, Work, Pleasure. Craftsmen resisting absorption into the proletariat had created a system of literary communication. Oral discussion and propaganda were supplemented by leaflets, letters, journals and books. Wilhelm Weitling came from these ranks. Bourgeois scoffers condemned him as a "paragon of peasant ignorance and vanity" and a "deranged communist taylor", but when Karl Marx had read Weitling's book he wrote: "One must prophesy an athlete's figure for this Cinderella."

Workers respected the authority of the printed word, although there was always a danger that they might be fooled. After all, the experts who drew up contracts, for example, were not of their kind, but were paid, commissioned and monitored by other classes. It was as well to be sceptical, especially about fine words and incomprehensible paragraphs. That is why the labour movement always cultivated workers' ability to express their experience and interests for themselves, fighting against censorship and repression of opinions, producing its own literature, and helping workers with libraries, recommendations and reviews.

Nevertheless, workers continued to write, read and print less than the bourgeoisie and to place more emphasis on oral communication. It was not just a question of education standards. Workers laboured long hours and needed their rest, and that left them little time and opportunity for reading and writing. They did not need to exchange correspondence, like the owners of capital, to organize their teamwork in the factory. They disseminated their social experience orally in conversation, anecdotes, jokes and "philosophical folklore" (Marx) long before the fruits were reflected in literature.

Teaching and converting As the proletarians grew stronger in number and organizational strength, they began to pose a threat to the bourgeois order. Moreover, their poor standards of living and education were an initial handicap in the Industrial Revolution. It was in Britain that the first liberals sought to correct the damage which real conditions were inflicting on the workers by offering educational assistance. They were thereby to learn the skills which would serve industry and become decent citizens, if not in terms of wealth, at least in spirit and lifestyle.

The British Mechanics' Institutes were models of literary instruction for the workers. The first of them was founded in London in 1824, and by 1826 18,000 wage labourers had completed courses at 100 institutes of this kind. In 1827 Lord Brougham, a co-founder along with Bentham and Cobbett, set up his Society for the Diffusion of Useful Knowledge to distribute cheap literature of a useful and entertaining nature. The *Penny Magazine* was a particular success, with 200,000 subscribers and many more actual readers. Brougham argued that "the peace of the country, and the stability of the government, could not be more effectually secured than by the universal diffusion of this kind of knowledge". Education was a capital asset which raised the value of labour and led to higher wages, which would gradually bridge the gulf between the wealthy and the poor. Of course, workers should be taught "the true principles and mutual relations of population and wages"[134], in other words, of capitalist society. This initiative made a lasting impact on the technical skills of workers and their familiarity with scientific knowledge. It did not, however, turn them into members of the bourgeois estate, either in lifestyle or, usually, spirit.

237 Workers reading the latest news from America in Manchester's Camp-Field Free Library in 1862. Bourgeois reformers such as Brougham had campaigned for the free public libraries.

The strategy underlying this form of dissemination took the living conditions of proletarians as its starting point. Their literature had to be cheap and quickly readable. It had to foster intellectual faculties, but these must be bent "towards objects at once useful and sublime".

This meant that reading material had to be entertaining in order to motivate the reader. In spite of demanding labour and poverty, it must bestow "pleasure and improvement"[135]. Access would be through libraries, reading rooms, book clubs and reading societies. Talks and discussions would make it easier to absorb and interpret the content. Reading in convivial groups would constitute a palatable framework "purifying morals and ennobling the spirit and taste".

Zealous social educationalists even proclaimed the dissemination of good books to be a modern crusade for converting the heathens.[136] But literature for workers should not be concerned with politics or sensual pleasures. This might inspire political ideals which would cause them to lose their "peace of mind, honour and respect, even their liberty". Or they might be tempted into "sensual pleasures and pastimes, perhaps even base passions" which would be the ruin of themselves and their families.[137]

Whenever the ruling classes engaged in the dissemination of literature, they were trying to ward off the labour movement and the publications it produced as they had recognized the role of literature for the workers. This is illustrated by the secret edict which the Prussian Minister of the Interior issued to presidents, regional councillors and mayors on countering Social Democratic propaganda: "This will mean applying those same methods by which the Social Democrats primarily score success . . . Specifically, the diffusion of good printed material—leaflets, newspapers, people's libraries—is unavoidable given the growing demand for reading matter."[138]

Mass-produced illusions The first workers who took an interest in reading were either highly skilled and ambitious for personal betterment, or else politically committed to the class struggle. By the end of the century, however, reading was part of normal working-class life, even though many kept it to a minimum. The majority read for amusement rather than anything else. Their needs unharnessed a flood of quite specific literary products, churned out in series with the same heroes, plots and settings. The large editions were printed increasingly on industrial technology. They could be purchased by instalment, and suspense was heightened by waiting for the next issue. If they proved successful, publishers could prolong them indefinitely. If not, they finished them off. (On average they ran into 100 instalments and 3,000 pages.) They were peddled directly to homes, workshops and pubs. Social educationalists, both religious and secular, lamented the "sad sight repeated every Saturday afternoon, when great excitement prevailed until the messenger so longed

for arrived with the brochures to have them literally torn from his grasp as old and young hunted greedily together for the pictures"[139].

The bulk of subscribers were younger workers, women, and particularly those who had first encountered literature in domestic service. "Of course the young lads devoured the back-alley novels, with a murder on every page . . . The skilled 19- to 22-year-olds liked war stories or something a bit spicy, with as many pictures as possible of scantily clad women . . ."[140] Working women's hearts "bled for *Marlitt, Golden Else* and *Countess Gisela*, and shuddered at the *Mystery of the Old Maid*". They always waited "impatiently for the next instalment and discussed what would happen next"[141]. In these dynastic and romantic tear-jerkers social conflicts, instruction and pleas for humanity were resolved within private individual relationships without any concern to reality.

Men preferred heroic melodrama. The conventional knights and outlaws were joined by a host of new idols in their roles as saviours, doers of good deeds, peacemakers, guardians of virtue, avengers and judges. They were adventurers, globetrotters, detectives, pirates, men of the Wild West, inventors and explorers. Karl May's novels, now famous the world over, drew on almost all these roles, often combining them in one man. His heroes fought single-handed in foreign lands, confronting danger with pure ideals, to defeat the evil which derives from greed, be it among Europeans, Red Indians or Arabs. The author pinned his hopes on a nobler brand of humanity, and his goals were social and international reconciliation.

Fiction was the easiest way for workers to forget their everyday proletarian existence and enter an imaginary realm where they encountered great passion, human probity, daring and success,

134 Brougham & Vaux (Henry, 1st baron): *Practical observations upon the Education of the People, addressed to the working classes and their employers (1824)*. London, 1825, p. 5.

135 *Ibid.*, p. 10.

136 This was, for example, the opinion of the German Benjamin Preusker who was inspired by the British pattern.

137 Preusker, K. Benjamin: *Andeutungen über Sonntags-, Real- und Gewerbeschulen, Cameralstudium, Bibliotheken, Vereine und andere Förderungsmittel des Gewerbefleisses und allgemeiner Volksbildung*. Leipzig, 1835, p. 23.

138 Quoted from: Siebert, Erich: *Kurze Geschichte der Bibliotheken in Deutschland. Lehrbrief*. Ed. by Fachschule für Bibliothekswesen "Erich Weinert". Leipzig, 1977, p. 84.

139 Springer, August: *Arbeiter und Kunst*. Stuttgart, 1911, p. 26.

140 Bromme, Moritz W. Th.: *Lebensgeschichte eines modernen Fabrikarbeiters*. Jena, 1905. Quoted from: *Proletarische Lebensläufe. Autobiographische Dokumente zur Entstehung der Zweiten Kultur in Deutschland*. Vol. 1: *Anfänge bis 1914*. Ed. by Wolfgang Emmerich. Reinbek near Hamburg, 1974, p. 293. (The Social Democrat Bromme helped to sale such literature in the workshop thus financing his advanced reading.)

141 Heimburger, Arthur: *Um die Jahrhundertwende: Erinnerungen eines Veteranen*. Berlin, 1977, p. 39.

238 This romantic novel was inspired by the Dreyfus Affair. Cheap literature borrowed its material from any source, including the latest events. Here everyday life was disrupted by exciting destiny, and social phenomena were encapsulated in personal relationships.

justice and reward, and the unknown life of distant climes and superior classes. This literature helped them to experience things which were beyond the bounds of their circumstances. The greatest enthusiasts were those whose work was tiring and monotonous, and who enjoyed little communication and few social contacts. Skilled and politically committed workers were less receptive. Literature of this kind used crude tools to project sentimentality and heroism. The plots followed easily recognizable patterns. In a subtle blend of the ordinary and extraordinary, social phenomena were transformed into personal relations, making the social element appear reasonable, as if under individual control.

Anyone who attempted to find a model for real life in this literature would have been utterly disorientated. For that reason the labour movement was sharp in its condemnation. Wilhelm Liebknecht wrote in 1872: "The cheapest of the entertainment rags, which are read primarily by the common people—and I include those novels which are peddled by instalment—are almost without exception—I think one could say are without exception—wretched trash as far as the form is concerned and in content opium to the intelligence and poison to morals."[142] The movement could teach workers how they might really improve their lot.

Yet this trivial fiction cannot have functioned solely as a narcotic if Pastor Apel believed it posed a threat to the Germany of Kaiser William II. It was, he scandalized, not "truly outstanding figures and human benefactors who play the major roles in these novels, but criminals . . . and people who come into contact with them . . . In spite of their misdeeds the criminals are portrayed as heroes, as noble men, as the martyrs of a good cause, as avengers of the oppressed", whereas "the representatives of the superior classes, the rich, the genteel and the educated [are] charged with the contemptible roles, scoundrels, deceivers, leeches and seducers". Surely this must "of necessity incite readers to class hatred, to discontent with the existing social order, with human laws and God's order on Earth"[143].

Theoretical weapons The labour movement set great store by the literate worker. Although it protested when ruling circles tried to restrict suffrage to those who could read and write, mass-scale organization with conscious, long-term aims required readers and its own literature. This ranged, according to strength and conditions, from manifestos, rules, minutes, reports and correspondence via leaflets, daily newspapers and magazines to theoretical articles, campaign mobilizations and entertaining texts geared to many concrete situations and sections of the population.

239 This advertisement for "very interesting books" appeared in *Süddeutscher Postillon* in 1908. There had always been erotic literature for upper-class connoisseurs, but in the 19th century these intimacies reached the common people.

142 Liebknecht, Wilhelm: "Wissen ist Macht—Macht ist Wissen," in: *Kleine politische Schriften*. Leipzig, 1976, p. 149.
143 Apel: *Die Verbreitung guten Lesestoffs*. Berlin, 1896, pp. 1–7.

One "paper agitator", especially a party or trade-union newspaper, could replace "a dozen competent flesh-and-blood agitators . . . moreover more thoroughly, as the printed word" could always be retrieved.[144] Great energies were invested in the battle against lack of money, bans and arrests. The Chartist campaign against the Stamp Tax was exemplary, when a tax on newspapers was designed to price them out of the worker's reach. And later the German Social Democrats fought a successful trench war against the ban on distribution of their party organ, distributing it without interruption against all the odds. "How often the heart of this old revolutionary laughed," praised Engels, "to see that beautifully oiled and silent interaction of dispatcher, editor and subscriber, that businesslike revolutionary work functioning week by week, year in, year out, with the same dependability!"[145]

Freedom of the press was a high priority, as the press was a key to organizing a mass movement. In 1906 87.4 per cent of Berlin's 48,352 Social Democrats subscribed to the party newspaper. In 1912 75.5 percent of the Berlin electorate voted for the Social Democrats, and 50 per cent of them were regular readers of party publications. Apart from the party and trade-union organs, there were special magazines for women, young people, cyclists, chess players and many other groups.

Labour-movement publications were born of modest beginnings, when the writing, printing and distribution all had to be done after a day's work. Articles were few and editions had to be small. In the early half of the 19th century only the occasional leaflet or magazine reached a mass readership. By the end of the century, however, the labour movement had set up facilities for producing a constant, systematic flow of literature in editions that at least matched the bourgeois competition. The publishing house set up by Heinrich Dietz in 1881 became the hub of book production for the German Social Democrats. It was here that Marxism acquired the printed form which brought it a certain influence over the labour movement. His publications were the "encyclopaedia of militant socialism", embracing "the entire history of Marxist ideas almost without a gap", and offering "an internally cohesive history of German culture based on the new, pioneering principles" of the historical approach elaborated by Marx and Engels. Not even a critical observer could fail to be impressed by the production and dissemination of literature in the German labour movement. "It has gradually built up a popular literature, the size of which can be judged from the catalogues of Social Democratic bookshops, with a content which popular books have never before dared provide, admittedly more superficial and injudicious than the previous works of religion and pa-

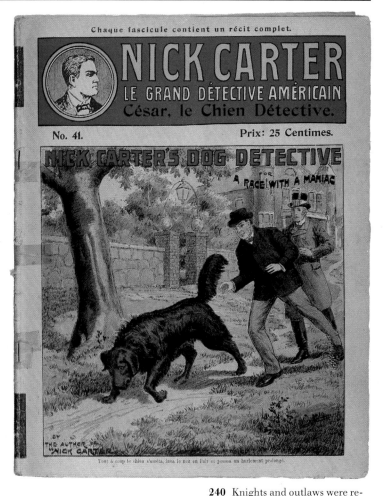

240 Knights and outlaws were replaced as enterprising heroes by detectives like Nick Carter and men of the Wild West, such as Buffalo Bill and Old Shatterhand.

144 Cf. "Protokoll über den sechsten Kongress der sozialdemokratischen Arbeiterpartei, abgehalten zu Coburg am 18., 19., 20. und 21. Juli 1874." p. 74.
145 Engels, Friedrich: "Letter of Farewell to the readers of the *Sozialdemokrat* of September 1890," in: Marx, Karl, and Friedrich Engels: *Werke*. Ed. by Institut für Marxismus-Leninismus beim ZK der SED. Vol. 22. Berlin, 1956–68, p. 77.

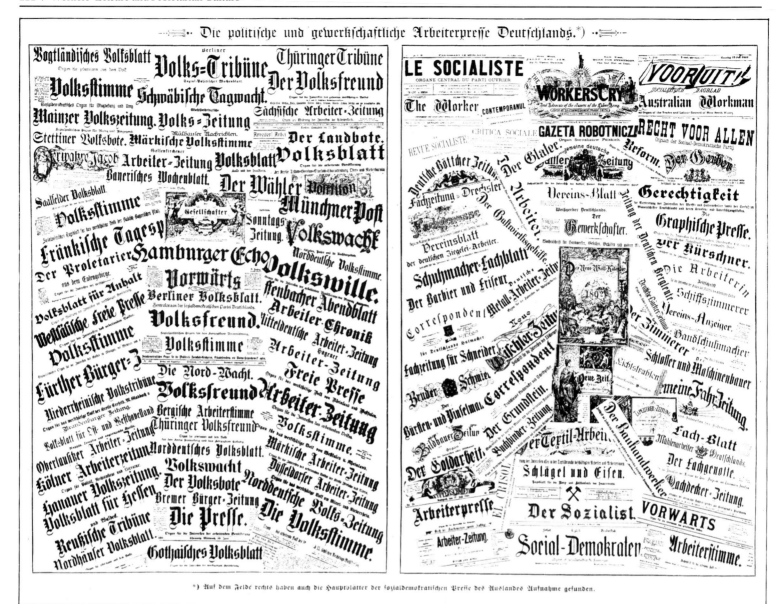

241 Titles of German and international working-class newspapers. The press was the key instrument of communication for mass organizations against a backcloth of rapidly changing situations.

242 "Reading the Newspaper." Lithograph by Konstantin Fedorovich Yuon. Workers, too, adopted the newspaper as an important vehicle of mass communication.

triotism, yet no less popular than these and new, modern, contemporary as neither of those has been. It has undertaken what they have neglected: with a bold flourish it has popularized modern science ... This is how the latest people's literature was created, a unique attempt, and daring in its nature, at combining dissemination of the party's new radical teachings on economics and politics with sweeping all the old education and culture, Christianity and the Bible, from the hearts and minds of the masses and from the face of the Earth."[146]

The labour movement always saw itself as a school for workers with varying abilities in reading and writing. It was no accident that, until the sixties, political organizations and workers' education associations existed hand in glove. The education associations taught workers how to use literature, starting with the alphabet, and they evolved into eloquent officials, editors and writers. There was help, too, in interpreting texts, with discussions in the organization and critical reviews, both for a general audience and in small groups.

146 Göhre, Paul: *Drei Monate Fabrikarbeiter und Handwerksbursche. Eine praktische Studie*. Leipzig, 1891, pp. 192ff.

243 *"Der Wahre Jacob* has come!" Drawing by Otto E. Lau. The German Social Democrats began publishing their satirical magazine in 1884, and it had the biggest circulation of all their press organs, with 366,000 subscribers in 1914.

244 Heading of *Die Neue Welt*. This entertaining supplement catered for the tastes of workers and working-class housewives. It included novels, short prose, sketches from nature and society, and essays on history and the arts, all of which were aimed at promoting the "transition from the old world to the new world". It was inserted free into many socialist newspapers, and by 1911 had a circulation of 550,000.

The need for literary entertainment posed problems for the labour movement. In this field the adversary was king, for capital was able to invest in mass-produced fiction. The labour movement tried to respond with diverting novels of its own, but there were some ideological scruples about hitting the enemy with his own stick. Would not workers in a socialist society have quite different needs and be satisfied only with the best? Could aesthetic standards be geared to "fist-clenching labourers"? Could they be reconciled with political content? Was Naturalism, with its depictions of milieu, an appropriate style if it did not enhance a worker's self-respect and fighting spirit? Perhaps Schiller's moral idealism had more to offer? These were topics which even concerned the Gotha Congress of German Social Democrats in 1896. The most widely-read fiction writers who were accepted and distributed by the labour movement at the turn of the century were: Honoré de Balzac, Edward Bellamy, Wilhelm Busch, Miguel Cervantes, Alphonse Daudet, Charles Dickens, Theodor Fontane, Maxim Gorki, Gerhart Hauptmann, Henrik Ibsen, Gottfried Keller, Guy de Maupassant, Karl May, August Otto-Walster, Wilhelm Raabe, Fritz Reuter, Walter Scott, Theodor Storm, August Strindberg, Bertha von Suttner, Jonathan Swift, Leo Tolstoi, Jules Verne and—top of the list—Émile Zola.

245 *King Mammon and Liberty*, one of the first children's books produced by the Social Democrats in an attempt to influence a younger readership. This volume was published in Leipzig in 1878 by a printers' co-operative.

246 The socialist labour movement respected the cultural heritage of the past. Socialists in Germany were drawn to the humanitarian idealism of Friedrich Schiller, a man who opposed all tyranny. The centenary of his death in 1905 gave the labour movement a chance to express its cultural aspirations. Illustration from *Der Wahre Jacob*, May 1905.

Everyday Art

Proletarian aesthetic senses were fashioned by house fronts, stations, cinemas, stairways, billboards and columns, shop windows, newspaper illustrations, reproduced prints, films and mass literature. By the end of the 19th century workers, for all their limited resources, were consuming films, pictures, hit songs, books, fashionwear, wall ornaments, stage performances, variety, circus acts and a host of other delights.

Over the last third of the century, industrial forms of production increasingly set their stamp on the leisure and entertainment opportunities available to the public. Art was now churned out in series: penny dreadfuls, light music, films, colour prints, sketches and songs for music halls, operettas. In fact, the consumers were subjected to regular bombardment by peddlars, advertisements, store displays and associations. Industry offered a range of goods to cater for mass demand, from enamel paintings to reproductions of the Renaissance masters, from political and technical magazines to romantic novels.

As new production and reproduction technologies advanced, new genres were created, such as cinema, posters, short prose for newspapers, and commercial art. The literary and fine arts now flooded the market at low price thanks to industrial methods.

The physical and nervous strains of industrial labour generated a strong need for relaxation, recreation, entertainment, distraction, and impressions totally remote from the proletarian world of work, housing and daily life. Time passed quickly and enjoyably for workers at the cinemas and people's theatres, with a book or a group hobby, at a show or a dance. Films and novels provided what the proletarian usually lacked in the daily routine. They satisfied curiosity and thirst for knowledge, inspiring the imaginations of their audience or readers. Here were popular panaceas to fulfil a worker's daydreams and banish rudimentary cares for a brief while.

On the whole, workers at the turn of the century were seeking access to all the leisure opportunities which the capitalist market could offer. They went to exhibitions, the theatre and the cinema, painted, read, attended lectures and concerts. Not all these things inspired the same passion, but: "The modern worker expected . . . to participate in the pleasures of life."[147]

Working-class songs Workers sang together at festivals, meetings and congresses. They made use of revolutionary songs on demonstrations and during strikes to back up their political demands. Singing and playing music together encouraged confidence and group identity. Militant words and tunes filled workers with courage or with the strength to accept defeat and venture into conflict with the class enemy yet again. "Then, comrades, come rally—And the last fight let us face!—The International unites the human race." Songs were like symbols of identification which brought comrades and friends together across great distances.

The workers in the songs marched in struggle to "the sun, to liberty and light" as the future glimmered from the dark ashes of the past. It was easier to understand the class struggle in terms of these graphic images, encouraging those who still stood aloof from politics to identify with labour-movement goals.

Songs and music in yards, pubs and clubs Organ-grinders and courtyard minstrels were familiar figures on the streets of working-class districts. They had to know the latest lyrics and play the best-known tunes to please their public. In the last thirty years or so of the 19th century, many landlords prohibited courtyard singing: "No beggars, hawkers or buskers". Only war invalids and the elderly and crippled obtained licences to perform in public in Germany after 1870. Other travelling musicians stood little chance.

Apart from the organ-grinders, there were fiddlers, guitar and banjo players and pipers making music on the streets of European and North American cities. Vocalists would try their luck in one courtyard after the next. The songs they sang, from ballads to tangos, usually consisted of a popular melody or dance rhythm with a short-lived, ever-changing text, often suggestive, sometimes downright lewd. Although steeped in local atmosphere, they quickly spread across national borders. The Berlin ditty *Komm, Karlineken, komm* was soon heard in Warsaw as *Pójdź Paulinko* and in Paris as *Viens, poupoule*. In Buenos Aires it was not only the organ-grinders who popularized the latest tango, but also the horse-tram conductors with their horns.

Apart from the ditties, the yards, doorways and streets of working-class districts resounded with the cries of street-sellers, knife-grinders and rag-and-bones men, the rhymes of children at play, and the ditties of serving maids. But music was not confined to the back yards, streets and squares; it could be heard in pubs, music halls, restaurants and theatres. Light music reached a mass audience thanks to fairground orchestrinas and pub juke boxes. The favourites were sentimental folk songs about faraway homes, lost youth, lovers parting and rejected sweethearts.

Workers would often hear military music echoing down the road, too, with its riveting march rhythms.

It was only at the end of the century, as a pleasure industry developed, that the dance music, popular songs, sentimental ballads, music-hall ditties and operetta arias found a truly mass audience. This industry commissioned light music and songs for bills which were already international in composition. They listed French dances, Scottish and Irish folk songs, Italian arias, Latin American dance music, the "gutter songs" of Berlin and Viennese waltzes. Garden restaurants and ballrooms were quick

---

147 Bromme, Moritz W. Th.: *Lebensgeschichte eines modernen Fabrikarbeiters.* Jena, 1905, p. 223.

247 Two organ-grinders about to play the same tune simultaneously. They have sold song sheets and the audience are requested to join in. The barrel organ was able to imitate and reproduce orchestral music, bringing it to workers on the streets, yards and fairgrounds. The gramophone then brought concert music into homes, but working-class families could not yet afford them.

248 "Living pictures" stimulated the spectator's imagination, conjuring up scenes of danger and romance and re-creating settings which workers would otherwise never experience, such as the salons of the wealthy or far-off places. The tricks of the camera provoked optical experience of a new kind.

249 Rose's Berlin theatre, 1914.

250 Refreshment stall, 1901. Workers were already acquainted with the fairground, the circus and variety hall, but now "serious" theatre began to make overtures in their direction. The working class took its own initiative with the "people's theatres", which sprang up in many towns to bring "quality" drama to proletarian audiences. They were not geared solely to aesthetic pleasures, as the Rose Theatre in Berlin illustrates.

to absorb the best-known works of Offenbach, Suppé, Johann Strauss, Millöcker, Zeller, Lincke and Gilbert into their repertoire.

Europe imported totally new sounds and dance forms from America, especially after the World Exhibition in Paris in 1899. The tango and ragtime were the most popular. These American imports set the tone in European light music up until the First World War.

Twixt amusement and knowledge Cinema at the close of the century was more than a technical wonder. It often began as an additional attraction in pubs, but soon turned into a rival. The cinema provided entertainment for the whole family, and it was cheap and easily accessible. Films supplied fun, diversion and pleasure, just like the out-of-town theatres, romantic novels, circuses, variety shows and music halls. Alongside the pub, many regarded a "visit to the cinema as the only period of complete removal from grinding daily routine"[148]. Films opened up new vistas of experience to workers, illustrating their unfulfilled dreams, bridging time and space as no other art could. The dream world of the feature film cast a veil over reality, offering a refuge to workers plagued by insecurity and worry.

The new medium was rapidly accepted, assisted by the location of cinemas at fairgrounds, in variety theatres and in pubs, and by the depictions of everyday life which dominated the earliest films. The mass appeal was doubtless due in part to the graphic images, the direct, unambiguous message and the universal comprehensibility. Film-makers took account of the pleasure an audience derived from seeing and experiencing. Cinema "brought workers as close as possible to reality and comfort"[149] in visual form. It was cheaper than the other entertainment on offer, did not rely on a particular frame of mind or suit of clothing, and could begin and end at any time. It provided what workers wanted most during their free time: diversion, variety, entertainment, information. Workers did not go to the cinema simply to see a particular film. The cinemas in working-class areas were meeting-places, where workers could enjoy themselves together and talk.

In some countries the labour movement objected to the cinema, fearing that it would devour all the workers' meagre free time and keep them away from political meetings and campaigns. Until the labour movement could make or commission its own films, it was hard to see the connexion between "mere amusement" at the flicks and a new medium which conveyed information and knowledge.

An ornament for the mantelpiece Working-class homes around 1900 were adorned by knick-knacks, advertisements,

251 The petty-bourgeois household was blessed by the image of a saint and a motto, such as "The early bird catches the worm" or "Home sweet home". Workers chose slogans from the labour movement: "We want peace, freedom and justice. Let no man be slave to another. Labour is the duty of all, that none shall want bread."

252 Workers seldom hung pictures of saints or rulers. They preferred countryside settings and angelic maidens. They would have been the first to acquire paintings with critical overtones. One of the most famous examples was Robert Koehler's "The Strike," 1886.

148 Altenloh, Emilie: *Zur Soziologie des Kino*. Jena, 1914, p. 53.
149 Panowsky, Walter: *Die Geburt des Films*. Würzburg, 1944, p. 57.

253 Workers all over the world felt a close affinity to songs. Anyone could repeat them simply from memory during their everyday labours, at social gatherings or at mass meetings. The militant songs of the labour movement conveyed basic ideals in vivid imagery. Singing together reinforced group identity. In 1915 the working-class choral associations of Germany had 165,000 members. In spite of the traditional language and metaphor, these old songs still make a symbolic impact on friend and foe of the labour movement alike. "Wherever a class-conscious worker may roam, wherever his destiny takes him, and however alien he feels, with no knowledge of the language, no familiar faces, far from home, the well-known melody of the *International* will win him comrades and friends" (Lenin, 1913). The banner of the choral society Vorwärts Gelingen, 1910.

254 Wall ornaments in a working-class Berlin flat. New reproduction techniques meant that workers could now hang pictures in their homes. Ornaments included photographs, magazine illustrations, industrially produced prints of art works, embroidered mottos and bric-a-brac. Thanks to photography proletarians, too, could now display portraits of their relatives. Photo by Heinrich Lichte & Co., Berlin, 1919.

calendars, magazine inserts and oil prints. Arranged in a jumble, they were important to the owners as family or individual souvenirs, or because of other personal associations. There were certificates to recall key events in life, photos of people they liked or admired. Pictures often acquired a special value either because they had been given by someone close or because they showed something familiar or desired.

Paper reproductions of paintings and mass-produced vases and wall plates could be purchased in department stores and furniture shops. Hawkers encouraged the spread of unframed oil prints in working-class households. Apart from their value as mementoes, these prints, photographs, posters, watercolours, copper etchings, wall plates, plastic wall medallions, calendars, plaster figures, antlers and deer heads demonstrated a higher living standard. Sometimes they were only bought to cover up a blemish in the wall. In the front room workers might hang "oil prints with plain landscapes, poaching scenes which seemed at first sight to present an exciting . . . image, pictures of guardian angels"[150], but also "diplomas awarded . . . at the sports festival for many years of loyal membership in some association or other. Then wedding certificates, confirmation certificates, blessings, battle scenes"[151]. Workers also hung reproductions of "Rembrandt, Rubens, Titian, even Raphael . . . and Meunier and Millet"[152]. If they were politically committed they would have a picture of the July Revolution, a portrait of Marx, or a caricature from a satirical magazine. Next to these there might very well be a saint, the queen or kaiser, Bismarck or some other government minister.

Sociable entertainment It became customary for workers to organize their own festivals and to foster their own patterns of sociability, with family excursions, summer get-togethers in allotment colonies, Christmas parties, concerts, dances and plays. Married workers were the driving force behind evenings of family entertainment. This description of a Christmas celebration organized by German Social Democrats in 1911 is a good example of such events: "Workers' choral societies embellished the festivity. The participants were enthusiastic about a tombola with hundreds of prizes which comrades had collected from the traders. Children took part in the programme, recited poems and put on little plays. One amateur actor, a party member, performed a sketch, and I can still hear some of his words today: 'As long as Bethmann rules the land, not one worker will lift a hand. As long

---

150 Springer, August: *Arbeiter und Kunst*. Stuttgart, 1911, p. 51.
151 *Ibid.*, p. 52 f.
152 *Ibid.*, p. 54.

255 *The Song of the German Social Democracy*, written by Georg Herwegh.

256 Every working-class organization had its banner. Banners were
elaborately embroidered and painted
in the craft tradition.

257 1 May celebra-
tions called for official
programmes of events,
including recitation,
drama and orchestral
music, commemorative
prints, title pages of the
press and postcards.
The worker on Max
Slevogt's lithograph of
1903 bears the symbols
of vigilance and strug-
gle. The caption was a
verse by Ferdinand
Freiligrath proclaim-
ing the proletarian as
the smith forging a fu-
ture state.

as the holes in our belly linger, not one worker will lift a finger.'"[153] Parties and celebrations like this strengthened the bonds between workers and attracted new members. Unaffiliated workers were drawn into political work through the close interaction of recreation, entertainment and discussion. Social events bore the marks of an independent proletarian culture and posed an alternative to the amusements which the capitalist market offered.

Workers and photography Photographic techniques for capturing and reproducing an image were first developed in the first half of the 19th century. Portrait studios soon opened in every industrial country. To begin with, it was expensive. Portrait photos became more widespread from the fifties, when the large formats were replaced by a visiting-card size. Fairgrounds offered workers their initial chance to have a souvenir picture taken, although the quality was usually poor.

But before everyone could afford to have themselves photographed individually, workers were captured almost accidentally by camera plates taking prestige shots of modern industry. They were an ornamental extra, hovering like dwarves beside locomotives, ships and other gigantic structures which the entrepreneurs paid photographers to document for contemporaries and posterity. Picturesque portraits of domestic servants, craftsmen and traders were more common before the sixties, afterwards there were also group pictures of soldiers and factory and construction workers. Anniversaries were a good excuse to hire a photographer. In 1864, for example, countless workers crowded round the 500th steam engine to be produced by the Bavarian company Maffei. Everyone had to keep absolutely still for the photographs to work, and they had to be taken in the open air before new advances permitted the camera to operate in a studio or on the shop floor. Spindler's, a laundry and dyer's just outside the gates of Berlin, published photos of this kind, still in the manner of paintings, in a publicity brochure produced in 1896 for the big trade exhibition. The workers were perceived and depicted as a component of the production site. The first person to take photographs of *déclassé* elements was a Dane living in New York. Jacob A. Riis published his book *How the Other Half Lives* in 1890, depicting the immigrant slums. The flashlight exposures could not yet be printed. In 1892 a newspaper reproduced them as drawings. Another pioneer of everyday photography was the Scot John Thomson. He took London street scenes in the seventies showing traders and tramps.

The spectrum of camera subjects was expanded in the nineties by class, wedding and confirmation photos and mounted portraits of soldiers. Around this time factory workers would occasionally visit a city studio to be snapped in their Sunday best against a painted backcloth with all the accessories typical of the period. Because of the way these portraits were always made, they found themselves adopting the poses customary for bourgeois clients, and in some respects many of these artificial shots testify to the workers' new-found confidence.

By 1900 portrait photos adorned working-class homes, and workers were sending picture postcards. It was not long before they were reading newspapers and magazines with photographic illustrations. Thus photography gradually found its place in everyday life, until eventually workers managed to afford their first box camera.

Private Dreams and Utopias

By the end of the century, more and more workers in the industrial nations of Europe felt a connexion between their own aims in life and the socialist aims of the labour movement. The mass parties in all these countries had followed the example set by the German Social Democrats and worked with the trade unions to lay the foundations for this identification, combining a revolutionary objective—transferring the key means of production into social ownership in the state of the future—with "legal" struggles which brought about immediate improvements in the current economic and political condition of the workers.

Contemporary studies of workers' aspirations and dreams demonstrated that, in formulating a vision of the socialist future, workers took their present hopes as a starting point. The workers questioned repeatedly listed better immediate living conditions and a dignified existence for themselves and their children as their goals for the future. Certain hopes and desires cropped up again and again. For example, they dreamt of having plenty to eat at last, wearing better clothes, staying in good health and not having more children than they really wanted. They wanted to be paid a decent wage and respect for difficult and dangerous work; they wanted their sons and daughters to enjoy a happy childhood; they wanted a proper training; and they wished all their children could have a bed of their own. They did not want their wives to have to work at the mill or wash clothes for "posh families". They wanted enough income to buy a bicycle or a pocket watch, to make their home really cosy, to buy a garden allotment or a little house, and to subscribe to a newspaper. They all wanted to work fewer hours (six to eight) so that they would have time to sleep as much as they wanted, and more time for the family, for pleasure, walks, modelling, painting, playing music, reading, learning and trade-union or party work. Many registered a longing to travel away for a summer holiday, and there was a continual wish for a carefree old age.[154]

Workers coupled these day-to-day yearnings with hopes which transcended the existing social order. A thirty-eight-year-old German weaver from Forst who had to feed six children on 22 marks a week said: "My sole wish is that the time should not be so far off when the socialist world order is introduced, when there will be no more hungry people and no more prodigals. So that a human being can be human at last and not an animal any longer."[155]

Other workers were anxious for the final great freedom struggle, so that the working class could settle accounts with their parasites and burst the fetters of slavery, and so that they themselves would live to see the victory of Social Democracy and the socialist state of the future, a world without wars where justice, equality and human dignity prevailed. Sociological research also noted proletarians who expressed private ambitions for themselves and their children. "That my children don't have to be slaves as I am," was a frequent wish. As labourers they were thinking primarily in terms of the career ladder and of becoming a skilled worker or foreman. Often, however, they set their sights elsewhere: an independent craftsman, an academic profession such as teaching, the law, the Church, a musician, or a government employee working for the post office or the railways with pension rights.[156]

Rodolphe Broda of Paris and Julius Deutsch of Vienna compiled a lengthy work of social psychology in 1910 called *The Modern Proletariat*. In this work they summed the position up as follows: "The very best of what can be found in proletarian hearts is expressed in this belief in a future of sunshine. The human dignity which is forced to the ground by the yoke of daily life rises with this belief in the future of the class . . . The individual who has no future takes courage from belief in the future of the class. The proletariat's faith in the future has assumed a quite specific form: socialism . . . The workers are devoted body and soul to socialism . . ."[157]

Communicating through utopian literature Workers showed the urgency of their hopes for social transformation by taking a deep interest in any blueprint for future life. Those passages in August Bebel's work of cultural history *Women under Socialism* where he paints a picture of life and work under future conditions had done much to promote international interest in

---

153 Faulhaber, Max: "Jahrgang 1904," in: *Kürbiskern. Geschichtsbilder.* Instalment 1 of 1981. Munich, 1981, p. 140.

154 Cf. Levenstein, Adolf: *Die Arbeiterfrage. Mit besonderer Berücksichtigung der sozialpsychologischen Seite des modernen Grossbetriebes und der psychologischen Einwirkungen auf die Arbeiter.* Munich, 1912, pp. 213–242.

155 *Ibid.,* p. 229.

156 Bernays, Marie: *Auslese und Anpassung der Arbeiterschaft der geschlossenen Grossindustrie. Dargestellt an den Verhältnissen der "Gladbacher Spinnerei und Weberei" AG zu Mönchen-Gladbach im Rheinland. Schriften des Vereins für Socialpolitik.* Vol. 133. Leipzig, 1910, p. 231, p. 242f.

157 Broda, Rodolphe, and Julius Deutsch: *Das moderne Proletariat. Eine sozialpsychologische Studie.* Berlin, 1910, pp. 125ff.

the book. Reading workers in general tended to like science fiction.

These entertaining short stories and novels with their fantasy settings provided excitement, action, suspense and adventure. It was fun exploring "other worlds" or future centuries where life was better or the challenges more stimulating. The fascination of science-fiction utopias for workers and the socialist movement is well illustrated by the success story of one book: the novel *Looking Backward: 2000–1887* by the American writer Edward Bellamy was an international bestseller, and there are many accounts of the massive impact it made.

The author, a progressive humanitarian of bourgeois origins, describes a harmonious society of freedom and peaceful co-operation among the peoples of the world. He contrasts a kind of communism in the imaginary year 2000 with the social contradictions of capitalism in the late 19th century. The book met with an enthusiastic reception, even though the labour movement in countries such as Germany had already taken the "step from utopia to science". The workers accepted this literary text with its vision of the future as an expression of their own goals and interests and took it very seriously. Over 400,000 copies were quickly sold in the United States, and from there the book set out to conquer the world.[158] Bellamy Clubs were formed in the United States, fanning the flames of the Nationalist movement for government ownership with slogans such as "The People versus the Trusts" and "Man versus Money".[159]

In Britain William Morris was inspired by Bellamy's novel to write a utopian work of his own. In *News from Nowhere* (1890), he painted a picture of the future in which "pure communism", as a naturally-orientated alternative to industrial capitalism, has been realized as the "only reasonable basis for society".

Several publishers marketed Bellamy's book in the Imperial German *Reich*. Clara Zetkin translated it for Dietz. Leading Social Democrats such as Wilhelm Liebknecht, Karl Kautsky and Franz Mehring paid tribute to the work in a plethora of articles. Conservative and reactionary writers who objected to this communist brand of visionary socialism responded with counter-utopias. These rebukes—the best-known being the malicious tracts by Eugen Richter and Emil Gregorovius—could not detract from the interest and understanding shown for Bellamy's blueprint by working-class readers and socialist leaders. They

---

158 Bellamy, Edward: *Looking Back: 2000–1887.* Introduction by Cecilia Tichi. London, 1982, p. 7f. and p. 27.
159 *Ibid.*, p. 22f.

258 Model of a phalanstery based on the ideas of the French utopian socialist Charles Fourier (1772 to 1837). About 2,000 people would live in the community, producing and consuming as a co-operative. They would require about 1,200 hectares of land, with homes, accommodation for animals and other buildings connected with the economy at the centre, along with a palace of culture and a church. Members would develop their productive inclinations by working consecutively in each trade and in the sciences and arts. Lithograph by Louis Jules Arnoux, *c.* 1840.

Der verhängnißvolle Weg.

Die Handwerker, Kleinbauern, Meister,
Sie ziehen in Maſſen heran.
Es lockt ſie der Sang der Sirenen
Auf eine gefährliche Bahn.

Er lockt ſie hinein in den Rachen
Des ſchrecklichen Götzen, des Baal,
Dort fallen ſie wehrlos zum Opfer
Dem mächtigen Großkapital.

Doch warnend tritt ihnen entgegen
Ein Weib aus der Freiheit Land:
„Nicht weiter auf dieſem Pfade!
Zur Linken die Blicke gewandt!

Hier ſtürzt Ihr hinab ins Verderben,
Wo gräßlich der Opferbrand loht,
Dort winkt Euch auf lichten Höhen
Erlöſung von Qual und Noth!"

259 This cartoon from *Der Wahre Jacob*, 1891, illustrates the "fateful path" of small peasants, craftsmen and traders into the grinding maw of the awful capitalist idol, to the musical accompaniment of National Liberals, Conservatives and reactionary mining magnates. In the background, by contrast, the Ancient temple of socialism rises symbolically with a statue of Nike, goddess of victory, bearing the wreath of justice in her left hand. The classic slogan on the architrave reads: Liberty, Equality, Fraternity.

felt they could support the book for the far-sighted meaning and hopeful orientation which it bestowed upon their own values in the arduous conflicts of day-to-day politics.

By describing a practicable socialism, Bellamy was reinforcing the spontaneous attraction which workers felt towards socialist ideas. Bellamy's novel made such a tremendous impact that it was cited as a "Crown witness" in the German parliament in 1893 during the heated debates about the aims of Social Democracy, the state of emergency and social visions.

Parliaments debate utopias Controversial discussions in the supreme national assemblies of Germany and France illustrated how proletarian consciousness of an alternative future society had spread and was influencing political activity.

In early 1893 the leading representatives of the German labour movement in the *Reichstag* rejected accusations by their opponents in the conservative parties that Social Democrats were unpatriotic adventurers and anarchists who lacked morals and ideals, revealed economic incompetence, aspired to the rule of force and sought to impose ineffective egalitarian values.

August Bebel, Wilhelm Liebknecht and Franz Egon Frohme were the chief counsels for the defence. They outlined the socialist view of the future and described how history had followed a course of evolution and revolution, in which certain junctures in socio-economic and political processes had always led to a qualitative change in social relations "in keeping with the iron laws of development" (Wilhelm Liebknecht). A new society would arise out of the bourgeois order, and the switch to socialism would inevitably come when capitalism was "in greatest flower" while *betraying* "all its evils". August Bebel stressed that the "Social Democratic movement . . , [is] a civilized movement of the first order, to which humanity's future belongs . . . The forces of production have long since outgrown our society, so that it shall and must of necessity perish from its own internal contradictions. For bourgeois society—and this is its internal contradiction—begets poverty and deficiency out of abundance. It is all summed up in this one sentence. But when a new organizational form allows the masses to benefit from this abundance, the verses sung by Heinrich Heine on this matter over 50 years ago will achieve fulfilment:

There's bread enough on Earth
For every human creature,
Roses, beauty, myrrh and mirth,
And peas—the kind that's sweeter!—
For everyone to feast on.
Just think of that, my darlings!
And Heaven we'll abandon
To the angels and the starlings.

(Great disturbance on the right and in the centre.) That, gentlemen, is our manifesto. The future belongs to us and us alone . . . (Lively applause from the Social Democrats. Hissing right.)"[160]

260 The English painter Walter Crane worked the demands of the labour movement into a flowering wreath in a commemorative print for 1 May.

261 A 1 May postcard showing workers in a smithy. All they forged was dedicated to their ideals: a future of liberty and peace.

Wir weihen was wir schmieden
Der Freiheit und dem Frieden

262 The special May edition of the satirical *Süddeutscher Postillon* in 1894 supported the demand for an eight-hour day. This would leave eight hours each for recreation and sleep which, in contrast to the good-for-nothing existence of the parasite depicted above, were well earned by the labouring man.

A few years later, in June 1906, alternative future societies were being discussed in the French parliament, too. This time it was Jean Jaurès, as the leader of the French socialists, who described the potential for a socialist transformation of society: "The basis we ascribe to socialism is not simply, or not especially, the purpose of realizing the idea of superior justice, but the fact that it represents the development and perfection of all previous cultural effort by humanity. (Very good! on the extreme left.) It is precisely because humanity, and particularly humanity in the recent age, has won a little light and a little liberty that it is aspiring upwards through this light and this liberty towards a superior justice. Because science and technology have created great mechan-

„Denke Dir, liebes Weibchen, welche Neuigkeiten!"

264 This optimistic family idyll which appeared in *Der Wahre Jacob* in 1892 reflects the worker's idea of a decent daily life: a comfortable home, the children well cared for, a tidy and attentive wife, and a politically committed husband fighting for his family's security.

263 Social Democracy as a hearty female setting the points for a cheerful journey into the new era. Revolutionary progress is portrayed allegorically as the locomotive of historical movement. Illustration from *Der Wahre Jacob*, 1898.

ical devices which embrace and unite the energy of humanity, the workers now understand the potential for a social order in which humanity works together in peace. . . . We are . . . as passionate about reform as we are about class struggle. Our methods are reformist, our aim, the entire transformation of the social order, is revolutionary. (Very good! on the extreme left.)"[161]

Abolishing the rule of capital and profit would, he declared, have tangible effects on the lives of the working population: a programme of housing construction "to increase the number of healthy and spacious homes", increased agricultural output using funds freed from elsewhere in order to improve food provisions, care for the elderly, accident insurance, higher living standards for working people thanks to steadily rising incomes, and administration of public affairs by a democratic state "which has the entire nation behind it".[162]

160 *Stenographische Berichte über die Verhandlungen des Reichstags. VIII. Legislaturperiode. II. Session 1892/93.* 2nd vol.: *Von der 32. Sitzung am 28. Januar 1893 bis zur 60. Sitzung am 7. März 1893.* Berlin, 1893, p. 820.
161 Speeches by Jaurès, Vaillant and Clemenceau in the Chamber of Deputies, June 1906. Quoted from: *Die Zukunftsdebatten im französischen Parlament* (Translated by Max Quarck). Frankfurt am Main, 1906, pp. 22, 25, 40.
162 *Ibid.*, p. 9f.

The Culture of Organization

More free time enabled workers to join together in organizations of their own. The solidarity born of economic motives developed into a complicated fabric of institutions. Proletarian organizations defended working-class interests against the employers and the state. For the individual worker, belonging to an organization meant finding a community of like-minded fellows. It brought advantages in the daily struggle for survival. The worker was able to draw on advice and assistance, saw his demands expressed, and encountered the respect of the group. And yet membership of a trade union or party could also entail disadvantages. It cost money and time and incurred the risk of a bad reputation, dismissal, or even exile, as in Germany under the law against socialists. The more members an organization had and the stronger it grew, the more security it achieved for his individual existence and the sooner his living standards managed to rise.

Workers' organizations were a forum where they could compare their daily experience and ascertain how much of it was generally relevant and what goals could be achieved. They taught workers that their plight was not the outcome of personal failure, and pointed the way to winning demands. Workers who joined independent labour organizations and adopted their ideas were treated differently by the state and by employers, with greater animosity and also greater respect than their unaffiliated peers. They also developed as personalities, acquiring confidence, a sense of purpose about their personal values on life, and the skill to defend their social interests.

In some countries, such as Russia, associations of workers were purely political fighting alliances. In the United States, coalitions of trade unions wielded a certain economic influence without giving birth to parallel political organizations. Class organization in the German-speaking lands was highly versatile. Apart from representing the political, trade-union and co-operative interests of the workers, it provided a framework for leisure. Associations offered a broad range of opportunities for cultural activity. Politics and social life combined on the evenings when dues were collected and at monthly meetings in the pub. Cultural institutions like the people's theatres and the Friends of Nature granted workers access to the realms of bourgeois culture, from the arts to mountain walks. These processes generated proletarian policies on culture and local government which lobbied for working-class leisure needs with rural and urban councils and with the government.

The foundations of proletarian organization Labour organizations usually originated from pub gatherings. Later on, workers would meet in trade-union clubs and people's houses where labour "officials" had their offices.

The labour organizations influenced how members spent their time. The evenings when dues were paid developed into a regular feature, with discussion on problems of everyday life and labour and a sense of group solidarity.

At first it was usually the younger, as yet unmarried men who could afford to pay regular dues or take on the risks of a career working for the organization.

Workers with more pronounced needs who demanded their share of society's wealth and were by no means averse to the growing range of consumer goods on offer hoped that collective campaigning would enable them to acquire and enjoy more social fruits. Only those workers who could read and write understood what was in the manifestos and read the association newspapers. They took advantage of the educational events, which also indirectly improved their career prospects. They learnt how to keep lists of members, compose leaflets, deliver speeches and thereby strengthen the organization.

The labour movement had its own calendar of festivities, including 1 May, American Labor Day in September, trade-union anniversaries and the Christmas parties held by German and Austrian socialists.

Cultural work Joining a class organization redeemed a worker from solitary anonymity: individual energy acquired weight from the organized mass. The organizations which parties and trade unions set up to run education and artistic activities were not the only bodies to play a cultural role. These mass organizations themselves were centres of sociability and assistance which promoted a code of solidarity and confidence. Organized workers differed from their unaffiliated fellows in thought, language and gait. They looked their bosses squarely in the eye, made no attempt to conceal their views, walked tall on the streets and in the factories, and sported a red carnation on 1 May.

Workers encountered features of the future society in their organizations. Their songs and the speeches given by their leaders extolled the human virtues which would prevail in tomorrow's community: diligence, honesty, pride, education, courtesy, loyalty, integrity, modesty and dependability. The standards prevalent in these organizations were to foster such characteristics. Leisure opportunities were an added attraction, drawing fresh members into the political movement. They offered people with less of a political schooling a chance to take part in creative activity. Consumer, production and housing co-operatives taught the workers to distinguish between what they wanted and what they could actually achieve. Every organization was a kind of testing-ground, introducing workers to the tasks of administration and cultivating skills that would be crucial to the government of the future society.

The diversity of proletarian organizations The labour movements of most countries evolved diverse forms of organiza-

265 A 1 May print by Walter Crane. The labour movement aspired to internationalism and resisted nationalistic thinking.

tion. Almost everywhere there were educational associations, solidarity funds, co-operatives, trade unions and socialist parties. The German movement was both ridiculed and admired internationally for its fanatical clubbability. It was exemplary, both in the framework it provided for workers' leisure and in the size and strength of its nationwide cultural organizations. Before the First World War broke out, for instance, the working-class athletic associations had almost 200,000 members. Only the workers' choral societies achieved a membership comparable with their bourgeois rivals (165,000). The New Free People's Theatre sold cheap tickets to 50,000 workers and organized its own performances. Some 6,000 working-class Samaritans cared for victims of accidents, watched over the sick and arranged transport to take patients to see their doctors; they provided First Aid at meetings. There were Esperanto and Ido societies to promote working-class internationalism by encouraging the use of a world language. About 6,000 proletarian freethinkers attempted to emancipate their class from the Church. They drew up secular rituals for naming babies, celebrating adolescence and burying the dead. They also campaigned for the right to cremation and for so-

Achtung! **Achtung!**
Bergarbeiterstreik!

In dem hiesigen Revier befinden sich die Berg- und Fabrikarbeiter in einem Lohnkampf!

Kameraden, Arbeitsbrüder! **Fallt den kämpfenden Bergarbeitern nicht in den Rücken!! Nehmt keine Arbeit auf!!** Uebt Solidarität, Gerechtigkeit und Brüderlichkeit!

Baczność! **Baczność!**
Strejk górników!

W tutejszym rewirze znajdują się górnicy i robotnicy fabryczni we walce zarobkowej.

Robotnicy! Nie zdradzajcie walczących o lepszy byt górników! Nie przyjmujcie pracy kopalnianej! Trzymajcie się solidarności, sprawiedliwości i braterstwa!

266 Strikers in Senftenberg, Germany, issued this leaflet in 1897 to warn others against accepting their work. If workers wanted to receive the value of their labour power, they had to prevent competition amongst themselves so that wages could not be beaten down. Their only weapons in the fight against the owners of capital were organization, solidarity, discipline and an awareness of their own interests.

267 A strike breaker is expelled and blacklisted by his union. Solidarity was a supreme moral imperative and infringements were rigorously punished. Many considered a non-unionized fellow-worker to be a man of no honour.

The above individual, THOMAS M. HUGHES, was expelled from St. Louis Typographical Union, No. 8, July 4, 1875, for a gross violation of his obligation as a member thereof, in having deliberately perjured himself by soliciting and obtaining work at less rates than those established by the scale of prices of said Union, thereby ratting a fair office, and justly subjecting himself to the scorn and contempt of all men who value the sanctity of a solemn and binding obligation, freely and voluntarily assumed. This Judas Iscariot, like his infamous prototype, is a professed Christian, and assumes the cloak of religion to hide his hypocrisy, thereby deceiving the unwary. He will be easily distinguished by his loud-mouthed professions of loyalty to Union principles whenever occasion demands it, and readily recognized by the following personal

DESCRIPTION:

Said THOMAS M. HUGHES is apparently between fifty and fifty-five years of age, about five feet seven inches in height, will weigh about one hundred and fifty pounds, and wears a short, dirty brown or reddish chin whisker, intermixed with gray. In manner he is plausible and oily, with a high appreciation of his ability as a workman, and, as a "Professor," is quite a success. As to his merits in that line, the paper which he has disgraced speaks volumes.

He deposited a Memphis traveling card at the April meeting of this Union, being the unworthy recipient of the charity of that sister organization in the shape of donations in money and tickets for himself and family from that city to St. Louis.

By order of

St. Louis Typographical Union,
No. 8.

St. Louis, July, 1875.

268 The banner of the Crimmitschau building workers, 1912. No labour organization existed for long without its standard. It symbolized group solidarity and rallied members on demonstrations. Carrying it, and if necessary defending it, was an honour. Thanks to the labour movement the red colour acquired a well-defined, appealing significance.

cial instruction in schools. 5,000 teetotal workers fought alcohol and took care of alcoholics.

Not a horde of wild savages Factories taught workers the basics about collective action according to firm rules. From the pecking order at the mill they learnt how to behave in a disciplined manner and recognize hierarchies. School and then military service drummed obedience into them. Guild parades and religious processions showed workers that mass displays of group power could be quite effective. In Germany the sports movement, which liked to exercise in squad formations, demonstrated the self-discipline required to make a mass parade succeed. The labour movement was able to make good use of all this experience.

Members of organizations, after all, had to accept tasks, sit quietly in meetings and listen, pay their dues on time, attend meetings of their own free will and acknowledge the rules. Besides, organized workers wanted to prove that they were a force to be reckoned with and not a horde of wild savages. A typical instance was reported to the British government from Lancashire in the summer of 1819. Workers were assembling in a field in the evenings and on Sundays and exercising like military units. They wanted "to accustom themselves to salutary physical drills in cleanliness, sobriety and discipline so that they could be permitted to appear with greater dignity than hitherto at big meetings in the future". As a result of these exercises, the Chartists hoped to develop from an untidy band into "a mass which strides and feels in unison"[163].

The symbols Germans who fled to the United States in 1848/49 and 1878 were a major influence on the early American labour movement. Their fondness of clubs and social gatherings motivated them to establish the kind of organizations that they had known in Germany in the industrial centres of the northern states. These organizations tended to be transitory, however, as the chance to buy land in the West tempted many to abandon their working-class existence. Efforts to negotiate the sale of labour as a group were crushed again and again by the army, trigger-happy Pinkertons and blackleg associations. In response, the American labour movement developed a militancy all of its own.

Like the French labour movement after the Paris Commune of 1871, the Germans during the bans on socialism from 1878 to 1890, and the Russians after the 1905 Revolution, the American workers were prompted by this constant state of emergency to devise their own cultural forms of solidarity. Apart from setting up a general administration, the Conference of Industrial Unionists in Chicago in 1905 decided to symbolize unity by producing rec-

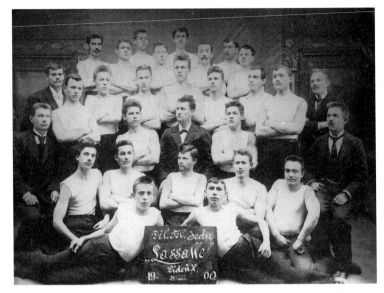

269 Lassalle Sports Club in Videń, Prague, 1900. While political organizations and trade unions, which were basically tools of social struggle, also provided communal activity, communication, good company and a platform for individual talents to develop, leisure associations for athletes, singers, chess players and musicians brought workers into contact with the militant labour movement.

270 The band of Unity Workers' Sports Club in Pisek, today Czechoslovakia. Photo of 1911.

163 Guttmann, Bernhard: *England im Zeitalter der bürgerlichen Reform*. Berlin, Leipzig, 1923, p. 229.

271 German Social Democratic leaders in Jena in 1899. Second and third from left in the front row are August Bebel and Paul Singer. That is not Karl Marx, of course, but presumably an actor from a tableau, then a popular fashion. The picture testifies to the links between Marxism and the labour movement in everyday party life.

272 A class at the party college set up in Berlin by the German Social Democrats, where socialism was taught as a science. Photo by Heinrich Lichte & Co., 1911.

273 A tableau illustrating various social groups and the ideals of the labour movement.

ognizable badges, buttons, transfer slips, application forms and dues stamps. As the railway companies would not carry workers who had no employment contract, roving labourers were obliged to travel illegally as stowaways. They therefore donned a standard pictogram. The Wobblies used secret markings like this to signalize potential danger and help to one another. This was the start of their mutual collaboration. The Industrial Workers of the World was born at the beginning of the 20th century out of a mixture of grass-roots organizations and the leftovers of the American Federation of Labor. It was the first proletarian organization on the Continent to address every ethnic group and recruit immigrants. Its publications and stickers appeared in various languages.

All national labour movements had flags, signs, songs and journals as vehicles and symbols of communication. The best-known of these was the old freemason symbol of joined hands. It was first introduced after the French Revolution by a bourgeois social club in Hamburg. From 1848/49 it had been adopted all over Germany and widely in Europe and America on flags, badges and stamps to express the workers' desire for unity.

Proletarian science   The key to the proletariat's success in social conflicts lay in their growing numbers. "But numbers count only in the balance, if united by combination and led by knowledge." Thus Karl Marx summed up this fundamental experience in his Inaugural Address to the International Working Men's Association in 1864. One consequence was that the secret sects of communist artisans and loose association of Chartist masses evolved into labour movements which united the ranks, with independent parties, trade unions, co-operatives, journals and societies of every kind.

Another consequence was that the workers who belonged to these organizations were able to process their daily experience and forge an independent awareness of their situation, their conditions, their opportunities and their working-class identity. "Anyone who wants to judge the worker's situation properly must be a worker himself . . . or at least it is better to be one than to want to do nothing about it," declared the taylor Wilhelm Weitling, later a key theoretician, propagandist and organizer of the early German labour movement, in 1841. "The first requirement for a worker who wishes to participate in the self-redemption of his class is that he should let himself be told nothing, but know for *himself*," concluded the tanner Joseph Dietzgen, a philosopher of the working class.

One function of the labour movement was that it transformed working-class consciousness, both for the individual and for the class. This is where experiences were expressed and information was pooled, making it possible to formulate generalizations and concepts which anywhere else would have been undesirable, forbidden, evaded or interpreted differently. This is where initiatives were unfolded which taught their own lessons about how to

274/275 During the Industrial Revolution, liberal reformers pressed for workers' education. They founded Mechanics' Institutes in England and *Bildungsvereine* (education associations) for workers in Germany. These evolved into other forms within a working-class cultural movement. Ticket for the *Bildungsverein* for workers and dues stamps.

assert working-class interests. In 1870 Theodor Yorck defined strikes as the "schools of socialism". A few members of labour organizations had to be freed from direct, capital-dependent labour to analyze the experience systematically and supplement the knowledge obtained with that of other classes. Individual perceptions and the opinions of the overall movement were communicated across a network of branch meetings, dues collections, rallies, newspapers and theoretical publications.

As the labour movement acquired mass character and stability, with industrial workers as its pillar of support, so it drew on deeper scientific principles. On the surface it seemed that free and equal partners in the social contract were making an equivalent exchange, but there must be some hidden truth which enabled the owner of the means of production, and not the owner of labour power, to dispose of the surplus wealth. Knowledge and expertise were necessary, for the modern working class had no desire to renounce the civilizatory gains of capitalism. On the contrary, they wanted to make full use of them. The responsibility for millions of workers was at stake. Socialism itself must become a science, not only in its comprehensive social understanding, but in order to defend working-class interests in the trench warfare of union negotiations, legislation, labour rights, and local politics. The labour movement set out to be scientific in the sense that Engels had attributed to the German Social Democrats: "Here there is no concern for careers, for profit-making, or for gracious patronage from above: On the contrary, the more ruthlessly and disinterestedly science proceeds the more it finds itself in harmony with the interests and aspirations of the workers."

Nr. 698   Mai-Nummer des Wahren Jacob   1913

H.G.J. 1913

Prometheus.

— Ja, du redest immer von Gleichheit und Güterteilen, allein ich setze den Fall, wir haben geteilt, und ich, ich spare meinen Teil, doch du verschwendest den deinigen, was dann?
— Ganz einfach! dann teilen wir wieder.

276 The cartoonist of *Fliegende Blätter* in 1846 did not see proletarians as workers, but as unkempt degenerates, lechers and revellers who detested law and order, as implied here by the Phrygian cap, which was popularized by the French Revolution in 1789 as a symbol of liberty. The cliché expressed here that communists prefer sharing wealth to working was obstinately propagated for years to come.

277 The proletariat, as the architect of culture, is compared with Prometheus chained by Zeus. He was a Titan who enabled mortals to evolve a culture by bringing them fire, but his deed incurred the wrath of new gods. From *Der Wahre Jacob*, 1913.

—You talk of equality and sharing wealth, but what if we have shared it out, and I save mine while you squander yours, what then?
—Why, simple! We share it out again.

278 "Hands off!" Cartoon by Honoré Daumier, 1834. A print worker defends freedom of the press. On the left it is threatened by the "bourgeois king" Louis Philippe. The scene on the right recalls the fate of Charles X, who had tried to hamstring the press. For the first time we see the power of an entire class projected onto the proletarian figure, turning him into a larger-than-life hero.

279 Three typical symbols of working-class consciousness on a union membership card: the tools are the means of production which workers use to create wealth and culture; the joined hands represent solidarity, which makes the movement strong; and the sun shines down from a better future.

Marxism in particular did scientific spadework for the labour movement. It developed in the nineties into the most influential theory within the labour organizations of Europe. In the early 19th century, the proletarian condition was so inhuman that condemnation was quickly followed up by action or plans for a non-capitalist society as envisaged by a handful of theoreticians. Karl Marx, on the other hand, had undertaken a critical study of existing philosophy, economics and socialist doctrine, then proceeded to analyze the situation of the working class, drawing on a wealth of specific material, and derived prospects for the working class from the trends in social development to date. Only a few workers had actually read his *Capital*, especially when the first edition of a thousand copies came out in 1867, the first volume for an entire week's wage after 12 to 14 hours' sweat a day. But they heard about it through the theoreticians, and the work influenced labour-movement strategy, becoming an arsenal of scientific arguments to state their case.

The basic insights reached the masses through popular essays and through their practical application to concrete working-class problems. Anyone who called the owner of the means of production a "capitalist" had heard the echo of *Capital*. Engels's book *Anti-Dühring*, meanwhile, was an introductory compendium to Marxism in the fields of philosophy, economics, morality, labour-movement history and socialism. August Bebel's book *Women under Socialism* reached a vast audience. The author had derived features of the future socialist society and its lifestyle from the history of social relations, productive technology and living conditions under capitalism.

"The greatest cultural movement" Workers could not expect to achieve much by being modest and abstemious. The labour movement aroused and fostered needs and expectations. Ferdinand Lassalle blamed the German workers for not noticing their sad plight as soon as their fellows in France and Britain: "That comes of your damned lack of wants!" It was the greatest misfortune for a nation to have no wants, he said, "for these are the *spur to its development and culture*". Virtue for workers meant "having as many wants as possible, but satisfying them honestly and honourably".[164]

It was a "knife-and-fork question", a "bread-and-cheese question", as preacher Joseph Rayner Stephens impressed upon the Chartists in 1839 to the constant indignation of the culturally privileged.[165] But the demands rose, went on growing and did not even stop at "neckties, visiting cards and bicycles"[166]. They ranged from work which could be experienced as a need, via the kind of knowledge which liberates humanity, to luxury of the sort which was considered wasteful for workers to enjoy even occasionally. Workers wanted more out of the civilization they had facilitated "than is essential to the satisfactory fulfilment of their functions in the economic and social process of bourgeois society"[167]. "The free development of each is the condition of the free development of all."[168] That was an aim formulated by various authors.

The moral purification and, as it were, remedial education urged by bourgeois philanthropists were rejected in favour of "social conditions for free cultural development"[169] for workers. "Knowledge itself is power," Francis Bacon had said. Wilhelm Liebknecht turned the phrase on its head and declared: "Power is knowledge. We must stride ahead of state and society . . ., power for us means knowledge! Without power we have no knowledge!"[170]

Workers had doubts about the justifications for a culture to which they had no access or which was meaningless to their lifestyle. Liebknecht was taking this argument to its logical conclusion when he called the dominant culture "the reverse of culture", "barbarism overlaid with the sequins of humanity", because it "contemptuously withholds the treasures of culture" from the mass of the people. "Yes, we do want to destroy it, because it is hostile to true culture,"[171] was the most radical declaration of battle.

In contrast, when the fourth estate assumed the reins of government it would "usher in blossoming morality, culture and science . . . such as never witnessed before in all history"[172]. This had been a widely held conviction among Social Democrats in Germany since Lassalle's day. Since workers had no privileges to defend, they would implement entirely the highest of all cultural and moral concepts, "universal human solidarity"[173].

The Social Democrats—and not only in Germany—believed that there was lasting cultural value in their "great feats" of arousing proletarian class consciousness, organizing the proletarian class movement, establishing the scientific basis for socialism, educating the labouring masses politically, propagating science and art among the proletariat, and creating new social working-class institutions.[174] Certainly, these advances had changed the workers by fostering confidence, needs and an ability for social action. They had given workers a greater share and influential voice in culture, through struggle and by creating practical responses. Art and literature had "no truer or more trustworthy guardians than the class-conscious proletariat"[175]. The labour movement was "the greatest cultural movement which the Earth had ever born"[176].

The slogans which adorned the walls when Germany's Social Democrats met for their 1896 Congress reflected their cultural confidence: "Socialism is peace"; "The holy alliance of the international proletariat against the unholy alliance of capitalist powers"; "The liberation of labour is the liberation of mankind"; "The flames of liberty are not fanned by the blood of the tyrants, no, but by the hearts of a people who know their worth"; "Mass ignorance is our most hated enemy"; "We do not live to work—we work to live"; "See, now, a new world in bud!—The class of labour shall soon be lord.—Not without struggle, yet without blood:—The mind is mightier than the sword."; "Socialism is the soil of all culture".

280 "Liberty's last refuge." After a drawing by Théophile Alexandre Steinlen, 1894. The links between the worker and Liberty, personified as a woman in a Phrygian cap, were a recurrent image. Usually workers followed as Liberty marched ahead, or else were depicted paying her homage. The new element here is that Liberty is seeking the worker's protection.

164 Lassalle, Ferdinand: "Arbeiterlesebuch. Rede Lassalle's zu Frankfurt am Main am 17. und 19. Mai 1863 nach dem stenographischen Bericht." 6th edition. Berlin, 1876, p. 33.

165 Quoted from: *Von Cobbett bis zu den Chartisten. Auszüge aus zeitgenössischen Quellen.* Ed. by Max Morris. Berlin, 1954, p. 108.

166 Luxemburg, Rosa: "Stillstand und Fortschritt im Marxismus," in: *Gesammelte Werke.* Vol. 1/2. Berlin, 1972, p. 367.

167 *Ibid.*

168 Marx, Karl, and Friedrich Engels: "The Communist Manifesto," in: *Collected Works.* Vol. 4. Berlin, 1959, p. 482.

169 Luxemburg, Rosa: "Stillstand und Fortschritt im Marxismus," in: *Gesammelte Werke.* Vol. 1/2. Berlin, 1972, p. 367.

170 Liebknecht, Wilhelm: "Wissen ist Macht—Macht ist Wissen," in: *Kleine politische Schriften.* Leipzig, 1976, p. 133 and p. 173.

171 *Ibid.*, p. 121.

172 Lassalle, Ferdinand: *Arbeiterprogramm. Über den besonderen Zusammenhang der gegenwärtigen Geschichtsperiode mit der Idee des Arbeiterstandes.* 2nd edition. Zurich, 1870, p. 34.

173 Liebknecht, Wilhelm: "Zu Trutz und Schutz," in: *Kleine politische Schriften.* Leipzig, 1976, p. 99.

174 Kampffmeyer, Paul: *Die Sozialdemokratie im Lichte der Kulturgeschichte. Eine Führung durch die sozialdemokratische Bewegung und Literatur.* 3rd edition. Berlin, 1907, p. 4.

175 Mehring, Franz: "Ideale Güter," in: *Gesammelte Schriften.* Vol. 14. Berlin, 1964, p. 566.

176 Braun, Adolf: *Ziele und Wege.* Berlin, 1906, p. 4.

Aus der Zeit – für die Zeit.

ARBEIT und FREIHEIT

Mammon ist der Gott des Tages —
Doch die gold'nen Säulen bében,
Wie Jupiters Säulen fielen;
Andre Zeit bringt andres Leben.

Beuge, Volk, dich nicht dem Götzen,
Dem sie heute Ruhm erzeigen,
Sorge, daß der Freiheit Göttin
Möge bald den Thron besteigen.

281 Capitalist society and the workers from an illustration in *Der Wahre Jacob*, 1894. The god Mammon and the golden calf are surrounded, not only by a speculator, a well-fed capitalist, an officer chasing a dowry, a matchmaker and her innocent commodity, and a cocotte, but also by a painter, an actress, a jockey, a lackey, a scholar and a journalist. Below, the procession of workers now strides out of the darkness. They set about ripping apart the rotten structures of the old society, ignoring the cultural trumpery.

282 During local elections in 1911 *Der Wahre Jacob* satirized the bogeyman image of the socialist worker promoted by the ruling classes.

283 The centrepiece of a 1 May post-card printed by German Social Democrats in the late 19th century. Liberty personified hands over her spiritual sword. It shall be borne with the knowledge which makes humanity free. Marx, Darwin and Lassalle represent the sources. The message to the labour movement is that the struggle should be based on understanding, not blind destruction.

This enthusiasm for the cultural mission of the socialist movement, however, implied a few problems. If the mind really was mightier than the sword and no blood had to be lost, did that mean that the working class could be liberated by enlightenment and persuasion? Intellectuals who found their way into the labour movement were usually at pains to pass the culture which they themselves had assimilated on to the workers in the nobler guise of true, genuine, ideal culture. These intellectuals felt slightly offended if workers did not accept their standards and swap the pub for the library, Karl May for Schiller, and material wants for ideal aspirations. When it came to the crunch—a revolution was in the offing or a world war needed preventing—many labour-movement leaders were so conscientious in their attachment to existing culture that they preferred to defend it rather than fight for the workers' interests.

In the judgment of the enemy   The cultural accomplishments of the labour movement were even acknowledged in the "judgment of the enemy"[177], although this was only voiced in exceptional cases and usually under duress: "We must say this of the red comrades: they have a sturdy organization and we might envy them it. They know what they want; they understand the goal which socialism has set for itself."

(*Trierische Landeszeitung*, voice of reactionary mining magnates, late July 1904.)

"The theory of value and surplus value devised by Karl Marx, that dazzling apologia for human labour, lent scientific expression to the sub-conscious sentiment of millions. Abject labour—the source of all value and increased value; the oppressed working class—sustainer of all mankind. Could any economic system offer a better platform to the personal dignity and confident honour felt by the worker?"

(*Der Holzarbeiter*, Christian trade-union newspaper, Nos. 24 and 25, 1908, in an article on "Workers' Honour and Sense of Class".)

"What the reds manage to offer young people is also noteworthy: Sunday excursions, daily athletics, cheap swimming lessons, youth centres open on winter Sundays, different kinds of instruction, visits to museums and exhibitions, concerts and plays, social assistance and a youth magazine."

(Pastor Schubert in the Christian *Kreuzzeitung*, quoted from the Social Democratic newspaper *Vorwärts*, No. 128 of 4 June 1910.)

"And I maintain today that German and Swiss industry owes a part of the prosperity it has since witnessed to the Social Democratic organizations. They have won better pay, shorter hours, a better lifestyle and improved skills for the workers. Even the

284 The worker sits at the feet of Enlightenment in harmonious alliance with Welfare, Art, Science and Education. A tableau based on this print was enacted at the Social Democrats' Congress in 1890.

---

177   Quoted from: *Die Sozialdemokratie im Urteil ihrer Gegner*. Berlin, 1911. (The references given there were taken over in a slightly altered form.)

strikes and the defensive action under the law against socialism, the support which they rendered, were instrumental in cultivating the workers' best intellectual qualities. All that has been useful to them in their labour."

(Rudolf Meyer, conservative social politician, in *Zukunft*, March 1897.)

"The best energy of the people lies in the working-class family which strides towards the future; the best fathers, who raise their sons well, are the most zealous Social Democrats."

(Pastor Classen of Hamburg in a lecture. Quoted from *Vorwärts*, late February 1907.)

"Art, science and education in Germany have been forced to hide under the wings of the Social Democrats!"

(Prof. Hans Delbrück in *Preussische Jahrbücher*, conservative, May 1900.)

"The working-class journals . . . have taught their readers the idea: read the best that is available, for you will grow by it; read it, even if it is not easy at first, in order to raise yourselves; realize that there are two kinds of entertainment: killing time and pleasure which nourishes, and do not be content with killing time."

(F. Avenarius in *Kunstwart*, 1907, first August issue, responding to a publisher's lament about obtuse bourgeois newspaper readers.)

"Social Democracy has changed the image of the people. The initiate quickly notices on a journey whether the region he is travelling through has been subjected to serious Social Democratic treatment, or whether the old ideas still prevail. Most Social Democrats wear a facial expression that is defiantly free, the voice is coarse and cheeky, and the conduct seems uncouth. The physiognomy of the others is substantially different. They are friendlier, and their friendliness often contains a trace of obsequiousness."

(The Reverend Liebster of Leipzig in his essay on "The Church and the Social Democrats", 1909.)

From the turn of the century, the right and the left within the labour movement disagreed about how to evaluate these achievements. Did they indicate that the working class could continue uninterrupted to advance up the cultural scale of capitalist society? And was this a necessary path to follow because the working class had not yet acquired sufficient culture to lay the basis for a classless society? Or had the working class, for all its cultural progress, always remained outside "today's culture"[178], even though they had achieved the cultural level they required to conquer political power? Was this power not the first condition for workers to develop their culture freely?

---

178 Luxemburg, Rosa: "Stillstand und Fortschritt im Marxismus," in: *Gesammelte Werke*. Vol. 1/2. Berlin, 1972, p. 676.

Victory and Defeat

When the era of industrial capitalism dawned, not a single labourer regarded proletarian existence as a permanent lifestyle. Economic pressure drove former peasants, farm hands, herdsmen, dairy maids and day labourers, and notably women and children, into industrial wage labour. Many of them only stayed while they were young, or until they had overcome their severest poverty and found another livelihood, or until their energy was exhausted or falling demand made their labour superfluous. Masters and journeymen who stood to lose their independence resisted being drawn into the proletariat, by breaking machines, forging utopian plans, working harder and learning new skills to ward off a proletarian existence. Philanthropists were happy to regard proletarians as human beings pure and simple, offering them help against proletarianization. Even conservatives among the upper classes supported workers against the industrial bourgeoisie because they saw the proletariat as a threat to the social order.

Even the factory artisans in the Conspiracy of Equals and League of the Just were unable to perceive a future force in the proletariat of the early 19th century, extensively exploited, disenfranchised and poorly organized as this class was. Nevertheless, they were the first to develop that confidence which enabled workers, instead of measuring themselves against the existing culture, to measure the existing culture against their own needs. But they still held proletarian life and civilized culture to be two incompatible opposites. They thought the proletariat was the result of a mistaken course, false morality or insufficient understanding. They believed its existence was meaningless and they wanted to eliminate it. They could not see that the proletarian existence held potential. Drawing on the utopian ideals of Saint-Simon, Fourier, Owen and other socialists, they made detailed cultural plans for a completely new society built by workers. These cultural dreams were born of their imaginations, and not of elements in the proletarian lifestyle itself. This incurred the risk that they might infuse their blueprints with retrogressive models borrowed from the craft economy, or conceive future culture simply as the reverse of present culture.

And yet by the turn of the century the proletariat had spread across the globe and constituted the largest social class in the industrially developed countries. It contributed the bulk of material production and focused increasingly in large factories, settling in industrial districts and cities. It was not only the number of workers which increased, but also their average skills. Their living standards rose from meagre beginnings. They had more free time and could satisfy more than their basic needs. The existence of this human category influenced settlement patterns, transport, consumer articles, education, concepts of justice, and philosophies. Wherever there were workers, organizations were founded to defend their interests. They were no longer secret sects, but numbered hundreds of thousands of members in many lands. They saw their congresses as working-class parliaments, with exclusive rights to determine the interests and aims of the working class. Elections turned into demonstrations of their power.

In 1912 the free trade unions of Germany had 2,553,000 members. On the eve of the First World War the Social Democrats numbered 1,086,000 card-carrying comrades, 4,250,000 voters and 110 parliamentary seats. There was not a single major town without a Social Democratic daily newspaper, consumer cooperatives, and working-class athletic and cultural associations. Marxism had become the most influential theory in the international labour movement in one land after the next. Millions of workers now called their employers capitalists and knew the slogan "Proletarians of all countries, unite!" off by heart. Their song, *The International*, was sung in countless languages.

Working-class living conditions created a culture which differed from that of the bourgeoisie, petty bourgeoisie and peasants in lifestyle and life agenda, institutions and norms, language and customs, hopes and aims. It was a culture of industrial labour, personal independence among masses, and organization based on solidarity rather than force or cash payment. It contained strategies for work and leisure, settlements and homes, family and community, communication and education, defence of social interests and indulgence in pleasures, and for perceiving and interpreting proletarian reality.

Ideas about culture were now developed which could be put into practice on a mass scale in response to almost all aspects of proletarian life. Experience had been gained from cultural work in the labour organizations and from the outcome of struggles for reforms in existing culture. These independent strategies for culture were derived from features of proletarian living itself, and the goal was that they should be able to evolve freely. Where small sects with doctrinaire plans had once presumed to define

society and culture, mass organizations with practical experience now declared the working class to represent the nation and to possess the skills required for ascending to a new historical plane of culture.

There were always some workers who felt they were better than their fellows, who refused to admit their proletarian identity and hid behind alien lifestyles and ideas. But the majority of workers acknowledged their situation. The proletarian way of life had proved to be the most effective in history for the toiling strata in terms of creating wealth and culture and also laying claim to a share of these things. Most wealth was still concentrated in the hands of those who owned the means of production. They decided how it should be spent. Working-class rights were restricted or else could not be utilized because of economic dependence. But the proletarians had gained confidence in themselves. Most of them no longer felt any urge to deny their proletarian status and replace it with simpler, pre-proletarian relations. They made use of their living conditions and organized to fight for their improvement. The labour movement had raised their consciousness and strengthened their ability to assert themselves socially, accomplishing improvements in proletarian conditions.

285 Leading German Social Democrats in 1900. At the centre are (seated) August Bebel and (standing) Wilhelm Liebknecht. They were committed to revolutionary class struggle. That was the sense in the words above their heads: In war, too, and in its communal conduct, a people truly becomes a people.

286 Armed people's militia on the streets of Moscow in 1905. The Russian Revolution of 1905 was a signal to both the labour movement and its enemies. It demonstrated the potential power of a twentieth-century mass movement, and the soviets, or councils, which it introduced served as an example of how to structure direct popular rule.

287 Revolutionary soldiers and sailors of Petrograd in 1917. These were workers and peasants in uniform. They had chosen the most radical form of class struggle by turning their weapons on their social enemy. Many Social Democrats had predicted that existing society would not outlive the First World War. In Russia their prophecy came true. Russia did not have the material or cultural foundations for a socialist society, but the chain of imperialist countries broke at its weakest link. The bourgeois democratic February Revolution and the socialist October Revolution unleashed a series of national and social uprisings and revolutions in many countries. The Bolsheviks saw their October Revolution as the dawn of a world revolution and hoped to win the support of the working class in more advanced nations. The fighting spirit and success of the Social Democratic Workers' Party of Russia (Bolshevik) lent it an aura of authority and raised the hopes of the oppressed everywhere.

288 "Fraternizing after a long enmity" was the caption under this souvenir photo of 1918. The international labour movement's commitment to peace was shattered in 1914.

After years of bloodshed, Russian and German workers took matters into their own hands and ended the hostilities.

Political parties, trade unions and leisure associations provided features of a lifestyle which was removed from capitalist influence, and the movement strove to extend free time so that workers could develop. Organized labourers were proud to regard their movement as "the greatest cultural movement" and socialism as the "soil of all culture". Marxism had become the most influential ideology for interpreting the workers' condition and the strategy of their movement. Bourgeois contemporaries registered this fact with the deepest unease. The conviction grew in the labour movement that if the proletarians of all countries united, they would be capable of changing the world.

That became a keen challenge around the turn of the century. Electricity and management methods increased productivity and socially disposable wealth. The monopolies accumulated economic power, stretched their tentacles across frontiers, and took control of the state. Concessions to the working class alternated with brute force. The imperialist governments carved the world up anew and headed for disaster. Many contemporaries felt an overwhelming sense that the epoch was in crisis. The

289 The boiler men of the mutinous crew on board the *Prinzregent Luitpold* in August 1917. Of all the war machinery, a battleship was most like a factory, with a concentration of skilled workers, many of whom were Social Democrats. In Germany, the sailors were the first to act against the war. They in fact initiated the November Revolution of 1918. The process began on 2 May 1917, when the crew of the *Prinzregent Luitpold* refused to obey orders, set up an illegal organization and went on strike. Lenin believed beyond a doubt that "in Germany the beginning of a revolution is obvious, especially after the shootings of the sailors".

290 Sailors of the *Helgoland* at an illegal 1 May celebration in 1916. Although the leaders of the big working-class parties had not engaged in any independent labour politics since the outbreak of war, the memory of labour-movement thinking on capitalism and war lived on, as did organizational experience and patterns of expression.

291 Revolutionary Berlin workers on the left of the labour movement pose on the factory floor in November 1918. They have clearly regained their self-confidence and optimism. Photo by Otto Haeckel.

292 A sailor of the German Navy marches at the head of a demonstration along Berlin's Unter den Linden on 9 November 1918. The Revolution began on 3 November 1918 with an armed rising of sailors and workers in Kiel. The aims were: power to the workers' and soldiers' councils, peace and socialism. Photo by Otto Haeckel.

293 Armed workers outside Munich Station during the *Räterepublik* (republic of workers' and soldiers' councils) of 1919. It was proclaimed in April by the Independent Social Democrats and the Anarchists. When the army attempted to topple the new republic in a coup on 13 April, the Communists came to its defence and joined the governing council. Bourgeois associations were disarmed, a Red Army was formed, the police force was disbanded, the banks were taken into social ownership and the bourgeois press was banned. Factory councils supervised production and took on local government functions.

294 The Hungarian Republic was proclaimed on 16 November 1918 at a mass rally on Budapest's Ortnaglaz Square. The Hungarian Councils' Republic followed in March 1919. As in 1848, the Hungarian Revolution was one of the most rigorous.

working class would be the determinant force of the future. The labour movement was sure of that.

The right wing of the movement hoped that they would be able to preserve what the workers had achieved while implementing reforms more easily in the "organized capitalism" of the future. Many others expected capitalist society to collapse and the working class to acquire substantial political power, thereby helping to fulfil the old demands for better proletarian living conditions. The left wing saw the moment approach when an onslaught could be launched on the political power of capitalist society, leading to the definitive liberation of the working class in a world revolution.

This was a period when new forms of class struggle were tested. The bourgeoisie began to increase the rate of exploitation by intensifying labour and raising prices for consumer goods, and at the same time they introduced programmes of reform designed to win the hearts of the men who led the big labour organizations. Many trade-union officials concerned with defending living standards from attack inevitably found this kind of integration attractive.

Huge political strikes and mass demonstrations showed that the labour movement could respond to the merger of state and monopoly power. When the Russian tsar thought he had to counter a peaceful demonstration of over 100,000 Petersburg workers in 1905 by using military force, this bloody repression unleashed the first political revolution of the new century. It was a power struggle which forced the labour movement to elaborate its own strategy and tactics for military class struggle and armed uprising. Tsarist rule of force remained entrenched for a few more years, but the Russian proletariat had given a signal which could not be ignored. It was now clear that the labour movement could lead the dissatisfied and rebellious masses and that in future it would function as the prime agent of democratic movement and revolution. Moreover, the Russian workers had invented and tested an organizational model for the "self-determination of the people": the soviet, or workers' council.

The bourgeoisie still lacked experience in making masses hungry for revolution turn against their own interests, and responded by militarizing society and indulging in nationalistic demagogy. They were also pressed in this direction by the incipient anti-colonial unrest in the peripheral zones of their rule, and above all by escalating competition among themselves. When the Second International met for its Stuttgart Congress in 1907, all the parties present voted for a resolution drawn up by Lenin, Martov and Rosa Luxemburg outlining how the organized workers of all countries should react to these trends in the interests of their class: "If war should threaten to break out, the working classes and their parliamentary representatives in the countries involved are duty bound to muster every strength, supported by the co-ordinating activity of the International Bureau, to prevent an outbreak of war by applying those means which appear to them most effective . . . Should war still break out, it is their duty to work for

295 "Spartacus at work!" A poster to blacken the Communists, whose party evolved from the Spartacus League. Revolutionary workers and communists were unscrupulously damned as bloodthirsty killers, who would destroy culture, the nation and the family, by the very same forces who were busy murdering thousands of workers.

296 A prisoner is led away during the fighting on Berlin's Alexanderplatz on 8 March 1919. Right-wing Social Democrats were content with a bourgeois form of capitalism which they felt they could exploit to gain gradual political and economic concessions to the working class. They joined forces with the Supreme Command to crush the revolutionary workers who wanted complete, direct power for working-class councils as a step towards a socialist society. Photo by Willy Römer, 1919.

297 The funeral procession for Rosa Luxemburg on 13 June 1919. Many factories and all labour organizations sent delegates. Germany's socialists had hoped that the mind would prove more powerful than the sword. Now thousands fell victim, like Rosa Luxemburg and Karl Liebknecht, to the systematic cruelty of right-wing repression. Photo by Willy Römer, 1919.

a speedy termination and to invest every effort towards making use of the economic and political crisis provoked by the war to mobilize the people and thereby accelerate the abolition of capitalist class rule."

Evidently the right wingers in the international labour movement were only paying lip service to this strategy for class struggle elaborated in 1907, for later they did not by any means do everything in their power to prevent an outbreak of war. But the basic mood of the workers and their organizations was hostile to the war. Until August 1914 the working-class parties of every country campaigned against the looming conflict. But when the imperialist rulers acted, the logical outcome and historical implications of the theoretical split among leaders of the labour movement were clear to see. Lenin's section of the Russian Social Democrats were the only ones who remained faithful to the resolution of 1907. All the other party leaders—either gritting their teeth or waving the flag—joined in the chauvinist delirium of those years.

The labour movement took time to recover from that defeat. When workers began to resist the oppressive state of emergency and speed up an end to the war, most leadership bodies of the great working-class parties were still jockeying with their national bourgeoisie. Eventually the hostilities had to be terminated abruptly, as the working masses and soldiers were exhausted and had begun to protest, but only the Russian proletariat had built a new type of class organization which was able to take advantage of this crisis and not only assume power, but even keep it. This victory, like the bitter defeat suffered by the other revolutionary workers, heralded a new stage in the history and culture of the class.

Appendix

Bibliography

Abendroth, Wolfgang: *Sozialgeschichte der europäischen Arbeiterbewegung.* Frankfurt am Main, 1965.

Achten, Udo: *Illustrierte Geschichte des 1. Mai.* Oberhausen, 1978.

Adelmann, William J.: *Haymarket revisited.* Chicago, 1976.

Alt, Robert: *Das Bildungsmonopol.* Berlin, 1978.

Die andere Kultur. Volkskunde, Sozialwissenschaft und Arbeiterkultur. Ed. by Helmut Fielhauer and Olaf Bockhorn. Vienna, Munich, Zurich, 1982.

Arbeiter im Industrialisierungsprozess. Herkunft, Lage und Verhalten. Ed. by Werner Conze and Ulrich Engelhardt. Stuttgart, 1979.

Arbeiter in Deutschland. Ed. by Dieter Langewiesche and Klaus Schönhoven. Paderborn, 1981.

Arbeiter und ihr Leben. Von den Anfängen der Arbeiterbewegung bis zum Ende der Weimarer Republik. Selection and introduction by Ursula Münchow. Berlin, 1976.

Arbeiterexistenz im 19. Jahrhundert. Ed. by Werner Conze and Ulrich Engelhardt. Stuttgart, 1981.

Arbeiterinnen kämpfen um ihr Recht. Autobiographische Texte zum Kampf rechtloser und entrechteter "Frauenspersonen" in Deutschland, Österreich und der Schweiz des 19. und 20. Jahrhunderts. Ed. by Richard Klucsarits and Friedrich Kürbisch. 2nd edition. Wuppertal, 1981.

Arbeiterkultur. Ed. by Gerhard A. Ritter. Königstein (Taunus), 1979.

Arbeiterkultur im 19. Jahrhundert. Ed. by Jürgen Kocka. Göttingen, 1979.

Arbeiterleben um 1900. Group of authors under the leadership of Dietrich Mühlberg. Berlin, 1983.

Arbeitertübingen. Zur Geschichte der Arbeiterbewegung in einer Universitätsstadt. Tübingen, 1980.

Ashraf, Phyllis M.: *Englische Arbeiterliteratur vom 18. Jahrhundert bis zum ersten Weltkrieg. Entwicklungstendenzen im Überblick.* Berlin, Weimar, 1980.

Balser, Frolinde: *Die Anfänge der Erwachsenenbildung in Deutschland in der ersten Hälfte des 19. Jahrhunderts. Eine kultursoziologische Deutung.* Stuttgart, 1959.

Baron, Gerhart: *Der Beginn—Die Anfänge der Arbeiterbildungsvereine in Oberösterreich.* Linz, 1971.

Bausinger, Hermann: "Verbürgerlichung—Folgen eines Interpretaments," in: *Kultureller Wandel im 19. Jahrhundert.* Göttingen, 1973.

Beiträge zur Kulturgeschichte der deutschen Arbeiterbewegung 1848–1918. Ed. by Peter von Rüden. Frankfurt am Main, Vienna, Zurich, 1979.

Bewegung und Klasse. Studien zur österreichischen Arbeitergeschichte. Ed. by Gerhard Botz et al. Vienna, 1978.

Bilder und Dokumente in der deutschen Turn- und Sportgeschichte. Berlin, 1956.

Bolognese-Leuchtenmüller, Birgit: *Bevölkerungsentwicklung und Berufsstruktur. Gesundheits- und Fürsorgewesen in Österreich 1750–1918.* Vienna, 1978.

Brügel, Ludwig: *Soziale Gesetzgebung in Österreich 1848–1918.* Vienna, Leipzig, 1919.

Brügel, Ludwig: *Geschichte der österreichischen Sozialdemokratie.* 5 vols. Vienna, 1922–1925.

Buhle, Mari J.: *Woman and American Socialism.* Urbana, Chicago, London, 1981.

Cole, George D. H.: *A Short History of the English Working Class Movement.* 5 vols. London, 1925–1927.

Deutsch, Julius: *Geschichte der österreichischen Gewerkschaftsbewegung.* 2 vols. Vienna, 1929 and 1932.

Deutsche Sozialgeschichte. Dokumente und Skizzen. Vol. I: *1815–1870.* Ed. by Werner Pöls; vol. II: *1871–1914.* Ed. by Gerhard A. Ritter and Jürgen Kocka. Munich, 1976.

Dokumente und Materialien zur Kulturgeschichte der deutschen Arbeiterbewegung 1848–1918. Ed. by Peter von Rüden and Kurt Koszyk. Frankfurt am Main, Vienna, Zurich, 1979.

Dokumente zur Bildungspolitik und Pädagogik der deutschen Arbeiterbewegung. Instalment 1: *Von den Anfängen bis zur Pariser Kommune.* Berlin, 1982.

Duis, Perry R.: *The Saloon. Public Drinking in Chicago and Boston. 1880–1920.* Urbana, 1983.

Ehmer, Josef: *Familienstruktur und Arbeitsorganisation im frühindustriellen Wien*. Vienna, 1980.

Die Eigentumslosen. Der deutsche Pauperismus und die Emanzipationskrise in Darstellungen und Deutungen der zeitgenössischen Literatur. Ed. by Carl Jantke and Dietrich Hilger. Munich, 1965.

Engelberg, Ernst: *Deutschland von 1849 bis 1871*. Berlin, 1962.

Engelberg, Ernst: *Deutschland von 1871 bis 1897*. Berlin, 1967.

Die Erste Internationale 1870–1876. 2 parts. Moscow, 1981.

Fabrik, Familie, Feierabend. Ed. by Jürgen Reulecke and Wolfhard Weber. Wuppertal, 1978.

Fahrenkrug, Hermann W.: *Alkohol, Individuum und Gesellschaft. Zur Sozialgeschichte des Alkoholproblems in den USA*. Frankfurt am Main, New York, 1984.

Fassbinder, Horant: *Berliner Arbeiter-Viertel 1800–1918*. Berlin (West), 1975.

Flanner, Karl: *Die Anfänge der Wiener Neustädter Arbeiterbewegung 1865–1868*. Vienna, 1975.

Flecken, Margarete: *Arbeiterkinder im 19. Jahrhundert*. Weinheim, Basel, 1981.

Foner, Philip S.: *History of the Labor Movement in the United States*. 5 vols. New York, 1947–1978.

Foner, Philip S., and Reinhard Schultz: *Das andere Amerika. Geschichte, Kunst und Kultur der amerikanischen Arbeiterbewegung*. Catalogue of the exhibition of the Neue Gesellschaft für Bildende Kunst. Berlin (West), 1983.

Frauen suchen ihre Geschichte. Historische Studien zum 19. und 20. Jahrhundert. Ed. by Karin Hausen. Munich, 1983.

Fricke, Dieter: *Die deutsche Arbeiterbewegung 1869–1914. Ein Handbuch über ihre Organisation und Tätigkeit im Klassenkampf*. Berlin, 1976.

Fussball. Soziologie und Sozialgeschichte einer Sportart. Ed. by Wilhelm Hopf. Rentheim, 1979.

Fussball-Weltgeschichte. Munich, 1973.

Geist, Johann F., and Klaus Kürvers: *Das Berliner Mietshaus 1740 bis 1862*. Munich, 1980.

Geist, Johann F., and Klaus Kürvers: *Das Berliner Mietshaus 1862 bis 1945*. Munich, 1984.

German Workers in Industrial Chicago, 1850–1910. A Comparative Perspective. Ed. by Hartmut Keil and John B. Jentz. Illinois, 1983.

Geschichte der deutschen Arbeiterbewegung. 8 vols. Berlin, 1966.

Geschichte der deutschen Frauenbewegung. Ed. by Florence Hervé. Cologne, 1983.

Geschichte der Zweiten Internationale. 2 vols. Moscow, 1983.

Glaser, Hermann: *Maschinenwelt und Alltagsleben. Industriekultur vom Biedermeier bis zur Weimarer Republik*. Frankfurt am Main, Vienna, 1981.

Griessinger, Andreas: *Das symbolische Kapital der Ehre. Streikbewegungen und kollektives Bewusstsein deutscher Handwerksgesellen im 18. Jahrhundert*. Frankfurt am Main, Berlin (West), Vienna, 1981.

Grundmann, Siegfried: *Die Stadt. Gedanken über Geschichte und Funktion*. Berlin, 1984.

Günter, Roland: *Fotografie als Waffe*. Reinbek near Hamburg, 1982.

Gutman, Herbert G.: *Work, Culture, Society in Industrializing America. Essays on American Working-Class and Social History*. New York, 1966.

Guttsman, Wilhelm L.: *The German Social Democratic Party 1875–1933. From Ghetto to Government*. London, 1981.

Handbuch des Büchereiwesens. Ed. by Johannes Langfeld. Wiesbaden, 1973ff.

Hanisch, Ernst: *Der kranke Mann an der Donau. Marx und Engels über Österreich*. Vienna, 1978.

Häusler, Wolfgang: *Von der Massenarmut zur Arbeiterbewegung. Demokratie und soziale Frage in der Revolution von 1848*. Vienna, 1979.

Hautmann, Hans, and Rudolf Kropf: *Die österreichische Arbeiterbewegung vom Vormärz bis 1945. Sozialökonomische Ursprünge ihrer Ideologie und Politik*. 3rd edition. Vienna, 1978.

Hiepe, Richard: *Riese Proletariat und grosse Maschinerie. Zur Darstellung der Arbeiterklasse in der Fotografie von den Anfängen bis zur Gegenwart*. Erlangen, 1983.

Historische Familienforschung. Ed. by Michael Mitterauer and Reinhard Siedler. Frankfurt am Main, 1982.

Höppner, Joachim, and Waltraud Seidel-Höppner: *Von Babeuf bis Blanqui. Französischer Sozialismus und Kommunismus vor Marx*. Vols. 1 and 2. Leipzig, 1975.

Die internationale Arbeiterbewegung. Fragen der Geschichte und der Theorie. Ed. by Boris N. Ponomarev. Vols. 1 and 2. Berlin, 1980 and 1981.

Jahrbuch für Volkskunde und Kulturgeschichte. Berlin, 1974ff.

John, Michael: *Wohnverhältnisse sozialer Unterschichten im Wien Kaiser Franz Josephs*. Vienna, 1984.

Kannonier, Reinhard: *Zwischen Beethoven und Eisler. Zur Arbeitermusikbewegung in Österreich*. Vienna, 1981.

Kasson, John F.: *Amusing the million. Coney Island at the turn of the century*. New York, 1978.

Kerbs, Diethart: *Kind und Kunst. Zur Geschichte des Zeichen- und Kunstunterrichts*. Catalogue of the exhibition. Berlin (West), 1976.

Klassenkampf, Tradition, Sozialismus. Von den Anfängen der Geschichte des deutschen Volkes bis zur Gestaltung der entwickelten sozialistischen Gesellschaft in der DDR. Grundriss. Berlin, 1978.

Klenner, Fritz: *Die österreichischen Gewerkschaften. Vergangenheits- und Gegenwartsprobleme*. 1st vol. Vienna, 1951.

Knilli, Friedrich, and Ursula Münchow: *Frühes deutsches Arbeitertheater 1847–1918. Eine Dokumentation*. Berlin, 1970.

Konrad, Helmut: *Das Entstehen der Arbeiterklasse in Oberösterreich*. Vienna, 1981.

Konrad, Helmut: *Nationalismus und Internationalismus. Die österreichische Arbeiterbewegung vor dem Ersten Weltkrieg*. Vienna, 1976.

Den Kopf tragt hoch trotz allem! Englische Arbeiterautobiographien des 19. Jahrhunderts. Leipzig, 1983.

Kramer, Dieter: *Freizeit und Reproduktion der Arbeitskraft*. Cologne, 1975.

Kuczynski, Jürgen: *Die Geschichte der Lage der Arbeiter unter dem Kapitalismus*. Part I: *Die Geschichte der Lage der Arbeiter in Deutschland von 1789 bis zur Gegenwart*. Vols. 1 to 21. Part II: *Die Geschichte der Lage der Arbeiter in England, in den Vereinigten Staaten von Amerika und in Frankreich*. Vols. 22 to 35. Berlin, 1960ff.

Kuczynski, Jürgen: *Geschichte des Alltags des deutschen Volkes. Studien 1 to 6*. Berlin, 1980–1985.

Kultur und Lebensweise des Proletariats. Kulturhistorisch-volkskundliche Studien und Materialien. Ed. by Wolfgang Jacobeit and Ute Mohrmann. Berlin, 1973.

Kultureller Wandel im 19. Jahrhundert. Verhandlungen des 18. Deutschen Volkskundekongresses in Trier vom 13.–18. September 1971. Ed. by Günter Wiegelmann. Göttingen, 1973.

Lammel, Inge: *Das Arbeiterlied*. Leipzig, 1970.

Lammel, Inge: *Arbeitermusikkultur in Deutschland 1844–1945. Bilder und Dokumente*. Leipzig, 1984.

Lange, Annemarie: *Berlin zur Zeit Bebels und Bismarcks. Zwischen Reichsgründung und Jahrhundertwende*. Berlin, 1972.

Lange, Annemarie: *Das Wilhelminische Berlin. Zwischen Jahrhundertwende und Novemberrevolution*. Berlin, 1976.

Langewiesche, Dieter, and Klaus Schönhoven: *Arbeiterbibliotheken und Arbeiterlektüre im Wilhelminischen Deutschland*. Bonn, 1976.

Läuter, Peter: "Die Anfänge der sozialistischen Verlagstätigkeit in Deutschland (1844–1900)," in: *Beiträge zur Geschichte des Buchwesens*. Vol. 2. Leipzig, 1966.

Listen der Ohnmacht. Zur Sozialgeschichte weiblicher Widerstandsformen. Ed. by Claudia Honegger and Bettina Heintz. Frankfurt am Main, 1981.

Literatur und proletarische Kultur. Group of authors under the leadership of Dietrich Mühlberg and Rainer Rosenberg. Berlin, 1983.

Die Londoner Arbeiteraufstände 1831 und 1834. Ed. by Kurt Holzapfel. Berlin, 1984.

Mesch, Michael: *Arbeiterexistenz in der Spätgründerzeit. Gewerkschaften und Lohnentwicklung in Österreich 1890–1914.* Vienna, 1984.

Mitteilungen aus der kulturwissenschaftlichen Forschung. Ed. by Lehrstuhl Kulturtheorie an der Humboldt-Universität zu Berlin. Nos. 4 and 5: *Materialien der wissenschaftlichen Konferenz "Geschichte der Kultur und Kulturauffassung der Arbeiterklasse" am 22. und 23. November 1978.* No. 9: *Materialien des IX. Kulturtheoretischen Kolloquiums "Kulturgeschichtliche Probleme proletarischer Lebensweise" am 26. und 27. November 1980.* No. 14: *Kulturtheorien und Lebensweise.* 1985. No. 15: *Kulturgeschichtsschreibung.* 1985.

Mommsen, Hans: *Die Sozialdemokratie und die Nationalitätenfrage im habsburgischen Vielvölkerstaat.* Vienna, 1963.

Morton, Arthur L.: *Die englische Utopia.* Berlin, 1958.

Morton, Arthur, and George Tate: *The British Labour Movement 1770–1920.* London, 1956.

Mottek, Hans: *Wirtschaftsgeschichte Deutschlands. Ein Grundriss.* Vol. 2: *Von der Französischen Revolution bis zur Zeit der Bismarckschen Reichsgründung.* Vol. 3: *Von der Zeit der Bismarckschen Reichsgründung 1871 bis zur Niederlage des faschistischen deutschen Imperialismus.* Berlin, 1969 and 1975.

Münchow, Ursula: *Arbeiterbewegung und Literatur.* Berlin, Weimar, 1981.

Oberkofler, Gerhard: *Die Tiroler Arbeiterbewegung. Von den Anfängen bis zur Gegenwart.* Vienna, 1979.

Perfahl, Brigitte: *Marx oder Lassalle? Zur ideologischen Position der österreichischen Arbeiterbewegung 1869 bis 1889.* Vienna, 1982.

Pforte, Dietger: *Von unten auf. Studien zur literarischen Bildungsarbeit der frühen deutschen Sozialdemokratie und zum Verhältnis von Literatur und Arbeiterklasse.* Berlin (West), 1979.

Plaul, Hainer: *Illustrierte Geschichte der Trivialliteratur.* Leipzig, 1984.

Poore, Carol J.: *German-American Socialist Literature 1865–1900.* Bern, Frankfurt am Main, 1982.

Proletarische Lebensläufe. Autobiographische Dokumente zur Entstehung der Zweiten Kultur in Deutschland. Ed. by Wolfgang Emmerich. Vol. 1: *Anfänge bis 1914.* Reinbek near Hamburg, 1974.

Quellen zur Geschichte der Erziehung. Berlin, 1975.

Rach, Hans-Jürgen: *Bauernhaus, Landarbeiterkate und Schnitterkaserne.* Berlin, 1974.

Rausch und Realität. Drogen im Kulturvergleich. 3 vols. Ed. by Gisela Völger and Karin von Welck. Reinbek near Hamburg, 1982.

Reck, Siegfried: *Arbeiter nach der Arbeit.* Lahn-Giessen, 1977.

Reisberg, Arnold: *Von der I. zur II. Internationale. Die Durchsetzung des Marxismus im Kampf um die Wiederherstellung der Arbeiterinternationale.* Berlin, 1980.

Reulecke, Jürgen: *Vom blauen Montag zum Arbeiterurlaub. Vorgeschichte und Entstehung des Erholungsurlaubs für Arbeiter vor dem ersten Weltkrieg.* Bonn, 1976.

Roberts, James S.: *Drink, Temperance and the Working Class in Nineteenth-Century Germany.* Boston, London, Sydney, 1984.

Rosenbaum, Heidi: *Formen der Familie. Untersuchungen zum Zusammenhang von Familienverhältnissen, Sozialstruktur und sozialem Wandel in der deutschen Gesellschaft des 19. Jahrhunderts.* Frankfurt am Main, 1982.

Rosenzweig, Roy: *Eight hours for what we will. Workers in leisure in an industrial city, 1870–1920.* Cambridge, New York, 1983.

Rühle, Otto: *Illustrierte Kultur- und Sittengeschichte des Proletariats.* Vol. 1. Berlin, 1930. Vol. 2. Lahn-Giessen, 1977.

Sandgruber, Roman: *Die Anfänge der Konsumgesellschaft. Konsumgüterverbrauch, Lebensstandard und Alltagskultur in Österreich im 18. und 19. Jahrhundert.* Munich, 1982.

Schäfers, Hans-Joachim: *Zur sozialistischen Arbeiterbildung in Deutschland in den Jahren vor dem ersten Weltkrieg.* Diss. A. Leipzig, 1965.

Schenda, Rudolf: *Volk ohne Buch. Studien zur Sozialgeschichte der populären Lesestoffe 1770–1910.* Munich, 1977.

Schivelbusch, Wolfgang: *Geschichte der Eisenbahnreise. Zur Industrialisierung von Raum und Zeit im 19. Jahrhundert.* Frankfurt am Main, Berlin (West), Vienna, 1979.

Schmidlechner, Karin M.: *Die steirischen Arbeiter im 19. Jahrhundert.* Vienna, 1983.

Siebert, Erich: *Kurze Geschichte der Bibliotheken in Deutschland. Lehrbrief.* Ed. by Fachschule für Bibliothekswesen "Erich Weinert". Leipzig, 1977.

Skambraks, Hannes: *"Das Kapital" von Marx—Waffe im Klassenkampf. Aufnahme und Anwendung der Lehren des Hauptwerkes von Karl Marx durch die deutsche Arbeiterbewegung (1867–1878).* Berlin, 1977.

Soder, Martin: *Hausarbeit und Stammtischsozialismus. Arbeiterfamilie und Alltag im Deutschen Kaiserreich.* Giessen, 1980.

Sozialgeschichte der Freizeit. Ed. by Gerhard Huck. Göttingen, 1972.

Das Sozialistengesetz. Illustrierte Geschichte des Kampfes der Arbeiterklasse gegen das Ausnahmegesetz 1878–1890. Berlin, 1980.

Stará dělnická Praha. Život a kultura pražských dělníků 1848–1939. Ed. by Antonin Robek, Mirjam Moravcová and Jarmila Stastna. Prague, 1981.

Stearns, Peter N.: *Arbeiterleben. Industriearbeit und Alltag in Europa 1840–1914.* Frankfurt am Main, New York, 1980.

Steiner, Herbert: *Die Arbeiterbewegung Österreichs 1867–1889.* Vienna, 1964.

Steiner, Herbert: *Karl Marx in Wien. Die Arbeiterbewegung zwischen Revolution und Restauration 1848.* Vienna, 1978.

Sturm, Hermann: *Fabrikarchitektur—Villa—Arbeitersiedlung.* Munich, 1977.

Teuteberg, Hans-Jürgen: *Urbanisierung im 19. und 20. Jahrhundert.* Cologne, 1983.

Thompson, Edward P.: *The making of the English working class.* Harmondsworth, 1976.

Thompson, Edward P.: *Plebeische Kultur und moralische Ökonomie. Aufsätze zur englischen Sozialgeschichte des 18. und 19. Jahrhunderts.* Selection and introduction by Dieter Groh. Frankfurt am Main, Berlin (West), Vienna, 1980.

Thompson, Edward P.: "Time, Work-Discipline and Industrial Capitalism," in: *Past & Present.* 38 (1967), pp. 56–97.

Tichy, Marina: *Alltag und Traum. Leben und Lektüre der Dienstmädchen im Wien der Jahrhundertwende.* Vienna, 1984.

Vester, Michael: *Die Entstehung antikapitalistischer Theorie und Praxis in England 1792–1848.* Frankfurt am Main, 1970.

Wahrnehmungsformen und Protestverhalten. Studien zur Lage der Unterschichten im 18. und 19. Jahrhundert. Ed. by Detlev Puls. Frankfurt am Main, 1979.

Webb, Sidney and Beatrice: *The History of Trade Unionism (1666–1920)*. New York, 1920.

Weber-Kellermann, Ingeborg: *Die deutsche Familie. Versuch einer Sozialgeschichte*. Frankfurt am Main, 1974.

Wendorf, Rudolf: *Zeit und Kultur. Geschichte des Zeitbewusstseins in Europa*. Opladen, 1980.

Wunderer, Hartmann: *Arbeitervereine und Arbeiterparteien. Kultur- und Massenorganisationen in der Arbeiterbewegung (1890–1933)*. Frankfurt am Main, New York, 1980.

Young, Percy M.: *A History of British Football*. London, 1968.

Zur Geschichte der Kultur und Lebensweise der werktätigen Klassen und Schichten des deutschen Volkes vom 11. Jahrhundert bis 1945. Ein Abriss. Berlin, 1972.

Zur Rolle der Frau in der Geschichte des deutschen Volkes 1830–1945. Eine Chronik. Leipzig, 1983.

Zwahr, Hartmut: *Zur Konstituierung des Proletariats als Klasse. Strukturuntersuchungen über das Leipziger Proletariat während der industriellen Revolution*. Berlin, 1978.

Sources of Illustrations

AEG-Telefunken, Frankfurt am Main 37

Akademie der Künste der DDR, Arbeiterliedarchiv, Berlin 201, 273

Akademie der Wissenschaften der DDR, Institut für Geographie und Geoökologie, Leipzig 65, 161

Archives et Musée du Mouvement Ouvrier Socialiste, Ghent / Archives d'Architecture Moderne, Brussels 222

Aufbau Verlag, Berlin 150

autopress, Neckarsulm 33

Bildarchiv Preussischer Kulturbesitz, Berlin (West) 16, 38

Breitenborn, Vera and Dieter, Berlin 226

Bröhan-Museum / Hans-Joachim Bartsch, Berlin (West) 80

Carl-Zeiss-Stiftung, Jena 225

coop Schwaben, Stuttgart 195

Deutsche Fotothek, Dresden 1, 12, 13, 17, 21, 25, 79, 89, 96, 113, 126 to 128, 136, 140, 146, 149, 157, 172, 173, 184, 191, 193, 194, 196, 214, 220, 237, 242, 258, 286

Deutsche Hochschule für Körperkultur, Leipzig 230, 231, 234

Deutsche Staatsbibliothek, Berlin 27

Dietz Verlag / Renate and Horst Ewald, Berlin 15, 29, 70, 97, 98, 102, 104, 110, 176, 178, 179, 210, 221, 254

Eulenspiegel Verlag, Berlin 212

Foto-Claus, Leipzig 41, 119, 163, 215

Freie Universität Berlin (West), Kunsthistorisches Institut 32, 35

Friedrich Krupp GmbH, Essen 23

Gedenkstätte Crimmitschauer Textilarbeiterstreik 1903/04 / Vera and

Dieter Breitenborn, Berlin 268

Gorman, John, Aimes Green / Waltham Abbey Essex 83, 84, 142

Gräfer, Hans, Berlin (West) 291

Hamann, Käthe, Hamburg 219

Harenberg Kommunikation, Dortmund / Vera and Dieter Breitenborn, Berlin 24, 60

Heimatmuseum Sebnitz 90

Humboldt-Universität zu Berlin, Bildarchiv der Forschungsgruppe Kulturgeschichte / Vera and Dieter Breitenborn, Berlin 171

Humboldt-Universität zu Berlin, Bildarchiv der Forschungsgruppe Kulturgeschichte / Thea Henkel, Berlin 5, 6, 19, 20, 34, 39, 42, 45, 51, 54–57, 59, 64, 67–69, 72, 73, 76 to 78, 81, 82, 100, 105, 109, 130, 131, 133, 135, 139, 145, 148, 162, 165 to 167, 177, 180, 183, 185, 192, 197 to 200, 211, 217, 236, 243, 256, 257, 262, 267, 276, 280, 284, 292

Institut für Marxismus-Leninismus beim ZK der SED, Berlin 26, 36, 46, 53, 116, 143, 147, 151–153, 155, 158–160, 168, 174, 182, 186, 188, 190, 223, 228, 232, 235, 260, 261, 265, 266, 271, 272, 279, 283, 285, 287–290, 293–297

Institut für Marxismus-Leninismus beim ZK der SED / Vera and Dieter Breitenborn, Berlin 7, 47, 141, 169, 170, 202, 203, 209, 239, 241, 244, 246, 259, 263, 264, 277, 281, 282

International Museum of Photography, Rochester 71, 75, 112

Kinderbuchverlag, Berlin 245

Koninklijk Museum voor Schone

Kunsten, Antwerp 120

Kulturamt Erlangen / Helmut Bauer, Ingolstadt 40, 114, 134

Kunstamt Kreuzberg, Berlin (West) 58

Kunstsammlungen zu Weimar / Klaus G. Beyer, Weimar 117

Landpersky, Harald, Tiefenbach 122

Library of Congress, Washington 86

Magyar Nemzety Galéria, Budapest 181

Märkisches Museum / Vera and Dieter Breitenborn, Berlin 8, 9, 28, 48, 61, 92, 94, 99, 101, 107, 125, 132, 137, 154, 156, 205–207, 227, 249, 250

Móra Ferenc Ifjúsági Könyvkiadó, Budapest 44

Münchner Stadtmuseum 218

Musée de la Vie Wallone, Liège 10

Museum der bildenden Künste, Leipzig 278

Museum für Deutsche Geschichte, Berlin 18, 43, 129, 252

Museum für Deutsche Geschichte / Vera and Dieter Breitenborn, Berlin 52, 229, 251

Museum of London 106

Museum of the City of New York 3, 4, 85, 189

Muzeum Klementa Gottwalda, Prague 175, 224

Österreichischer Bundesverlag / J. Fiegl, Vienna 93

Photothek Berlin (West) 87, 88, 103, 247

Public Libraries Department / W. G. Belsher, Birmingham 111

Publisher's archives 62, 63, 238, 240

Renno, Eberhard, Weimar 124

Rijksmuseum-Stichting, Amsterdam 255

Staatliche Kunstsammlungen Dresden, Kupferstichkabinett 204

Staatliche Kunstsammlungen Dresden, Kupferstichkabinett / Deutsche Fotothek, Dresden 118

Staatliche Kunstsammlungen Dresden, Kupferstichkabinett / Gerhard Reinhold, Mölkau near Leipzig 138

Staatliche Museen zu Berlin, Kupferstichkabinett 216

Staatliche Museen zu Berlin, Museum für Volkskunde 248

Staatliche Museen zu Berlin, Nationalgalerie 2, 30, 66

Staatsarchiv Ludwigsburg / Hauptstaatsarchiv Stuttgart 274, 275

Stadsarchief Antwerp 115

Stadtarchiv Berlin 31, 74, 144

Stadtarchiv Frankfurt am Main 50

Stadt- und Bergbaumuseum Freiberg, Saxony 11, 91, 164, 213

Starl, Timm, Frankfurt am Main 22

State Historical Society of Wisconsin 125

Történeti Múzeum, Budapest 108

Ústav Marxismu-Leninismu úv KSČ, Prague 14, 269, 270

Winter, Gordon, London 49, 121, 208

Württembergisches Landesmuseum, Stuttgart 233, 253

Zentralbibliothek der Gewerkschaften / Vera and Dieter Breitenborn, Berlin 187

Zentralbibliothek Zurich 95

Subject Index